Versatile Physicians

II

Physicians the Medical Historians Forgot

Fillmore Buckner, MD, JD

HERITAGE BOOKS
2009

HERITAGE BOOKS
AN IMPRINT OF HERITAGE BOOKS, INC.

Books, CDs, and more—Worldwide

For our listing of thousands of titles see our website at
www.HeritageBooks.com

Published 2009 by
HERITAGE BOOKS, INC.
Publishing Division
100 Railroad Ave. #104
Westminster, Maryland 21157

Copyright © 2009 Fillmore Buckner, MD, JD

Other books by the author:
Versatile Physicians

All rights reserved. No part of this book may be reproduced or transmitted in any form or by any means, electronic or mechanical, including photocopying, recording or by any information storage and retrieval system without written permission from the author, except for the inclusion of brief quotations in a review.

International Standard Book Numbers
Paperbound: 978-0-7884-4911-6
Clothbound: 978-0-7884-8237-3

Dedicated to:

the late Andrew Walkover,

Professor of Legal History and Family Law

at the University of Puget Sound School of Law,

who first interested the author in the history of a

profession.

TABLE OF CONTENTS

SUN YAT-SEN	1-31
SIR ARTHUR CONAN DOYLE	32-55
GERTRUDE STEIN	56-73
RICHARD JORDAN GATLING	74-85
W. SOMERSET MAUGHAM	86-124
JOSEPH IGNACE GUILLOTIN	125-137
THOMAS DOVER	138-153
ERNESTO GUEVARA de la SERNA	154-192
HUGH MERCER	193-203
OLIVER GOLDSMITH	204-213
EMIN PASHA	214-233
SIR LEANDER STARR JAMESON	234-242
THOMAS CLARK DURANT	243-261
WILLIAM HENRY HARRISON	262-272
AYMAN al-ZAWAHIRI	273-292
JEAN PAUL MARAT	293-304
JOHN KEATS	305-332
JOHN HENRY HOLLIDAY	333-350
ANTON PAVLOVICH CHEKHOV	351-373
FRANZ FANON	374-384
BIBLIOGRAPHY	385-399

PREFACE

As a student of medical history, the author has long realized that classic medical histories ignore physicians who make significant contributions to political, military, literary, artistic or economic history. This volume contains biographical sketches of twenty physicians who made or are, in one case, making significant impacts on history in areas other than medicine.

In the preface of the first volume of Versatile Physicians, the author stated that he would not include the biographies of either Arthur Conan Doyle or Gertrude Stein. Doyle because he has been detailed elsewhere so frequently, and Stein because technically she never graduated medical school. However, after these two biographies were published in the King County Medical Society Bulletin, the readers persuaded the author that the two should be included in the present collection.

As in volume one, there is one dentist included in the mix. His inclusion is controversial because his contribution to society is questionable at best. However, he is such a well-known and interesting historical character, his inclusion was hard to resist.

The collection is international with all five continents represented. It is also eclectic, with inclusions ranging from a terrorist, to a romantic poet, to a president of the United States. Nonetheless they all have one thing in common - - they studied medicine.

Mercer Island, Washington 2008

ACKNOWLEDGMENTS

The biographical sketches of Arthur Conan Doyle, Gertrude Stein, Ernesto Guevara de la Serna, Thomas Clark Durant, Hugh Mercer, and W. Somerset Maugham have previously been published in the *King County Medical Society Bulletin* and are published here with the permission of the Editor, William Spence, M.D.

The author would like to thank Kate Barber, King County Medical Society Librarian at the University of Washington Health Sciences Library, for her generous help in locating material. Thanks too to the many members of the King County Medical Society Historical Society who heard and read so many sketches, included and excluded; made comments and suggestions; and are primarily responsible for the production of this little volume.

Finally, many thanks to Harker Brautighan, who undertook the onerous task of editing this collection.

x

SUN YAT-SEN

Sun Yat-sen was born on November 12, 1866, in the small village of Ts'wi'heng in the Pearl River delta of Kwangtung Province. Kwangtung Province is on the South East coast of China and Canton is its provincial capital. His was a peasant family, members of a weak clan. Sun Yat-sen's father worked as a porter in Macao, the Portugese enclave in Kwangtung, until, at age 32, he had saved enough money to buy a half acre farm and marry. The couple had a total of six children. Sun Yat-sen was number five. His given name was Wen. Two siblings died in infancy. The father took employment as the village watchman for a little extra income. The household included two widowed aunts.[1]

There was not enough money to send Wen to school before age eight. Although the school taught Confucianism and Chinese Classics, Wen's teacher reportedly was a veteran of the Taiping rebellion (1850-1864) and also taught an anti Manchu message. Wen had barely two years of classic education when he left for Hawaii accompanied by his mother. Wen's eldest sibling, Sun Mei, had gone to Hawaii with a maternal uncle and had prospered there. Wen was left in Hawaii under the care of his older brother. The brother enrolled Wen in Iolani School, the Church of England elementary school, commonly known as the Bishop's School. The classes were in English and Wen only knew one or two words of pidgin English when he entered. However, Wen proved to be an excellent student and when he graduated he took the second prize in English grammar. The school required classes in Christian doctrine, daily prayers and attendance at Chapel, and Wen became interested in Christianity despite his big brother's objections.

---

1. Widows of the father's brothers who had gone to America during the gold rush. One had died before reaching California and the other had been killed in California.

After graduation from grade school, Wen spent a short time working for his brother on Maui, but then his brother enrolled him in the Punahou School, then the highest institution of learning in the Hawaiian Islands. The school was run by American Congregationalist missionaries. Again Wen was attracted to the Christian doctrine and was about to be babtized. This angered Sun Wei to the point he shipped Wen back to China in the summer of 1883.

Once back in his village, Wen began preaching the superiority of Western ways. He also desecrated the village's wooden image of the Northern God. His family was forced to spirit him away to Hong Kong and pay for restoration of the statue.

In Hong Kong, Wen enrolled in a Church of England high school and the Government Central School (Queens College). Although Wen, later as Yat-sen, claimed he studied Chinese Classics with a Christian Missionary from the London Missionary Society during this time, his claims of a classic Chinese education were always in doubt. During this time the Sino-French War raged, and Wen/Yat-sen later claimed the disasterous outcome to the Chinese was what started him on his career as a professional revolutionist. Certainly by this time his pro-west feelings had combined with and included anti Manchu attitudes.[2]

In 1884, he was finally babtized by the American Congregationalist Missionary, Dr. Hagar. At the time of his babtism, he abandoned his given name of Wen and adopted the name Yat-sen. By this time, his parents thought the furor in the village had died down enough for Yat-sen to return home for an arranged marriage. He went home long enough for the marriage, but outraged the village by assaulting the image of another god, and Sun Yat-sen scurried back to Hong Kong without his bride.

In 1885 Sun Yat-sen was admited to the Canton Hospital Medical School, an American Missionary School headed by Dr. John Kerr. Despite Sun Yat-sen's conversion to Christianity and anti-Manchu leanings, his brother Sun Mei had resumed his financial aid. Because of his fluent English, Sun Yat-sen was able to work as an interpreter in the hospital for his tuition and board. Again in later years, Sun Yat-sen was to claim he received instruction in Chinese Classics during this year, but the evidence for this instruction is even flimsier than durning his first stay in Hong Kong.

---

2. The Manchus were invaders from the steppes of the Northwest Frontier who had ruled the Hans (native Chinese) since 1644. They had completely absorbed the Chinese bureaucratic system and the Classic Chinese education system and had become tradition bound rulers.

It was during this period he began his associations with the criminal anti-Manchu secret societies, the Triads. It is hard to imagine Sun had time enough to work as interpreter, be a successful medical student, a self described full time revolutionist, and spend any appreciable time learning Chinese classics.

In 1887, Sun Yat-sen transferred to the recently opened College of Medicine for Chinese in Hong Kong. The school was run by Dr James Cantlie and Patrick Manson[3]. Sun Yat-sen gave many differing reasons for the transfer over the years, but the plain and simple reason appears to be that his antigovernment activities with the Triads had drawn the attention of the Emperor's secret police. Canton was Chinese and dangerous. Hong Kong was British and safe.

Even so, there is ample evidence Sun Yat-sen continued his anti-Manchu activities in Hong Kong and some local police reports indicate he experimented with bombs while he was a medical student. Besides his association with the Triads, Sun now fell under the influence of Ho Kai. Dr.

---

3. Patrick Manson was already famous for his pionier work in discovering the Malaria parisite in the stomach of the mosquito. He was to gain further fame later in the control of the mosquito in Malaria control.

Ho was an Aberdeen trained physician and attorney. He returned to Hong Kong and developed an extremely successful law practice. He had established the Alice Hospital in honor of his British wife who had died. Alice Hospital was the site of the College of Medicine for Chinese, and Dr. Ho was prominent in its administration and was a full time professor on its faculty. Dr. Ho too was an outspoken advocate of China's modernization.

Through Dr. Ho, Sun was introduced to a cadre of respectable western educated Chinese expatriates who were in sharp contrast to the underworld character of his compatirates in the Triads. Dr. Ho convinced Sun Yat-sen that his Western education qualified him to speak on all public affairs, not just matters of public health.

Dr. Ho's message, adopted almost verbatum by Sun Yat-sen in letters to bureaucrats during his medical school days, was that China's troubles were of its own making and not due to Western exploitation. Its backwardness, corupt government and legal system, based on a civil service system that chose leaders and administrators by examinations that excluded all but Confucian Classicists were the root of its problems. The problems could be solved by leaders who were western trained.

There were twelve students admitted to the first medical school class. It appears that Sun Yat-sen was a standout from the start. He rapidly became Dr. Cantlie's protégé as well as Dr. Ho's. Besides leading the class academically, he began demonstrating considerable surgical skill. Only two members of the class graduated in 1892. Sun Yat-sen took all the honors. However, when he attempted to practice medicine in Hong Kong, he was informed that the medical school did not meet the standards of the Hong Kong Medical Council. His license was denied. Dr. Ho had found that affluent Chinese preferred to go to traditional Chinese practitioners and that western patients preferred to go to western physicians. That was why he had practiced law and not medicine in Hong Kong.

On Ho's advice, Sun Yat-sen decided to combine herbalism with western medicine and set up a "Chinese-Western Apothecary" in Macao. It was extremely successful from the start. Before long, the Portugese authorities barred him from treating Portugese patients, and, soon thereafter, passed regulations forbidding pharmacies from filling his perscriptions.

Undaunted, Sun Yat-sen moved his operation to Canton. He set up several shops in Canton and its environs and hired herbalists to handle that aspect of the practice and confined himself to the practice of surgery. Dr. Cantlie reportedly helped him on his more complicated cases. Again his shops and practice were highly successful.

Suddenly, in 1894, he abandoned medicine and traveled North to present Li Hong-chang, China's leading statesman, with what Sun Yat-sen called a proposal. Today, we would be more likely term the document a manifesto. It called for five major reforms:

1) Rational exploitation of China's manpower and natural rescources;

2) Economic development (industrialization);

3) Adoption of Japan's nine year development plan;

4) Sever the culture bound choice of leaders and administrators;

5) Agricultural modernization and reform.[4]

Sun could not have picked a worse time to try to see Li. The Japanese had designs on Korea and there was an international crisis with a Japanese invasion force on the move. Li refused to see Sun Yat-sen. However, through his missionary connections, Sun Yat-sen's reform plan was widely published in the missionary papers in China and abroad.

---

4. It is interesting that Sun Yat-sen's last point made no mention of land reform. It was not until shortly before his death and when pushed by his Soviet supporters that he finally added land reform to his platform.

On the strength of that publicity, Sun Yat-sen left for Hawaii in the fall of 1894. His aim was to raise money from the 20,000 Chinese residents to support his revolutionary activities. He did poorly, but managed to set up a twenty man cell unter the title of Society to Restore China's Prosperity.

In January of 1895, Sun Yat-sen left Hawaii to return to Hong Kong. The Sino-Japanese war had left China in chaos. Sun thought he could set his revolution in motion. The revolution was set for October 26. It was ill-conceived, ill-planned and ill-executed. There were only about fifty individuals from several factions involved and Sun Yat-sen was only one of several leaders. By October 26, the police were well aware of all aspects of the scheme and all the leaders except Sun were captured and beheaded. Sun escaped to Hong Kong. There, despite help from Dr. Cantlie, he was advised to leave immediately. Even if not extradited to China, he was in imminent danger of assassination. His family left for Hawaii without delay to avoid any attempted retaliation.[5]

On November 12, 1895, Sun Yat-sen arrived in Kobe, Japan where

---

5. His father had died prior to the failed revolution. The relatives that went to Hawaii were his mother, his wife and his two children, a boy born in 1891 and a daughter born in 1895. Yet the author can find no reference to Sun Yat-sen returning to his village or his wife after 1884.

he was hailed as the leader of the Chinese Revolutionary Party. Sun immediately cut off his queue, assumed western dress and grew a mustache. He raised enough money to purchase passage to Hawaii where his brother, Sun Mei, was caring for his family. He arrived in January 1896 and stayed about six months[6]. He managed to raise enough money to get to the United States. He raised practically no money or support in the United States, and after three months left for England.

Sun Yat-sen arrived in London in September 1896. He was greeted warmly by Dr. Cantlie and became a guest in his home. The Chinese minister immediately contacted the British Foreign Office for permission to extradite Sun. The British Foreign Office refused to allow extradition. Chinese agents followed Sun everywhere. The Chinese Legation was located around the corner from the Cantlie home. Despite warnings from Dr. Cantlie and Dr. Manson to stay away, either Sun Yat-sen was indiscreet enough to enter the legation voluntarily or was lured there by promises of immunity. In any case, on October 11, 1896, he was taken prisoner and held in a locked room at the legation while the Chinese officials made arrangement to

---

6. A second daughter was born in November 1896.

smuggle him back to China by ship. Sun Yat-sen was finally able to convince a British porter to get a message to Dr. Cantlie. In fact, Dr. Cantlie had already been informed of Sun's capture by a British housekeeper. Cantlie and Manson contacted Scotland Yard, the Foreign Office, and the London Times. Lord Salisbury pursuaded the Times to sit on the story and ordered Scotland Yard to begin around the clock surveilance of the Chinese Legation and for the Thames River Police to survey all China bound ships.

Cantlie and Manson, distressed that nothing more substantial or immediate was being done to secure Sun's release, went to court to obtain a writ of Habeas Corpus. The London Globe picked up on the court action and the story broke in the Globe and the Times. An embarassed Foreign Office finally had to directly confront the Chinese Legation and force Sun Yat-sen's release. The story was carried in every major newspaper in the world outside of China. It made the world's most unsuccessful revolutionary a household name throughout the world.

Sun Yat-sen spent a total of nine months in England. Fifty-nine days of which were spent reading in the British Museum Library. It was during this time that he formulated his three principles of government for China: Socialism, Nationalism, and Democracy.

On July 2, 1897, Sun Yat-sen sailed for Montreal. He crossed Canada to Vancouver by train and immediately sailed for Yokohamma[7]. In Yokohamma, Sun Yat-sen was greeted by Miyazaki Torazo, an ardent Japanese nationalist and advocate of panaisianism. Miyazaki Torazo became a staunch supporter of Sun Yat-sen. Through Miyazaki Torazo, Sun Yat-sen gained powerful allies in Japan who hoped a successful revolution would gain them extensive concessions in China. Sun Yat-sen became wholly subsidized and was listed as a Chinese language teacher on the government payrolls.

In the meantime, a gentry reform movement was quietly being organized in China. The emperor appeared to be supportive, but the elite administrators and the Doweger Empress were adamantly opposed. The military backed the Dowager Empress and the administrators. The emperor was deposed and the Dowager Empress placed on the throne.

The Japanese hoped to unite Sun Yat-sen's movement[8] with the

---

7. Sun Yat-sen had been banned from Hong Kong in an order published March 1896, six months after the October 26 failed revolution.

8. Sun Yat-sen must have been something of a con man. His few supporters left in Hong Kong and Canton were unorganized, inactive and hardly constituted a cell. In no way could they be called a movement.

gentry reform movement. Always the opportunist, Sun Yat-sen readily agreed. The gentry movement, loyal to the Emperor and knowing Sun Yat-sen's anti Manchu stand, refused. In spite of this, Sun Yat-sen commitment to panaisianism won the Japanese over.

In 1898, Sun Yat-sen organized the support of Filipino insurgents against the United States in the Philippines. He arranged for shiploads of arms to be shipped from Japan. At least two ship loads were sent, though it is debatable whether either one successfully landed their cargo. The United States finally became aware of the Japan's support and Japan hastily put a stop to Sun Yat-sen's activities on their behalf. Nonetheless, Sun Yat-sen's profit on his Philippine activities allowed him to finance a new Hong Kong propaganda paper, the "Chinese Journal."

Also, in 1898, in central China, popular riots against foreign missionaries began. The riots expanded rapidly, extending to all foreigners by 1899, and became known as the Boxer rebellion. In May 1900, the attacks extended to foreign railroads, property and diplomats. A four-hundred man international force was sent to Peking to protect the foreign embassies. On June 20, 1900, the German Minister was shot and a siege of the foreign embassies in Peking began. A day later, China declared war on the foreign powers. By this time, twenty-three foreign warships were off the China coast and an allied expeditionary force of 48,000 men was being assembled.

The chaos of war was too much for Sun Yat-sen to ignore. He set sail for Hong Kong. He conferred with his followers in the harbor, and put three Japanese agents ashore to work with his group. He sailed on to Saigon and tried to persuade the French to supply him with arms and money to bribe Chinese troops. The French refused his request out of hand.

With clandestine approval of the British, Sun Yat-sen returned to Hong Kong and again tried to make an alliance with the deposed emperor's supporters. The deposed emperor's supporters wanted nothing to do with him. Sun Yat-sen and Dr. Ho then presented the foreign powers a proposal offering extensive concessions in China in return for support for Sun Yat-sen's proposed revolution. The local Hong Kong officials looked on the offer favorably, but it was promptly rejected by the British Foreign Office.

By September of 1901, the Boxer Rebellion had been put down by the foreign troops and the foreign powers had imposed a $300 million indemnity against China. The foreign powers instituted a lien against all Chinese taxes and duties and in many cases took over the duties of collecting the taxes. Sun Yat-sen decided that the popular antagonism against the foreigners and the resentment and discontentment over the indemnity made the population ripe for revolution.

Sun Yat-sen's plan was to have the Triads, acting as shock troops, attack from the outskirts of Kwangtung Provence to draw troops away from Canton. Then the cells in Hong Kong and Canton armed with weapons cached in Canton, would rally the coolies and crush the government troops between them. Again Sun Yat-sen's planning, preparation and execution was flawed. At the last minute it was obvious that the movement was uncoordinated, but it was too late to call it off. The revolutionaries remained active for two weeks before they were overwhelmed with twenty-thousand government troops, but they never succeeded in rallying the general population within or without Canton. Sun Yat-sen hastily retreated to the arms of his mistress in Japan.

Little is known of Sun Yat-sen's activities over the next two years. However, by 1903, there was evidence of a strong nationalist movement unrelated to Sun Yat-sen within China. This movement viewed Sun Yat-sen as an uncultured outlaw. He was unable to approach this group on an intellectual, ideological, political or military level. To remedy this, Sun Yat-sen convinced the Japanese military to set up a secret military academy to train Chinese officers for a nationalist revolutionary army. The course was only eight months, but included basic tactics and arms manufacture. Cheng Kai-shek was a member of the first class. Sun Yat-sen also tried his hand at writing for some of the papers controlled by the nationalists.

In late 1903 or early 1904, Sun Yat-sen returned to Hawaii with a new nationalist message and started a new organization, The Chinese Revolutionary Army. After years of alliances with the criminal groups, the Triads, Sun Yat-sen finally took their oath and became a Triad member. After about four months in the Islands, he entered the United States with forged documents. Again he failed to rally funds or support, but he did succeed in having an appeal to the American people published through his missionary contacts. There was no appreciable impact, and Sun Yat-sen left for London, Brussels, Paris, and Berlin. He spoke to Chinese students wherever he went. The students opposed his secret-society based movement and preferred the mainstream intellectual movement he was not a part of. He had to change his message to include the intellectual movement. He finally recruited a small number to his Revolutionary Army.

In 1905, he visited the Socialist International Headquarters and sold them on the idea of a nonexistant Chinese Socialist Movement and that he was Chief of the Chinese Socialist Revolutionary Army.

The Japanese rout of the Russians in the 1905 Russo-Japanese war, bolstered Sun Yat-sen's faith in his panasian theories. By July 19, 1905, he was back in Japan. He was greeted warmly because of his strong panasian stand. The Black Dragon Society, the ultranationalist, militant, right-wing Japanese political society invited all the various Chinese revolutionary factions to hear Sun Yat-sen plead for unity. Sun Yat-sen actually brought little to the table. Other than his well known name and his connection to the criminal-Triads, his movement was politically and financially bankrupt. However, his obvious Japanese support, especially that of the military, lent him stature. The various factions agreed to unify under Sun Yat-sen as the China Federal Association (AKA the China Alliance) with a four point platform:

1. Expulsion of the Manchus;

2. Restoration of Chinese Rule;

3. Establishment of a Republic;

4. Equalization of Land Rights.

Huang Hsing was elected second in command, and the recently formed student magazine "20th Century China" became their party publication.

For the remainder of 1905 the Alliance under Sun Yat-sen began a program of inciting local unrest and constructing a constitution for their proposed new government. The alliance immediately ran into problems with the proposed constitution. While all factions more or less agreed on the four point platform, there was wide disagreement on the nature of the country's new constitution. The problems were exacerbated by Sun Yat-sen's frequent departures on fund raising jaunts.

In December 1906, there was an uprising of peasants and miners. The rebels fought a guerilla war and held out against government forces for over one month. The uprising proved to the alliance that its attention should be directed to forming an organization that could mobilize, direct and sustain popular uprisings. Huang Hsing was far more adept than Sun Yat-sen in these areas and began taking an ever more prominent role in the Alliance.

By 1907, the Japanese no longer felt supporting the nationalist effort in China was to their advantage and expelled Sun Yat-sen and thirty-eight other nationalist leaders. The Japanese gave Sun Yat-sen a $25,000.00

golden parachute as he left for Hanoi[9] The money caused a great deal of disent among the leaders of the Alliance, but the group remained unified.

Sun Yat-sen remained in French-Indo-China throughout 1907 and used up his funding on fruitless attempts to stir up riots and uprisings over the border in China. On January 25, 1908, the French finally expelled Sun Yat-sen from Indo-China and banned his return. Sun left for another unsuccessful fundraising trip in Europe and then the United States. Sun spent countless hours flirting with a group of conspiritors that included Homer Lea, a self styled military expert[10]; Banker C.B. Boothe; W.W. Allen, a consulting engineer; and J.P. Morgan. The scheme came to naught when J.P. Morgan withdrew his support.

While Sun Yat-sen was away, Huang began recruiting elements of the military and police. After the deposed Emperor and the Dowager Empress died within a day of each other in mid-November 1908, Huang

---

9. Rumor has it that the actual amount was much more, but the exact amount, if any, he received under the table has never been revealed.

10. Lea's book on Japanese aims in the Pacific did predict Pearl Harbor. In return for sponsoring Sun's revolution the group wanted control of China's railroads for ninety-nine years, control of China's Central Bank, National mineral right concessions, and a twent-five year coinage concession.

began making serious inroads into both services.

Sun Yat-sen finally hit the financial jackpot in Vancouver, British Columbia on February 11, 1911. He sold bonds in the amount of $HK85,000.00 to Chinese expatriates. He took that amount and $HK100,000.00 that mysteriously appeared from Southeast Asia[11] and immediately purchased arms for the next uprising, scheduled for April 11,1911. However, on April 8, a miner killed a Manchu official and the revolution broke out without the planned coordination. The revolution failed, with over 100 of the Alliance killed. This was Sun Yat-sen's third failed attempt at revolution (his fourth if his activities in French-Indo-China were considered).

Another group, The Literary Society, not part of the Alliance and without foreign support or any connection to Sun Yat-sen, began organizing a secret army. On October 9, 1911. an accidental explosion blew up one of their arms caches in Hankow and stimulated a premature uprising. On October 10th they seized a strategic armory and won a decisive battle against

---

11. Sun always claimed the money was from his fund-raising activities in Southeast Asia. However, many believe it was the unofficial funds given him by the Japanese when he was expelled.

government troops. The victorious rebels went on to take Hankow and Hanyang. The Alliance took advantage of the troop diversion stimulated by the uprising and seized Canton and parts of Kwangtung Provence.

Sun Yat-sen was not part of either uprising. He was in Colorado on another speaking tour. He went home via Washington, DC and London and although he got support from several arms corporations, neither government would support him. In fact, the British Government already had recognized Yaun Shi Kai, the stategist of the revolution and in control of the military, as the one man capable of bringing order out of chaotic China. Sun Yat-sen, always the opportunist, wired that Yaun was acceptable to him and he would support him at a nationalist organizational meeting to be held in Shanghai.

Sun Yat-sen arrived in Shanghai on Christmas day, 1911, ahead of Yaun. As the best-known name connected with the revolution, he received a hero's welcome. The Alliance took advantage of the situation and Sun Yat-sen was elected president of the newly declared Chinese Republic. Sun Yat-sen knew the real power lay with Yaun and that he was a dead man if he did not make it clear he was merely acting as a stand -in until Yaun had finished assuming control of the remainder of China. He wired Yaun making it clear that once Yaun was ready, he would step down and Yaun would merely have to swear allegiance to the new republic to step into the presidency. The situation was such that Sun's performance as president could be nothing but underwhelming. Sun remained in office, as a figurehead, a mere three months.

Sun Yat-sen was now shunted off to be director of Railroad planning. A job that made him an international joke because he was so inept. He was a political nonentity and viewed as an impractical idealist whose only virtue was as a fund raiser. His popular nickname was "Big Noise Sun"

Yaun proved to be a disappointment to Sun Yat-sen and the Alliance. From the start he favored the status quo, The Alliance reacted by joining several splinter groups to form a new political party, the Kuomintang. Sun Yat-sen was one of the directors of the new party. As Yaun conslidated his power, he showed obvious disdain for the republic's constitiution and entered into a usurious loan arragement with the western powers without parliamentary approval. Then, in 1913, he assainated one of the Kuomintang leaders. The Kuomintang challenged Yaun on the loan and accused him of the killing. Yaun answered the challenge by firing Kuomintang Governors and placing his troops on alert.

A Kuomintang general started the second revolution. Yaun put the revolt down easily and was recognized internationally as China's leader. Again, Sun Yat-sen was able to escape to Japan. This time he was ignored. Without funds or followers he put together a few Chinese into a secret society he gave the grandoise name of "The Chinese Revolutionary Army" with, of course, Sun Yat-sen as leader. They adopted all of Sun's pre-revolution slogans and platforms.

In 1914, when WWI broke out, Japan siezed all of the German holdings in China and extended those holdings to include all of Schantung Provence. When China protested, the Japanese Government delivered Twenty-One Demands with the intention of becoming the preeminent foreign power in China. The Chinese were up in arms. An effective anti Japan boycott was started. Japan landed 30,000 troops. Sun Yat-sen once again sided with Japan and tried to regain some support in the panasian movement. Yaun used the crisis to declare himself Emperor.

On October 25, 1915, the forty-nine year old Sun Yat-sen married twenty-three year old Rosamonde Soong[12]. Rosamonde was an American

---

12. The the three Soong sisters all married politically powerful men. Sister Ailing (Sun Yat-sen's former secretary) married H.H. Kung, and sister Meiling married Chaing Kai-shek.

college graduate and the daughter of one Sun Yat-sen's close friends. His missionary friends and his father-in-law, were shocked by the fact he had never divorced his first wife who was still living in Hawaii and being supported by his older brother.

In November 1915, a revolt with no connection with Sun Yat-sen started in Southwest China. Japan sent Sun Yat-sen and advisors to assist the revolt. With monies supplied by Japan, Sun Yat-sen began bribing government troops and hiring mercenaries. With Japanese help the revolt survived, but did not prevail. On June 6, 1916, Yaun died of uremia. The central government troops disintegrated into a system of regional warlords and the republic ruled in name only.

Sun Yat-sen again was out of power. He wrote books, traveled, and spoke. He advocated China's neutrality in WWI[13]. Finally, in June 1917 he tried his hand at revolution again. A militarist had seized power and restored the Manchu Dynasty. Sun Yat-sen had some supporters in the Southern Naval Command. He boarded one of the vessels and the entire command sailed into Canton and seized the city. Sympathetic members of Parliament

---

13. There is some evidence that Sun Yat-sen was subsidized by the Germans for his antiwar stand.

moved to Canton and Sun Yat-sen formed a millitary government with himself as Grand Marshall. Again Sun Yat-sen had little real power and he was unable to gain alliances outside the city. By 1918 he had lost his title and what little power he had and again escaped to Japan.

In July 1918, he settled in the French Concession in Shanghai. There he continued to write, courted Lenin, studied the Russian revolution, and continued to play footsie with the Japanese.

By 1920, he had assumed an anti-Japan stand favored by the Soviets and had once again become active in the Kuomintang. He took control of the party in Canton and of the city itself. He declared his party was the legitimate government of China and became the figurehead for reform advocating a republic, democracy and socialism. He began moving north militarily and was soon defeated both on the field and within his party. This time Sun Yat-sen escaped to Hong Kong. Significantly, Chiang Kai-shek, his top military leader, remained loyal and he had scattered support within the Kuomintang throughout China.

Now with little support outside China, Sun Yat-sen again turned to Soviet-Russia. On December 21, 1921, Lenin sent J.F.M. Sneevliet as an emmisary to Sun. Sneevliet was a Dutch Communist who had previously set up a united front in French IndoChina, and earlier that year had started the Chinese Communist Party. Sneevliet was unimpressed with Sun Yat-sen's political thinking, but thought an alliance with the Kuomintang might serve both their purposes. Sun Yat-sen was not yet ready to renounce all efforts with the West or Japan and put Sneevliet off. However, within six months he realized that despite his personal popularity and name recognition in China, his political power was nil. On August 14, 1922, Sun Yat-sen agreed to a united front between the Kuomintang and the Chinese Communist Party[14]. From this time on Sun Yat-sen went public with his pro-soviet sympathies.

With Soviet advisors aboard, in January 1923 the Kuomintang adopted a new constitiution and added national self-determination and international equality to its platform. Its organization, however, was now modeled after that of the Communist Central Committee. In the same month, Sun Yat-sen and his supporters again took control of Canton. Immediately the U.S.S.R. pledged him support and recognized him as the voice of China.

---

14. At the time the alliance was made, the Chinese Communist Party probably numbered less than their claimed 300 members, and Sun undoubtedly believed they would be an insignificant fraction of the Kuomintang. The communists maintained dual memberships.

By 1923, the Soviets were subsidizing Sun to the tune of about $1,000,000.00 per year even though Sun's govenment only controlled Canton. The rest of Kwangtung Provence was firmly in the control of the warlords. Despite his ties to the U.S.S.R., Sun Yat-sen never stopped looking elsewhere for a better deal.

In the late Fall of 1923, the Soviets sent Michael Borodin and two Soviet Army officers to Sun. From then on Borodin became the Kuuomintang's guiding spirit. Borodin added land reform and modern labor laws to Sun's platform. He raised Sun Yat-sen's popularity in China and lowered it internationally by insisting Sun protest the collection of Chinese taxes by foreign governments[15]. On the strength of Sun's renewed popularity, Borodin pushed through a motion that made Sun Yat-sen the Kuomintang's leader for life.

By 1924, Borodin and his activities were beginning to cause friction within the party, but the alliance held into 1925. There were more than 1000 Soviet advisors working in Canton and additional trained agitators working with peasants and laborers all across China. There was a full blown war

---

15. The Western governments sent gun boats and laughed at him.

college manned by Russian officers and supplied with Russian arms. General Vasily Blucher arrived to advise Chiang Kai-shek, the Kuomintang's top general.

On September 12, 1924, the Kuomintang forces began to move north to take Kwangtung provence from the warlords. A second force was deligated to disarm the Canton Merchants' militia. Both moves were highly successful and Sun Yat-sen was now a force to be reckoned with. Sun was invited to Peking to take part in the formation of a new government. For reasons that have never been adequately explained, instead of leaving for Peking immediately, Sun Yat-sen set sail for Japan. Whatever his reasons for going were, he returned from Japan without any tangible results and arrived in Peking too late to contribute to the conference. He was in noticeably poor health.

By the end of December, Sun Yat-sen's health had deteriorated considerably. He was admitted to the Rockefeller Foundation's Peking Union Medical College Hospital. After an extensive work up, an exploratory laparotomy confirmed the diagnosis of incurable liver cancer. He died at home on March 12, 1925.

How Sun, whose only talent appears to have been persistant failure, came to become the icon he is today remains a mystery. Yet to both sides of the Taiwan straits, he is the George Washington, Thomas Jefferson and Thomas Paine of the Chinese Republic. The surgeon who cured his country.

SIR ARTHUR CONAN DOYLE:
Physician, Writer, Patriot, Spiritualist
&
The Man Who Hated Sherlock Holmes

I'll tell you a most serious fact,
That opium dries a mucous tract,
And constipates and causes thirst,
And stimulates the heart at first
And then allows its strength to fall,
Relaxing the capillary wall,
The cerebrum is first affected,
Lungs and sexuals don't forget.[16]

Arthur Conan Doyle was born in Edinburgh in May 1859. The Doyles were an old aristocratic Irish-Catholic English family. His Grandfather, John Doyle, was London's best known illustrator and satirical artist of his time. His two uncles were also well known artists and illustrators. Arthur's father, Charles Doyle, was the black sheep of the family and its only unsuccessful member. He lacked the talent of his brothers and had neither the ambition nor drive to find an occupation in

---

16. Verse scrawled on the margin of one of Arthur Conan Doyle's medical school textbooks.

another field. Through family connections, a job was finally found for Charles in the Edinburgh City administration. He was given the title of architect, but from his job description it appears he was little more than a draftsman in the city's engineering department. The family also arranged for Charles to board with a down-on-their-luck Irish-Catholic family, the Foleys. The income for boarding Charles was welcome. There was also a Foley daughter of marriageable age, Mary, and both families considered this as an extra incentive for the arrangement. Charles followed the path of least resistance and soon wed Mary. Arthur was the second of seven children born of this union and the oldest boy. Throughout his entire employment, Charles never received a raise in salary or an advancement in rank. The family was never poverty-stricken but was always on the economic edge.

By the time of Arthur's birth in 1859, Charles was seeking solace in the bottle. He contributed little or nothing to Arthur's upbringing. Although Arthur and his mother had a close emotional bond, she was overwhelmed with her ever-increasing family. and Arthur was essentially on his own. He was streetwise and tough. He attended local schools and was a voracious reader of adventure fiction, but his frequent fights, petty thievery and occasional brushes with local authorities seemed to mark him for an uncertain future. However, his mother believed he was bright and given the proper stimulus and guidance he could change direction. When Arthur was 10 years old, his mother went to his Doyle grandfather and uncles and asked them send Arthur to a private Jesuit school. The Doyles too thought Arthur was bright and agreed to finance his education.

The school was strictly regimented with a strict adherence to an extensive set of rules. Arthur rebelled at the antiquated curriculum and the strict discipline and was the frequent recipient of rather brutal corporal punishment. Despite his many run-ins with the Jesuit brothers, he excelled at his studies and was an outstanding school athlete. His instructors considered him to be a brilliant student. He began a regular correspondence with his mother that continued well into his adult life. He wrote poetry and essays. Much to the Jesuit's distress, he continued to be a voracious reader of adventure fiction. At age 16, Arthur graduated with honors.

He was eligible for entrance into the University, but the London Doyles thought Arthur was too young, and sent him to Feldkirch, a Jesuit school in Volarberg, Austria. The year was supposed to teach Arthur German and allow him to take some advanced courses. Arthur refused to mix with the European students. Taking only courses offered in English, he spent all of his time with fellow English students. Consequently, even though he got glowing reports from his instructors, he learned little or no

German. However, during this year, Arthur discovered Edgar Allan Poe and the birth of the detective story.

Arthur returned home with rather vague ideas about being a writer. His uncle, Michael Conan, was a well-known journalist and believed Arthur had great talent as a writer. His grandfather and Doyle uncles also thought he had great talent. His mother, however, thought writing was an uncertain way to earn a living. She wanted him to live at home and study medicine at the university in Edinburgh. Even though Arthur had absolutely no interest in medicine, he felt he could not disappoint his mother. He agreed to enter medical school.

Arthur described medical school as, "One long weary grind at botany, chemistry, anatomy, physiology, and a whole list of compulsory subjects, many of which have very indirect bearing on the art of curing." In his memoirs, Arthur Conan Doyle claims he spent his time chasing girls, engaging in sports at every opportunity and reading every adventure story he could get his hands on. He also had multiple fist fights and was considered an accomplished boxer.

Some time during his medical school years he began writing stories for extra money. He sold his first story, *The Mystery of Sasassa Valley,* to Chamber's Journal in 1879. *The Mystery of Sasassa Valley* most closely fits in the science fiction genre of today. He did not attach his name to this story or the next twelve or thirteen he wrote. It is uncertain why he published so many early works anonymously. The story was well received and his family seems to have known he wrote it.

Despite Arthur's description of medical school and his activities during his school years, he must have been an excellent student. He was hired by Joseph Bell, Professor of Surgery and the outstanding surgeon in Edinburgh at the time, as Bell's outpatient clerk. A position considered a great honor among the students. Bell was renowned for his tremendous deductive abilities. He was able to determine facts about patients and their diagnosis before they said a word about their problems. Arthur was fascinated by the man and his abilities.

Arthur also did some independent research as a student and published a paper entitled *Gelseminum*[17] *as a Poison*.

While Arthur was in the third year of medical school, his father was finally institutionalized with epilepsy and what was diagnosed as alcoholic dementia. The financial situation at home was desperate. His oldest sister, Annette, left home to become a governess in Europe and two younger sisters

---

17. Gelsemine = An alkaloid found in the Yellow Jasmine plant.

left shortly thereafter. Arthur decided to cram a year's studies into six months and work the remainder of the year. Through a fellow student, Arthur heard of a job as surgeon aboard the whaling ship, *Hope*. It sounded like the kind of adventure Arthur had been seeking all his life, and on the 28th of February, 1880, he stepped on board for a trip to the arctic.

Within fifteen minutes of boarding the ship, Arthur was embroiled in his first fist fight with one of the stewards. His prowess as a street fighter proved to be the catalyst for the crew accepting him as the surgeon. The ship turned out to be as much a sealer as whaler, but Arthur saw the North Coast of Norway and the ice fields of the Arctic. The trip was thrilling to him, and became one of the highlights of his life. The Captain of the *Hope* summed up Arthur Conan Doyles' service with these words, "You can fight, mend a broken leg or any other wound and write a true account of it when it is all over."

Arthur returned to medical school for his final year and received his Bachelor of Medicine and Master of Surgery degrees. He immediately took another job as a ship's surgeon on the ship *Mayumba*. However, this was the passenger ship, not a whaler. Its destination was Africa and not the Arctic. Arthur found the passengers much more demanding than the crew members of the *Hope*. His boxing didn't enhance his rapport with the passengers. The intense heat did not enhance his ability to cope or his tolerance. To make things even worse, he developed a tropical fever. Because Arthur was the only doctor, he had to care for himself and almost died. Several of the passengers died of the same fever during his illness. He returned to England convinced that he had to find a practice on shore.

In 1882, Arthur went to London to speak with his aunts and uncles[18]. They assured him that if he set up practice in London, the family's endorsement would immediately make him the most sought-after Catholic physician in the city. Although he knew such an endorsement would mean a large and lucrative practice, Arthur declined the family help. He stated that he did not want to deceive his family into unwittingly assuming he was Catholic. He had broken with the church years earlier. The family was appalled and withdrew all offers of help. A medical school friend, Dr. George Budd, asked Arthur to join his practice in Plymouth.

Budd was an unorthodox, charismatic, and very successful practitioner. However, his practice was based mainly on his own persona, and Arthur really never fit in. After about three months had elapsed, Dr. Budd asked Arthur to leave, but offered to help Arthur set up a practice of

---

18. It is not clear if his Grandfather had passed away or was just absent from the meeting.

his own.

Arthur set up practice in a vacant dental office in Portsmouth. Dr. Budd's promised help never materialized. Arthur had no contacts in Portsmouth - - no friends or other sources of patient referrals. His waiting room was empty. He continued writing as a way to keep some income coming in. Finally, because he excelled at sports, he thought he might make contacts within the sporting clubs. He joined a cricket club and a rugby club and then the Science and Literature Society. Through the clubs, he met the executive of a local insurance company and began acting as the company physician. In addition, he got some employment at the local eye hospital, although the exact nature of the work there is unknown. His practice began to grow slowly and although he was never prosperous, he began earning a living. One of his patients, Major General Dawson, was a spiritualist and introduced the subject to a very receptive Arthur Conan Doyle. Arthur was fascinated by spiritualism and it seemed to become a new religion for him.

By 1885, he felt secure enough to propose marriage to Louise Hawkins, the attractive sister of one of his patients. Louise ("Touie") remains a rather shadowy figure. Arthur's biographers have little or nothing to say about her, and Arthur never mentions her by name in his memoirs. This is even more strange given the fact that pictures of her show she was extremely attractive, and the few references there are to her, paint her as an intelligent, supportive, loving wife and mother. She also seems to have influenced Arthur's writing. Coincident with the marriage, Arthur's writing became more serious. His writing breakthrough came with the publication of *J. Habakuk Jephson's Statement* in Cornhill Magazine. This piece was based on the story of the ship *Mary Celeste* and, like his first published story, would probably be considered science fiction today. The sale of *J. Habakuk Jephson's Statement* paid for Arthur's office rent for an entire year. Arthur then tried two different novels. Neither of them could hang together well enough to satisfy Arthur, and both were eventually scrapped.

Finally, Arthur decided to write an Edgar Allan Poe like mystery novel based on the deductive abilities of his Edinburgh mentor, Dr. Joseph Bell. The result was the first Sherlock Holmes novel, *The Scarlet Letter*[19], published by Ward, Lock & Co. in 1887. Arthur received twenty-five pounds (25£) for the book. The book received great critical reviews but no lasting success or fame for its author. Arthur then tried his hand at a historical novel. *Micah Clarke* was published by Longmans Press in 1889. This novel was critically and popularly successful and Arthur's income from

---

19. The title was changed to *A Study in Scarlet* for publication in the United States to avoid confusion with Hawthorne's popular novel of the same name.

writing began to exceed his meager medical practice income. Over the next two years, Arthur was extremely productive. He published a second Sherlock Holmes book, *Sign of Four (The Sign of the Four* in the United States). Again, the book was well received by the critics in England but never created much of a stir. Notwithstanding its lack of popularity in England, the book was a runaway best seller in the United States and Canada. As many as twelve different pirated editions of the book were eventually published[20], but it is doubtful that Arthur received much financial gain from the book. In 1890, Arthur published his widely acclaimed historical novel *The White Company*. Critics acclaimed it the finest historical novel ever written. It was the English best seller Arthur had been waiting for. The book went through fifty printings during Arthur's lifetime and is still in print today. It can be found on the shelves of every library in England, Canada and the United States.

Arthur was now financially independent of his practice income. The royalties from *Micah Clarke* and *The White Company* offered Arthur and his family a higher standard of living than was ever possible from the meager

---

20. There was little or no copyright protection for English publications in America or vice versa.

medical practice. Arthur finally managed to complete his thesis,[21] and received his MD from Edinburgh. He then closed his Portsmouth office and, without much planning or consideration, went off to study Ophthalmology in Vienna.

Arthur's German consisted of a few schoolboy phrases and he was absolutely lost in the Vienna Eye Clinics. After a few weeks of frustration, he left. He spent some time with a Paris ophthalmologist he had an introduction to, and then more time with an oculist learning about lenses. He then went to London and opened an office as an ophthalmologist. He sat in an empty office and wrote stories to kill the time.

Fortunately for Arthur, the demographics of London were changing because of efficient rail transportation. More and more middle class London workers were living outside the city where there was less congestion and cheaper property and commuting by rail to work. Stories in small literary magazines were the preferred reading material of the commuters. The most popular of these magazines was Strand Magazine. In 1891, Arthur submitted two short Sherlock Holmes stories to Strand Magazine. The stories were an instant hit.

---

21. On Tabes Dorsalis.

Shortly after submitting the stories, Arthur developed a severe case of influenza and, while he was home recovering, decided he was a writer and not a doctor. He closed his ill-fated ophthalmology office and moved into a large house in one of London's suburbs.

Strand Magazine was desperate for more Sherlock Holmes Stories, but Arthur wanted to write another historical novel. Hoping to get the Strand Magazine off his back, Arthur quoted the Strand what he considered an unreasonable amount per story, £35. Much to his surprise Strand Magazine contracted with him for another six stories at that price. The Strand hired Sidney Paget to illustrate the stories. They had made a mistake. They really wanted Sidney Paget's brother Walter to do the illustrations, but became confused. However, the mistake immortalized Walter Paget. Sidney Paget used his brother Walter as his model for Sherlock Holmes, and that picture of Walter Paget is the Sherlock Holmes that still prevails today. Walter Paget always wore a deerstalker hat and Inverness cape when he was in the country and Sidney Paget placed Sherlock Holmes in the same dress, making the two items the Sherlock Holmes trademark.

As the publication of the last of the six stories approached, The Strand contacted Arthur for another six stories. Arthur eager to be finished with Sherlock Holmes and start a "more important work" quickly raised his price to £50 per story. The Strand readily agreed.

As soon as he completed the six promised stories for the Strand, he started a book for his American audience, *The Refugees*. He had barely started on *The Refugees,* when the Strand editors were back asking for a dozen more Sherlock Holmes stories. Arthur was sick of the stories and wanted to stop writing them. However, his mother loved them and urged him to continue writing them. Probably as much to please his mother as for the money he would receive, Arthur agreed to negotiate a new contract for twelve stories with Strand Magazine. For the ensuing twelve stories, Arthur demanded and received 1000 pounds(£1000), making him the highest paid writer in England. Nonetheless, Arthur had made up his mind to kill off Sherlock Holmes in this series of stories.

Asking for a delay in delivery of the new stories, Arthur and Louise left on a trip to Europe. In Switzerland he saw the Reichenback Falls and developed the plot for Sherlock Holmes' demise. When, in 1893, the Strand published the last story, *The Final Problem,* in which Holmes purportedly falls to his death in the falls, the public reaction was beyond anything Arthur or the Strand contemplated. Men wore black arm bands or hat bands. Arthur Conan Doyle received hate mail. The Strand's circulation dropped by 20,000 readers. Arthur Conan Doyle appears to have been the only person in

England glad to see the end of Sherlock Holmes.

1893 was a momentous year in other ways as well. Charles Doyle finally died and Louise was diagnosed with tuberculosis. Arthur immediately packed up the entire family and moved to Switzerland where the mountain air supposedly cured tuberculosis. Arthur, as full of energy as ever, loved the mountains. He hiked, climbed and, remembering the Norwegians he had seen on skis when he was on the whaling ship, sent for four pairs of skis. As Arthur suspected, Switzerland was ideal ski country. Skis were completely unknown in Switzerland and Arthur created quite a stir as he traveled far and wide on his skis. The four pairs of skis introduced by Arthur Conan Doyle were the seedlings of the entire Swiss ski industry.

By 1894, Louise appeared well enough for Arthur to leave her alone in Switzerland while he completed a long awaited lecture tour of North America. Arthur's fame in America had preceded his fame in England and he remained as popular, or even more popular, there than in England. The lecture tour turned out to be the most successful tour in the history of the United States. Attendance exceeded expectations everywhere Arthur appeared. His finances buoyed by the successful tour, Arthur returned to Switzerland and began writing a new historical fiction series for Strand Magazine. The series featured a Napoleonic army officer, Brigadier Gerard.

Brigadier Gerard stories were well received but had none of the rabid popularity of Sherlock Holmes.

Louise's health seemed to be steadily improving, and, when on a trip to England to settle some business affairs, Arthur heard that the air in Surrey had cured tuberculosis, he decided to move the family back to England. He bought a site in Surrey and arranged for a house to be built. While the house was being built, Arthur and Louise took a trip to Egypt and Sudan. Arthur's next novel, *The Tragedy of the Korosko* was based on the trip to the Sudan and the fictionalized seizure of a tour group by the Dervishes. Just as Arthur and Louise were about to leave Egypt, Kitchener began mobilizing troops for the march against the Dervishes and control of the Sudan. Arthur volunteered as a war correspondent, but was always at the wrong place at the wrong time and gave up the whole idea before there was any real action. Arthur and Louise returned to England in the spring of 1896.

Back in England, the family moved into their new home in Surrey. The next spring, at a local party, Arthur met and fell in love with Jean Leckie, the beautiful daughter of a wealthy Scottish family. Jean Leckie was equally in love with Arthur. Reportedly, the pair agreed not to consummate their affair until Louise died. The pair considered their admittedly morbid agreement the epitome of romantic chivalry. Unfortunately, Louise fooled them and lived almost another ten years.

Meanwhile, living in Southern England agreed with Arthur. In the next two years he wrote *Sir Nigel,* a sequel to *White Company*, and a historical play, *Waterloo*. Both were critical and financial successes.

In 1899, the Boer War broke out. Arthur, now forty, immediately volunteered for a combat command. The War Office turned him down, but because of his notoriety, finally thought it was good public relations to put him in charge of a field hospital. Arthur went to South Africa and served for one year. He kept meticulous notes and copies of orders, bulletins and dispatches and, upon returning to England, wrote *The Great Boer War*. *The Great Boer War* was considered the definitive history of the conflict at the time it was published. The last chapter of *The Great Boer War* was devoted to recommendations for modernizing the British Army. All of Arthur's recommendations were ignored, but, had they been adopted, would have saved countless British lives in World War I.

Following the Boer War, Britain was criticized throughout the world for its behavior against the Boers. It was accused of concentration camps, rape, torture, and a reckless burnt earth policy. Germany led the clamor against Britain. Arthur immediately entered the fray, and in 1902 published the 60,000 word *The Cause and Conduct of the War in South Africa*. The book sold close to 500,000 copies in all its translations, and was hailed universally as a fair and even-handed report of British conduct. The book seemed to quiet most of the overt criticism. Arthur was knighted later in 1902 for "services to the nation," almost certainly for *The Cause and Conduct of the War in South Africa*.

In 1901, Arthur got the idea for another Sherlock Holmes story. Hating to waste a good plot, yielding to popular demand, and against his better judgment, Arthur brought back Sherlock Holmes in *The Hound of the Baskervilles*. Holmes remained dead, but Dr. Watson tells the story as a serial in Strand Magazine. The magazine's circulation increased by 30,000 during the run of the serial. After the publication of *The Hound of the Baskervilles*, several factors seem to have combined to make Arthur change his mind about Sherlock Holmes' death. First, the reception of the story exceeded even Strand Magazine's expectations. Second, the American market was willing to pay top dollar for reprint rights of any future stories. And finally, and probably most importantly, Jean Leckie had been urging him to resurrect Holmes and had even suggested the mechanism. So, in 1903 an new series of Sherlock Holmes stories started in Strand Magazine with *The Adventure of the Empty House*. Arthur never attempted to kill off Holmes again and Sherlock Holmes stories appeared periodically until shortly before Arthur's death.

Louise Doyle died in 1906, and in 1907 Arthur married Jean Leckie. The marriage was an unusually happy one. Arthur and Louise's two children, Kingsley and Mary, now teenagers, knew and liked Jean and had expected their father to remarry. Arthur and Jean had three additional children, Denis, Adrian and Jean. Arthur wrote a book about their childhood, *Three of Them*. Jean was much stronger and more athletic than Louise and was a great companion to Arthur's outdoor activities. In 1911 the two of them engaged in a continental automobile race through France organized by Germany. Arthur finished the race certain that the Germans were bent on war, but his warnings seem to have fallen on deaf ears.

Following Louise's death, Arthur turned his attention to what he considered cases of miscarriage of justice and social reform. He was active in several prominent English court cases, and the English Court of Criminal Appeals was said to be established as a result of his work on the Edalji case.

His book *Crime of the Congo* was credited with bettering conditions in the Belgian Congo. However, not all his writing involved injustice. In 1912, Arthur reverted back to the original genre of his stories, science fiction. *Lost World* was the first of the dinosaur books. It formed the basis of the movie of the same name and was the forerunner of every lost continent, dinosaur movie up to and including Jurassic Park. The book was the first of a four book series and was followed by *The Poison Belt, When the World Screamed,* and *The Disintegration Machine.*

As World War I approached, Arthur Conan Doyle renewed his cries to reorganize the armed forces and warned of the danger to Britain of Germany's submarine fleet. But, again his warnings were ignored. In 1914 Arthur made another tour of the United States and Canada that was almost as successful as his first. When the War finally erupted in August of 1914, Arthur immediately volunteered and was turned down. Undaunted, Arthur formed a Civilian Reserve Corps. Although the government shut down this paramilitary group, it was the impetus for the formal reserve corps. While the war was still on, Arthur began work of a history of the War. His six-volume *History of the Great War* is still, by far, the clearest and most objective history of WWI one can find.

WWI changed Arthur's life in other ways as well. Jean's brother was killed as were his sister Connie's husband, Willie Hornung, and two of his nephews. The killed brother-in-laws were his closest friends. Then he lost his only brother and his son, Kingsley, in the Influenza Pandemic of 1918. These personal losses turned Arthur's complete attention to spiritualism. Arthur attributes this shift to spiritualism to a "Message from the Grave". Some speculate that Arthur and Willie Hornung had made an agreement to try to communicate to each other if one died, but no one is certain of exactly what Arthur meant by the "message from the grave." In any case, Arthur devoted the remainder of his life to trying to communicate with the dead.

Jean appears to have been as involved in spiritualism as Arthur. Those that knew the couple could not believe how they were taken in by the charlatans that approached them. Houdini, who was also interested in spiritualism and spent his later life debunking the frauds, called Arthur a monomaniac on the subject of spiritualism. Arthur could not believe Houdini did not have super spiritualist powers even though Houdini explained every trick he carried out. A classic story involves a message Jean gave Houdini, supposedly from his mother. The message was headed by a cross and was in perfect English. Houdini carefully explained why the message was a fraud. First, his mother was Jewish and would never have headed a message with a cross. Second, his mother only spoke Hungarian and Yiddish and never could have written anything in perfect English. Arthur never spoke to Houdini again, he was outraged that Houdini could doubt Jean. Although Arthur's writing was consumed for the remainder of his life with the thirteen or more books he wrote on spiritualism, he managed one more Sherlock

Holmes story, *The Adventure of Shocombie Old Place*, for Strand Magazine in 1927. Arthur Conan Doyle died of a heart attack in 1930 at the age of 71.

Much as Arthur feared, the name Sherlock Holmes is recognized by far more people than is the name Arthur Conan Doyle. In fact, more people believe in the existence of Sherlock Holmes than any other fictional character and more movies have been made about him than any other fictional character. The company that now occupies 221B Baker Street has to employ one person just to take care of the correspondence addressed to Sherlock Holmes. Other authors have continued Sherlock Holmes stories to the present day. Biographies of Sherlock Holmes have been published. Two types of Sherlock Holmes clubs exist in almost every country in the Western world. The first type of club celebrates Sherlock Holmes as the greatest fictional detective of all time. The second type of club maintains Sherlock Holmes was a real person with Dr. Watson retelling his cases and Arthur Conan Doyle being the mere scribe. It is up to the reader to decide whether this devotion to a fictional character is a tribute to its bigger than life author or whether the fictional character has diminished the meaning the author's life.

GERTRUDE STEIN

Most of us know enough about Gertrude Stein to at least connect her to her famous quotes from *A Long Gay Book* or *Sacred Emily,* "A day is a day is a day" and "A rose is a rose is a rose" respectively. Others would be able to identify her as the author of *The Autobiography of Alice B. Toklas,* but few know of her medical connection. Much of our ignorance probably stems from the fact Gertrude Stein was an unkempt, physically unappealing, and, to all but a favored few, a generally unpleasant individual. Thus commentators concentrated on her work and not the individual.

Gertrude Stein was born in Allegheny, Pennsylvania, which she described as a Pittsburgh suburb, on February 3, 1874 to Daniel Stein and his wife, the former Amelia Keyser. She was the youngest of seven children, only five living. Her grandparents were wealthy, although the exact nature of their business interests is unclear. Shortly after Gertrude's birth, her father quarreled with his family and severed whatever relationships he had with the family business. In 1875, Daniel packed up the family and moved to Vienna. Whatever his reasons for moving to Vienna were, it was an unwise decision. He struggled to make a living. Relations with his wife deteriorated, and the children were left to the care of servants. After three years and his wife's threats to leave him if he did not leave Vienna, Daniel moved the family to Paris. The move provided no relief. He had no more success in Paris than in Vienna. Gertrude, a toddler during most of this European wandering, attached herself to her brother Leo, two years older and her constant companion. After another unsuccessful year, Daniel moved the family to Baltimore in 1879. Things did not improve either financially or with his dissatisfied wife. Finally, in 1880, Daniel moved the family to Oakland, (East Oakland, in one account) California.

    He was finally in the right spot at the right time. San Francisco was in a boom and Daniel became a very wealthy man investing in the San Francisco street car systems, real estate, and playing the San Francisco Stock Exchange. The children lived in the lap of luxury, their every whim was catered to. However, neither parent spent time with them. Many years later, when a newspaper reporter asked her about her life in Oakland, Gertrude reportedly said, "There is no there there." The emotional tie between Leo and Gertrude became even stronger.

Leo, brilliant and good looking, became Gertrude's hero. Michael the oldest brother, was remote because of the age difference, but was probably a surrogate father in many ways. Simon and Bertha, the intervening brother and sister, were disliked by both Leo and Gertrude. They considered Simon simple-minded and incompetent and Bertha a pest. The relationship with Leo was so strong that the death of her mother from cancer when Gertrude was fourteen seems to have caused little disruption or grief in Gertrude's life.

A mere three years later, in 1891, Daniel died of what is described as a heart attack. Michael apparently handled the estate in an open, honest, evenhanded way, and each of the children became wealthy in his or her own right. Michael also made provisions for living arrangements for each of the younger four. Gertrude went to Baltimore with Bertha. However, Leo was to go to Boston to attend Harvard. Gertrude, who had never graduated highschool, applied to Radcliffe (Harvard Annex until 1894) as a special student and was admitted.

At Radcliffe, Gertrude took courses from George Santayana, Vaughn Moody, Josiah Royce and William James. William James in particular had a profound effect on Gertrude. James' unconventional teaching style and his original ideas intrigued Gertrude. She became interested in experimental psychology and worked in the Harvard Experimental Psychology Laboratory under Hugo Munsterberg. Within a year she had published a paper, *Normal Motor Automatism"* (With Leon Solomons) in the *Psychological Review*. She continued to work with Munsterberg and James while at Radcliffe and co-authored a second paper on automatic writing before graduating Radcliffe in 1897.

Leo graduated Harvard at the same time and decided to take postgraduate work at Johns Hopkins. Gertrude enrolled in the medical school at Johns Hopkins. The decision to go to medical school was influenced by William James. The decision to go to Johns Hopkins was determined by Leo's presence there. Leo was still Gertrude's security blanket.

By the time Gertrude entered medical school she had developed into a loner. Her physical appearance and aggressive demeanor had made her unpopular with her fellow students at Radcliffe, and did little to enhance her relations with her medical school classmates. She had a stocky build; was heavy; had her hair tied back in a poorly done bun; her clothes were unkempt and mismatched, she was aggressive and caustic in her dealings with others; and, as one classmate put it. "She was neither feminine nor charming." From most reports, Gertrude, while masculine in appearance and suspected of being homosexual, was essentially asexual while at Radcliffe. It was as if she had not yet either discovered sex or it was non-issue.

Gertrude's first year of medical school was a triumph. She took the top grade in anatomy and did well in her other subjects. She volunteered to make models of brain tracts for her professor of Anatomy, Dr. Franklin Mall. Gertrude also did neuroanatomy studies for Dr. Lewellys Barker, then in the anatomy department but later Osler's successor. Gertrude studied the nucleus of Darkschewitsh in young infants. Her work was of high enough caliber that Barker made several references to her in his book *The Nervous System and Its Constituent Neurones*.

Gertrude never again achieved the academic excellence she demonstrated in her first year, but she continued to do satisfactory work and was scheduled to graduate with her class of fifty-four in 1901. However, she was the lone member of her class not to be awarded a diploma. Records of the faculty meeting in which the decision was made reveal that Osler introduced the resolution that she not be granted her diploma and that the resolution passed despite her defense by Dr. Mall.

In researching the reason Gertrude did not receive her diploma, one encounters a number of different explanations for her failure. First, there is the long-perpetuated myth that she refused to take her examinations because she was only there to learn. This is the most common explanation given in the literary references and probably relates to an episode at Radcliffe. At the final examination in a course taught by William James, Gertrude scrawled a message that she didn't feel like taking an examination that day and left the examination room. James sent a subsequent message that he understood and Gertrude got the high mark for the course. However, the Johns Hopkins records show Gertrude took her medical school examinations and this widely accepted explanation is a myth.

Second, there was the conflict between Gertrude and John W. Williams, the professor of Obstetrics. There was genuine animosity on both sides, Williams liked to teach by using "war stories," stories of various cases embellished and told in a humorous and often lewd manner. Gertrude objected to Williams' off-color stories and told him so. Williams, on the other hand, couldn't stand Gertrude's appearance, sloppy dress and masculine manner[22]. Williams was supposedly antisemitic as well, and that might have increased the conflict[23]. Gertrude told Williams she was going to boycott his lectures in protest. Williams, in turn, told Gertrude that the lectures were an essential part of the course and that he would flunk her if she didn't attend. Gertrude did not attend and Williams did flunk her. Williams gave her the opportunity to take a summer course and try again. She refused. According to Williams, Gertrude thanked him for ending her medical career because medicine now bored her. This account is most likely true. Gertrude, Williams and Gertrude's classmates, while differing on details, all give a similar story, and Gertrude received her lowest grade in obstetrics, a 5 on a 4 point scale.

Then there is the account that Gertrude could not adjust to the clinical years and that she flunked four of her final examinations. It is true that her grades declined dramatically in the clinical years and that she failed

---

22. Not only was Gertrude overtly aggressive and masculine in appearance, but she worked out regularly with a professional boxer and supposedly gave a good account of herself. Female classmates stated they never feared being accosted in Gertrude's presence. In one version of the confrontation with Williams, Gertrude invited Williams to settle it in the ring.

23. Although it appears that the Stein family was undoubtedly Jewish, Gertrude had divorced herself from any religious commitment in early childhood.

three subjects[24] in addition to Obstetrics, and that she barely passed medicine and pediatrics. These points are confirmed by her records at Johns Hopkins. However, there are three widely differing accounts as to why the obviously bright enough Gertrude made such a dismal showing in her final year. The classmate version holds that Gertrude was poor with her hands, disorganized, untidy, belittling to patients and nurses to whom she obviously felt superior, and felt clinical medicine was beneath her intellectual superiority.

The literary critics who focus on Gertrude's homosexuality believe this is when she discovered her sexuality. There seems to be good evidence that while she was in the last two years at Johns Hopkins, Gertrude fell in love with a Bryn Mawr student. From various accounts it appears Gertrude had competition for the young lady's affections. Whether this competitor was male or female is unclear, but, in either case, Gertrude lost the lady to her competitor. According to this version, Gertrude was so obsessed with the failed relationship that she could no longer concentrate on school and thus failed.

The literary critics who focus on Gertrude's relationship with her

---

24. Dermatology, Laryngology and Rhinology, Otology and Ophthalmology.

brother Leo, have still another version. Leo was at loose ends at this point in his life. He was still a graduate student at Johns Hopkins. Although he was brilliant and had varied interests at which he excelled, he could not concentrate on one field of interest long enough to acquire the expertise necessary to make it his life's work. Leo talked about going to Europe to find himself. According to this version, when Leo went to Harvard, Gertrude went to Harvard Annex; when Leo went to Johns Hopkins, Gertrude went to Johns Hopkins; if Leo was confused and terminating his studies, Gertrude sympathetically rejected her studies and was ready to go to Europe with Leo.

Undoubtedly all three of these factors played a part in Gertrude's failure to graduate from medical school. But Gertrude's certainty that she did not want to practice medicine or do neuroanatomy probably played a much more major role than anyone realized.

Gertrude and Leo went to London and took rented rooms together. Gertrude spent endless hours reading in the British Museum Library. Through Leo's contacts, Gertrude met Bertrand Russell and other English intellectuals. However, Gertrude decided London was too damp and cold for her. Gertrude moved back to New York where she tried to come to terms with her homosexuality. Her frustrated romance with the Bryn Mawr student had convinced her that she was a lesbian. But she decided she was enough of a social pariah without adding a homosexual label and decided to keep her sexual orientation secret as long as possible. As an outlet for her frustration, she outlined a book she wanted to write about the whole Bryn Mawr affair.

With Gertrude in New York, Leo moved on to Paris to study painting. He rented a studio at 27 Rue de Fleurus and began haunting the museums and art galleries. He soon became known as an art collector of impeccable taste. He discovered Cezanne and began to collect his work and study him in depth. In 1903 Gertrude joined Leo for a vacation in Spain, North Africa and Italy and then moved in with him at his studio. Gertrude wrote the book about her affair with the Bryn Mawr student, *Q.E.D.*, and locked it away in a cabinet[25]. She then started another novella, *Fernhurst,* about a real life lesbian affair on the Bryn Mawr campus known as the Hodder/Gwin Affair.

Gertrude began accompanying Leo on his art excursions. With their combined incomes they bought quality art; Renoir, Delacroix, Toulouse-Lautrec, Gauguin, Cezanne, - - sometimes purchasing multiple paintings by an artist.

---

25. It was published only after her death.

Michael Stein and his wife Sarah arrived in Paris about this time, and with Leo's advice they also began collecting quality art. Michael and Leo discovered Matisse and thought he was a genus. Both bought his paintings He became a fast friend of the two brothers, and often visited at one or the other's apartments. Gertrude much preferred Picasso, and the two seemed fascinated with each other. Their friendship lasted for over forty years and in 1906 Picasso painted his famous portrait of Gertrude.

In 1905 Gertrude began writing *Three Lives* about three servant girls. The book was probably based on three Cezanne paintings. Leo was not pleased with the work. He felt it had no central theme and no sequential episodes. It also demonstrated Gertrude's racial and class prejudices to the world. To Gertrude, any one who criticized her was an enemy. In Leo's case it meant her idol had feet of clay. Leo's critique of her writing was the beginning of a rift between the siblings that would continue until her death. Gertrude thought she was demonstrating her genius to the literary world. The grammatical and syntactical experimentation that was to become her hallmark was underway. Although Gertrude was breaking new ground in English literature, her idea was not new. Guillaume Apollinaire, had been doing similar work in French for some time before Gertrude started. Stein had met him through Picasso, although it is almost certain she knew of his work for several years before she met him.

In 1907, Gertrude met Alice Toklas at her brother Michael's house. Alice was from San Francisco. Her mother had died when she was in her teens and she had kept house for her father. Alice was largely self-educated but well educated especially in music, theater, literature and opera. She was thirty and had come to Paris with a friend. Her family had known Michael and Sarah in San Francisco and soon after she arrived in Paris, she came to visit. Alice and Gertrude showed interest in each other almost immediately and Gertrude invited her to the studio the next day. It was evidently love at first sight. Alice continued to room with her friend but she spent days with Gertrude. She took over all the household management, acted as Gertrude's secretary and handled the constant stream of visitors. Unlike Leo, Alice loved Gertrude's work.

With Alice on the scene, the rift with Leo widened. Gertrude's overt homosexuality embarrassed Leo, but did not seem to bother him enough for him to make the break. Unfortunately, Leo was rash enough to criticize Picasso's early cubism. The die was cast. Over the course of the next thirty months, Alice moved in and Leo moved out. Gertrude severed all ties with

Leo. The art work was divided and their lives separated. Leo finally left Paris in 1913. He eventually married, but never did settle on a single area of interest. He died of cancer in 1947.

Gertrude, of course, assumed the role of husband in the relationship to Alice's role of jealous wife. They appeared to live in their own world of art and literature with little regard for the political happenings around them. When the first World War broke out they were visiting in London and were not allowed to return until Alfred North Whitehead managed to get them a special pass. They cleaned out their apartment in Paris and immediately moved to Spain. Unable to get funds from the U.S., Gertrude periodically sold art to cover their extravagant lifestyle. In 1917 the pair returned to France and began doing field work for the American Fund for French Wounded. Gertrude even learned how to drive so she could make deliveries.

After the war, Sherwood Anderson entered her circle. Anderson had praised her work in an article and Gertrude was deeply touched. Through Anderson, Gertrude met Hemingway. Hemingway and Gertrude had some weird sort of chemistry between them. Gertrude was attracted to him and Alice could sense it. Alice hated Hemingway from his first visit. Gertrude was a major influence on Hemingway. She convinced him to leave journalism and become a full-time writer. She also set up his first trip to Spain. Hemingway even used one of Gertrude Stein's quotes in *The Sun Also Rises:* "You are a lost generation." However, Stein couldn't tolerate Hemingway's success and best sellers. He was her buddy as an unknown reporter, but his greater fame as writer was intolerable. She would not speak to him after the publication of *A Farewell to Arms* in 1929. Gertrude prided herself on being cryptic and ambiguous and had never had a bestseller. Hemingway's style was short, direct and clear and he was turning out bestseller after bestseller.

Gertrude published *The Autobiography of Alice B. Toklas* in 1933. It was the story of Gertrude's early life in Europe. It was her one and only bestseller and saved her almost exhausted resources. The book was attacked almost as soon as it was published. Leo called her a liar. Matisse, Braque and a large group of other artists published rebuttals. Nonetheless, Gertrude basked in the limelight. With her usual modesty she claimed, "Einstein was the creative philosophical mind of the century and I am the creative literary mind of the century." This prompted the following review in the New York Times:

> Easy to read and easy to forget. It is now

obvious that Miss Stein's chief asset in writing is her colossal egotism and her inability to create character.

The rise of fascism in the 1930s did not disturb her. There is little doubt that Gertrude was a fascist at heart. She had been a snob since birth and firmly believed in her own superiority and privilege over the masses. Gertrude hated Franklin D. Roosevelt with a passion and was an ardent supporter of Franco. She remarked that she thought Mussolini was "good" for Italy and that Hitler was a romanticist. Even as WWII loomed on the horizon with the annexation of Austria and Czechoslovakia, she felt world affairs were of little significance. When Poland was invaded and she was advised to return to the United States, Gertrude saw no reason to leave the comfort of her home. Finally Gertrude and Alice moved to a rented house in Bilignin, France and took most of Gertrude's art work with them. Gertrude left the care of her Paris apartment and belongings to the Nazi collaborator, Bernard Fay. Bernard Fay was a former university professor[26] who came from a prominent Royalist right wing family. He limped from a

---

26. Malcom states he was a Harvard graduate and a specialist in American history.

childhood attack of polio. In 1940 he had been named head of the Bibliotheque Nationale and editor the Nazi antisemitic Paper, *La Gerbe*. He was one of Stein's few long term friends. His exact role in the French Nazi party and the role he played in Stein's survival are still unclear[27].

The war cut off all Gertrude's funds from the United States. However, despite many official warnings from the American embassy, Stein refused to return to the United States. Alice sold Gertrude's artwork for the pair to survive. They ignored the war. They had no radio and took no newspapers. Gertrude had complete faith in Pètain and the Vichy government. Rumor has it that she wrote speeches for Pètain.

Gertrude and Alice returned to their apartment after the war. Nothing had been touched. Bernard Fay had been a faithful guard of their property[28]. Gertrude had little time to enjoy her homecoming. In July 1946, while visiting a country inn outside of Paris, Gertrude took ill. She was admitted to the American Hospital in Paris. A laparotomy was performed and she was found to have an inoperable cancer. She died the evening of

---

27. Malcom spends considerable time on Fay and concludes he was a member of the Gestapo and waged the French campaign against Freemasons.

28. Stein wrote a letter to the French court in Fay's defense detailing his guardianship of her apartment.

surgery, July 27, 1946. Alice arranged Gertrude's funeral at American Cathedral Church of the Holy Trinity[29]. The body remained there for several months before space was found for it at Pere Lachaise Cemetery.

Gertrude left Picasso's portrait of her to the Metropolitan Museum of Art in New York City, her papers and manuscripts to Yale University Library and money to Carl Van Vechen to publish her unpublished works. Every thing else went to Alice in a life estate and then to her nephew, Allan Stein[30].

Alice Toklas continued to live on in the pair's apartment. She published her now famous cookbook in 1953. In 1963, she published her memoirs as *What is Remembered*. Alice died of unknown causes March 7, 1967. She was buried in Gertrude's tomb.

---

29. This was Alice's choice. Alice had flirted with Catholicism for many years and she believed if both she and Gertrude were buried in the Catholic Church there was a chance they would be together in the hereafter. Her conversion to Catholicism and her burial of Gertrude were supposedly encouraged and heavily influenced by Bernard Fay. The choice must have shocked Gertrude's friends and family, and would have shocked Gertrude ("Dead is Dead") had she been alive, but Alice prevailed. Gertrude had abandoned all connection with religion as a teenager and had never acknowledged her Jewishness even to herself, but a conversion to Catholicism was hardly on her agenda.

30. Allan is presumably Michael's son, but that presumption has not been confirmed.

RICHARD JORDAN GATLING

Gatling and gun have become joined in our minds like Siamese twins. Even pre-World-War II American underworld slang corrupted his name so that a "Gat" became the name of any repeating pistol. History has forgotten that the majority of Richard Jordan Gatling's inventions were for constructive purposes or that he was a physician. His Southern sympathies during the Civil War made him unpopular with the general public in the North, and little was written about him outside the South. Nonetheless, this interesting man's story is worth telling.

Richard Jordan Gatling was born on his father's plantation at Maney's Neck Township, Hertford County, North Carolina (about six miles south of the Virginia border) on September 12, 1818. His father, Jordan Gatling, an unsocial, stingy man had nursed 80 acres of undesirable farmland into a rich plantation of over 1200 acres. Jordan Gatling was an accomplished blacksmith and carpenter and had built the family home with his own hands. He carved intricate canes and walking sticks as a hobby. He was not only a successful planter, but an accomplished inventor, designing and constructing a wide variety of farm implements for his own use.

As a boy, Richard Jordan Gatling hunted and fished in the area around the plantation. He attended the Buckhorn School located about two miles north of the Gatling home. At age fifteen his education was over and Richard Jordan Gatling became a clerk in the office of his great uncle, Lewis Meredith Cowper, Clerk of the Court of Common Pleas and Quarter Sessions of Hertford County, North Carolina.

The job lasted one year and then Richard went to work on his father's farms. It was during this period of his teens that Richard helped his father develop a machine for sowing cotton and another machine for thinning the cotton plants. At age nineteen, Richard left the plantation and tried his hand at teaching school. He lasted one term and then returned to his father's farm.

At twenty, while on a business trip to Norfolk for his father, he attended an unsuccessful demonstration of a new steamboat propulsion system. Richard Jordan Gatling was convinced he could do a better job, and when he returned home began working in his father's blacksmith shop. He modeled his propeller after the farm's windmill. It had four angled blades and a central shaft. Richard wanted to patent the propeller but his father would not let him take time off to go to Washington to secure a patent. Seven months later he finally got enough time off to register his invention, only to find Erickson had beaten him to the patent by a matter of days.

Richard left his father shortly thereafter and opened a country store in Frazer Cross Roads, North Carolina. He ran the store for four years. At some point during his stay in Frazer Cross Roads he joined the Methodist Church, causing a rift with the remainder of the family who were staunch Baptists. While the store reportedly was quite successful, this occupation was no more personally satisfying to Richard than was teaching. Sometime between the time he began teaching and the time he left Frazer Cross Roads, Richard suffered a failed marriage, but no details are available.

In 1844, he turned his attention back to inventing. He returned to his father's blacksmith shop and developed a rice sower. The rice sower was really an improved modification of the cotton planter he had helped his father build. It was a moderate financial success. That same year he left for St Louis because he had heard there were great financial opportunities in the West. He was immediately hired as a store clerk and spent his time off observing the area. He immediately recognized that the Western Wheat Belt would be a terrific market for a wheat drill. He quickly modified his rice sower into a wheat drill. He hired a mechanic to make the wheat drills for him and sold the first batch in ten days for a $3000.00 profit. He quit his job in the store and began selling his wheat drill full time. The wheat drill was highly successful, it used less seed that old fashioned sowing and protected the wheat from the Western winters. Within five years he had amassed a fortune and Gatling essentially lived off the profits from that invention for the rest of his life.

In the winter of 1845, Gatling caught smallpox while a passenger on a steamship in the Ohio River. His case has been reported as Variola Major, but whether it was Variola Confluens or Variola Hemorrhagica was not detailed. In any case, it was nearly fatal. The steamship became ice-bound. Food was scarce and it was two weeks before he could reach medical help. He remained in isolation in Pittsburgh for three months. He was severely pockmarked and grew a beard to cover the marks somewhat. That experience convinced Richard that he should study medicine to protect himself and his family from any future lack of medical care.

In the meantime, Richard returned to North Carolina. His father had died while he was in quarantine and had left him a tract of land. The visit home was significant in that he became fascinated with the beautiful daughter of his older brother James Henry. Rebecca Gatling was the reigning beauty of Hertford County and, by all accounts, of Northern North Carolina. There seems to be little doubt Richard Jordan Gatling fell in love with his niece. Whether family pressure or his own moral code prevented the romance from progressing is unknown, but to the best of our knowledge the romance was never consummated. Richard remained devoted to Rebecca for the rest of his life.

Gatling began his medical training in 1847 at Indiana Medical College, LaPorte, Indiana. That same year he patented a machine designed to separate hemp fibers. At some point in his training he transferred to Ohio Medical College in Cincinnati. He graduated from Ohio Medical College in 1849. Although he never set up a formal practice, he used the title "Doctor" for the remainder of his life and medicine continued to be a background interest as he continued his other pursuits. After graduation he moved to Indiana.

In 1854, Gatling now thirty-six, married sixteen year old Jemima Sanders. Jemima was the daughter of John H. Sanders, MD, and the aunt of

General Lew Wallace who achieved fame as a Civil War Union general, but is best known as the author of *Ben Hur*. The marriage seems to have stimulated a new wave of creativity in Gatling. In 1857, he invented a steam plow, and, began helping his brother, John Henry Gatling, with John's flying machine. The steam plow was not readily accepted by farmers, and was not the great financial success Gatling had hoped for. John Henry Gatling resented Richard's intrusion into the his plans for the flying machine and it would appear all collaboration ended rapidly.

In 1860, Gatling patented a whole series of inventions. The machine for separating hemp fibers that he had invented in 1847 had been a moderate financial success, but he now improved it and named it a hemp brake. It became a staple in the hemp industry. He also patented a rotary plow, a cotton cultivator and a rubber washer for tightening gears.

With the outbreak of the Civil War, Gatling turned his attention from agricultural inventions to guns. Gatling supposedly saw his gun as substitute for large armies and huge numbers of casualties:

> In 1861, during the opening events of the war I witnessed almost daily the departure of troops to the front and the return of the wounded, sick and dead. The most of the latter lost their lives not in battle, but by sickness and exposure incident to the service. It occurred to me if I could invent a

machine-- a gun -- which could by its rapidity of fire, enable one man to do as much battle duty as a hundred, that it would supersede the necessity of large armies, and consequently, exposure to battle and disease be greatly diminished. I thought over the subject and finally the idea took practical form in the invention of the Gatling Gun.

Letter to Miss Lizzie Jarvis of Maney's Neck, NC from Richard Jordan Gatling in 1877. From Johnson & Stevenson

Richard Jordan Gatling received Patent #36836 for his gun on November 4, 1862. The original gun consisted of six rotating barrels. At the top of the rotation, a .58 caliber paper cartridge was dropped in the chamber. At the bottom of the rotation, the barrel was fired. When everything worked right, the gun could fire over 200 rounds per minute. Gatling ordered six guns from the Greenwood, Co. in Cincinnati, but the factory burned down before the guns could be delivered and Gatling lost his entire investment. Faced with Bankruptcy, Gatling appealed to his Indiana friends and business acquaintances. They rallied behind him and he was able to have twelve guns made instead of the lost six.

The Indiana Governor, Oliver P. Morton, became a supporter and asked the War Department to consider the gun. His request was denied, but the governor's request and favorable press stirred up enough public interest that the War Department eventually did have to evaluate the gun. Because of the fragility of the paper cartridge, the original model proved to be unreliable, and the conservative army ordinance department would not buy it[31]. Gatling continued to improve his gun throughout the war, and by the end of the war had two calibers of Gatling guns firing metal cartridges, a 1" and .50 caliber. In 1864, the guns were tested in battle by Union General Benjamin Butler who had bought the twelve original guns with his own money. General Butler fired a Gatling gun himself in the battle of Bermuda Hundred, near Richmond, Virginia. It proved to be an ideal infantry weapon and got glowing reports. However, the gun saw little use for the remainder of the war. The War Department finally adopted the 1" gun in 1865, but the first order was not placed until 1866 and was for on-hundred guns. However, the War Department mow wanted the order divided, fifty .50 caliber and fifty 1" guns.

Richard Jordan Gatling continued to work on improvement to the gun for the next thirty years. From rigid frames to frames that allowed lateral swings and vertical movement, from open to enclosed barrels, with calibers varying from one inch to .30 caliber and differing numbers of barrels. There

---

31. The Navy evidently bought some of the original models in 1862.

was the Camel Gun, the Torpedo Gun, the Bulldog and a wide variety of numbered models. He finally came up with a ten-barrel model that fired a .30 caliber metal cartridge that was cranked by an electric motor. It was capable of firing over 400 rounds per minute.

In 1867, Gatling traveled to the Paris Exhibition with his gun; by the end of his European trip, the Gatling gun was officially adopted by the ordinance departments of England, Russia, Hungary, and Egypt, and eventually it was adopted by almost every major country. The Gatling gun saw its first real service in the Franco-Prussian war of 1870-1871 where it was used mainly to protect infantry units' flanks. The American army used the Gatling gun extensively in the Western Indian campaigns, and eight Gatling guns saw service in Cuba during the Spanish-American War.[32] Gatling guns were deployed in the Philippines during the Insurrection. The Gatling gun's first major role was in the Russian-Turkish war of 1877, and it played a lesser role in the Chile-Peru war of the same year. England used the Gatling gun in its Egyptian Campaign of 1872, the campaign against the

---

32. Many observers credit the Gatling gun for the American's success in Cuba. The Spanish Mauser rifle was far superior the rifles carried by most US units and the Gatling guns made the difference in America's favor.

Ashantees in 1873, and the Zulu Campaign of 1879, [33]. The Gatling Gun Company[34] merged with Colt. The Gatling gun manufactured by Colt was the standard United States Army machine gun from 1866 until 1911 when it was replaced with the Maxim type machine gun.

For the entire time Gatling was trying to sell his gun to the Union Army, he was an active member of the Knights of the Golden Circle[35], a secret organization of Southern sympathizers and accused saboteurs. Gatling was eventually cleared of all charges of sedition, but became an unpopular public figure.

In 1888, Richard Jordan Gatling turned his attention to other inventions. The first of these was a long range cast cannon. The United States Army had great hopes for the cannon, but on the third shot of its initial test, it blew up. Gatling abandoned work on guns and patented a

---

33. Some foreign armies were still using the Gatling Gun in WW I.

34. The Gatling Gun Company probably never manufactured a gun. A Philadelphia company, Cooper Firearms, apparently made most of Gatling's early models, and by 1865 or 1866 Gatling's guns were already being made by Colt.

35. When the leaders of the Knights of the Golden Circle were arrested, it was reorganized as the Order of American Knights and when that organization was broken up, it became the Order of the Sons of Liberty.

bicycle that used both hand and foot power, a flush toilet, a machine plow, a torpedo boat and a steam cleaning system. None of these were great financial successes, although the mechanical plow had moderate returns for a few years.

Richard Jordan Gatling was a better inventor than he was investor. Most of his considerable fortune was lost in poorly conceived real estate transactions and failed railroad stocks. His fortune was gone long before he died. He did not live to see his machine gun replaced. During the winter of 1903 he developed influenza and then a series of secondary respiratory infections. He died on February 26, 1903 in his daughter Ida's home in New York City. He was 84 years old and destitute. Richard Jordan Gatling is buried in Crown Hill Cemetery, Indianapolis, Indiana. In 1943, the Government finally named the Destroyer, DD621, the USS Gatling after him. His electric motor operated multiple barrel gun has seen several modern rebirths and is in active service today, one-hundred-forty-three years after its conception by this talented physician.

W. SOMERSET MAUGHAM

Willie, Willie, Willie Somerset Maugham
You're at top of the literary form,
You'll be going on fine,
Till you're ninety-nine
Willie, Willie, Somerset Maugham[36]

"*If the whole truth were told about any human being, he would inevitably emerge as the most depraved of criminals.*"[37] No line is more apt when lent to the life of William Somerset Maugham. For William Somerset Maugham (WSM) spent his entire life attempting to hide his homosexuality

---

36. Cambridge undergraduate's verse published at time of WSM's 80th birthday. Reprinted from Raphel, *W. Somerset Maugham and his World*, at 106.

37. W. Somerset Maugham being quoted by S.N. Behrman in a letter to W.Somerset Maugham from Morgan, *Maugham*, at xiv.

and true character from the public. He even attempted to prevent a posthumous look at his life by instructing that his letters be burned after his death.

WSM was born on January 25, 1874 in the British Embassy in Paris. His father, Robert Ormond Maugham, came from a family of English lawyers, and Robert's firm had their Paris office across the street from the Embassy. The firm acted as the Embassy's solicitor. WSM's birth in the Embassy had been arranged to make sure WSM had English citizenship.

WSM's mother, the former Edith Mary Snell, was small and beautiful - - in contrast to her husband, twenty years her senior and considered the "ugliest man in Paris". The pair were known in Paris society as the beauty and the beast. However, the marriage seemed to be happy and WSM had three older brothers from the union. Robert Maugham was a book collector and had traveled extensively in the Middle East and North Africa. He had brought home and adopted a Moorish symbol that was to be WSM's trademark throughout his life.

WSM picked up the middle name he appears to have favored throughout his life from his godfather, General Sir Henry Somerset, a distant relative of his maternal grandmother. Although his family had made sure he was an English citizen, WSM had been born in France and French was the first language he spoke. He essentially grew up as an only child in a French household, because his three older brothers[38] were in English schools by the time he was three or four. WSM and his mother were very close and many observers believe this is the only mutually loving relationship WSM ever had.

Edith Maugham ran a popular salon in the afternoons and WSM was allowed to attend whenever he wanted. The salon was attended by the French political icons of the day. WSM was familiar to most of them. However, there is little evidence that any of them made a lasting impression on WSM. Edith Maugham suffered from tuberculosis. French physicians of the day recommended pregnancy as a cure. Edith had a stillborn when WSM was five, and he was eight years old when his mother died in childbirth with her seventh pregnancy.

Just two years later, his father died of stomach cancer. WSM hardly knew his two oldest brothers[39] and the one closest to him, Frederick, was still in Cambridge, where he was a brilliant student and an outstanding

---

38. There had been a fourth brother who died in infancy.

39. Charles, a lawyer in his father's firm, and Henry (Harry), who had given up the law to become a lyric poet.

athlete. The family decided the best place for WSM was with his father's brother, William McDonald Maugham. William was Rector of Whitstable, a small oyster port on the Kent coast. William's wife, Sophia, was a German hausfrau and the couple, although childless, seemed to accept WSM as a duty rather than a blessing. WSM's inheritance of £150 per year would cover most of his expenses.

WSM left Paris for Whitstable with his nurse. He spoke English poorly with a French accent. When he got to Whitstable he found his aunt and uncle no happier to see him than he was to see them. The nurse was sent back to Paris the next day. Coincident with the move to England, WSM developed a severe stammer that remained with him the rest of his life. The McDonald Maughams, as a couple, were stiff and had no idea how to raise a young boy. WSM hated his aunt and uncle and derided them horribly later in life. However, all the objective evidence shows they were kind, as generous as their limited means would allow, and always did what they thought was in WSM's best interest.

His uncle enrolled WSM in Canterbury's Kings School, a twenty-minute train ride from Whitstable. WSM was hazed over his short stature, his stammer, and his French accent. WSM, in turn, was angered at the arrogance and parochial attitude of the English students. WSM was not considered good- looking and was not an outstanding athlete. It appears that he developed crushes on other boys with those attributes. How far those crushes went is unknown, but there are no verified homosexual encounters while WSM was at King's School. One year short of graduating King's School, a pulmonary infection forced a period in the sun on the Riviera with a tutor. WSM discovered French literature and came back to King's School with an new interest in literature and writing. He spent another year at King's School.

Upon graduation, the question of a profession and his further education became a problem. The family had traditionally produced lawyers, but WSM's stammer was so pronounced that law appeared to be out of the question. His uncle suggested the church, but again the stammer and WSM's strongly voiced objection ruled out that possibility. Finally it was decided to send him to Heidelberg for a year. The exact reasoning for this year in Germany, other than Sophia's relatives being nearby, is not clear.

In Heidelberg, he met Ellingham Brooks, a young man who had abandoned the practice of law to study art and philosophy. Brooks introduced Maugham to great literature and great art. He also became

WSM's first confirmed homosexual lover. WSM left Heidelberg fluent in English, French and German and more convinced than ever that he wanted to be a writer.

Back in England, the question of a profession was still unsettled. Although WSM still had his £150 per year to support him, and could have tried his hand at writing, it does not appear that he even suggested such a possibility to his brothers or uncle. He was finally placed in a London accountant's office to learn accountancy. Maugham hated accountancy, but loved London. He left the accountant's office and returned to Whitstable and the rectory he hated.

The village physician suggested medicine to WSM. WSM was really not interested in medicine per se, but thought it would be a marvelous opportunity to view and experience life in the raw, and give him subject matter to write about. It would also get him back to London, a destination he cared about. He jumped at the suggestion and the family seemed pleased with the decision.

On September 27, 1892, WSM began the five-year medical student course at St. Thomas Hospital in London. He took rooms across the river from the hospital and began keeping a journal. We know he loved London and his access to books and the theater. However we know very little about what kind of medical student he was or how he felt about his medical training. His future writing treated physicians poorly, but his biographers indicate that he repeatedly brought up the fact that the French physicians were responsible for his mother's death and attribute this as its source.

We do know that two incidents during his medical training had a strong effect on his future life. The first was a vacation break Maugham took during his second year as a medical student. He went to Italy. It offered him complete relief from the wards and the tedium of his studies. He felt the trip rejuvenated him and gave him a new perspective and energy. Travel became a method of finding subject matter and rekindling his creative processes for the rest of his life.

The second incident was the trial of Oscar Wilde during WSM's third year as a medical student. Although we cannot verify any homosexual activity by WSM before Heidelberg, he had admitted to himself by this time that he was a homosexual. When Wilde was convicted and sentenced to prison, Maugham was frightened beyond all reason. He determined to maintain the public image of a heterosexual man about town whatever the cost. His paranoia persisted and he continued the facade for the rest of his life.

Sometime in 1895 he began writing stories. His first two stories were rejected as too short. However, during his obstetrical clerkship he did sixty-three deliveries in Lambeth, one of the worst and most dangerous slums in London. This clerkship appears to be the only one WSM admitted he liked. In 1896[40], drawing on the experience of his obstetrical clerkship, Maugham began *Liza of Lambeth*. In January of 1897, he submitted the manuscript to T. Fisher Unwin, a London publisher. Unwin's first reader didn't like it, but Unwin gave it to two further readers who thought it should be published. WSM signed his first contract while still a medical student. The terms were generally unfavorable to Maugham. It is variously reported that he got either no advance or £20 after the first 750 copies were sold. The book got a single favorable review, but the public liked it and it went through two editions. Unwin took an option on WSM's next two books.

1897 proved momentous in WSM's life for two other reasons. First, in September of that year, his uncle died. The vicar was loved in the

---

40. WSM gave many dates that could not be verified. Some he might have just been careless about or have had a poor memory of, but he consciously lied about dates if he thought it put him in a better light.

community and the funeral reportedly the largest seen in Whitstable. However, Willie and Henry are the only ones of the brothers who are known to have attended the funeral. Second, in October 1897, WSM passed his examinations and was awarded his diploma as a physician and surgeon. WSM must have done well as a student, because he was offered an appointment in the department of obstetrics and gynecology[41]. WSM, bolstered by the success of *Liza of Lambeth*, and with the two Unwin options in his pocket, turned the offer down and decided to become a full-time writer. He later stated that he regretted not accepting the appointment, but most biographers doubt the sincerity of that statement.

WSM hired an agent and went off to Spain and then Italy. He later wrote that he had an affair with a Spanish girl, however, there was no contemporary verification. WSM did use the trip for an unsuccessful travel book and wrote his second novel for Unwin, *The Making of a Saint*. WSM got a £50 advance, but the book did not do as well as *Liza*. Unwin was

---

41. There is some argument about the nature of the appointment. The offer may have been from one of his professors and not the hospital, however, there is agreement he was offered a faculty appointment. There is general agreement that he was considered a failure by the hospital staff even after he gained literary fame.

finally able to sell the book to an American publisher and it became WSM's first published book in America.[42]

In 1899, WSM returned to London. He combined the two rejected stories he had written as a medical student with two new stories and turned it into a book. Unwin published it as *Orientations*. The book had poor reviews and sold poorly. This was the beginning of a black period for WSM. After the success of *Liza* in 1897, he had ten years of poorly received and flatly rejected works. WSM kept up the appearance of a successful author and man-about-town. £150 per year and his pitiful royalties made this an almost impossible task, but somehow WSM managed to keep up appearances in both the literary and social societies of London. He continued to play the role of a heterosexual to the public even bragging about his conquests. However, according to Morgan, his only verified heterosexual affair during this period was with Violet Hunt, an older writer[43]. He began writing plays, frequently waiving his fees to get them produced, but the most successful only had a twenty-eight day run.

---

42. *Liza* was not published in America until 1921.

43. She was forty-one and WSM was twenty-nine. They remained friends, exchanged letters and dedicated books to each other.

In 1904, his brother Harry[44], the unsuccessful lyric poet, committed suicide. Although the brothers had never been close and Harry had openly resented WSM's success with *Liza*, the death seems to have moved WSM greatly. He had always been keenly conscious about being paid for his work, but now payment terms and audits became a minor obsession. He changed agents and made it clear he wanted to change publishers. However, at this point, none of the legitimate publishers were interested.

WSM had been closest to his brother Frederick, now a successful lawyer and politician, but, following Harry's death, he spent his closely held funds to go to Paris to see his brother Charles who had taken his father's place in the firm's Paris office.

WSM's big break came in late 1905. An American producer, George Tyler, was in England looking for material. He thought WSM's play, *Lady Frederick,* was a great vehicle for a female star. He offered $1000.00 for an option, providing WSM could spice it up. Tyler was unable to find an American star willing to take on the role and finally dropped the option. The $1000.00 was enough to send WSM to Egypt. There he met and started an

---

44. Henry Neville Maugham.

eight-year affair with Ethelwyn Silvia Jones, a promiscuous divorcee and daughter of playwright Henry Arthur Jones. WSM obviously knew he was sharing the lady's bed with several others of his circle, but at least one biographer states he proposed and was turned down.

By 1907, WSM had reached the point of financial bankruptcy. He had little or no income from writing and he had drained his meager inheritance. His London society life-style and affairs, plus presents for his male lovers had drained his resources. He talked to his family about going back to St. Thomas for a refresher course and then signing on as a ship's doctor.

Then a minor miracle happened. The Royal Court Theater had a surprise flop and needed a stopgap play for six weeks. One of WSM's friends sold the producer on using *Lady Frederick*, and Ethel Irving, a major English stage star, agreed to play the lead. The play opened on October 26, 1907 and ran for 422 performances in five west end theaters. It then moved to New York and had a 96 performance run there.

By mid 1908 WSM had four plays running simultaneously in London. His financial crisis was over with a bang. He was now truly wealthy. He was a member of the Garrick Club; a friend of Winston

Churchill; the owner of a house in Mayfair; a serious collector of theater art; and had become a serious bridge player. What he worked on or if he worked on any writing project over the next few years is unknown.

In 1910, he made his first trip to the United States. He loved New York and met Broadway producers and writers. He visited some cousins in New Jersey and then, rather hurriedly returned to London.

Sometime between 1911 and 1913, WSM re-encountered[45] the beautiful Syrie Bernardo Wellcome at a theater party. Syrie, thirty-two, was legally separated from Henry Wellcome of Burroughs-Wellcome Pharmaceuticals. Syrie was receiving £2400 year from Wellcome. She was known to have had a series of wealthy lovers and was either just ending or had just ended an affair with Selfridge of Selfridge's Department Store. Syrie was fascinated by Maugham and seemed to genuinely fall in love with him. Maugham, for his part, seemed to consider Syrie a beautiful desired woman who would be an ideal cover for his homosexuality. In any case, they began a hot and heavy affair. Syrie soon had a miscarriage. In the midst of the affair, WSM suddenly rented a villa in a homosexual colony on Capri.

---

45. WSM had first met Syrie some years earlier when she had still been with Wellcome.

Syrie who found she was now pregnant for the second time by WSM, wired she was coming to Capri. Maugham tried to stop her, but she came anyway. Some biographers hint that Syrie knew about Maugham's homosexual affairs from the time they met, while others claim she stumbled on them when she got to Capri. Syrie was obviously carrying WSM's child, and the two returned to England which had now entered World War I.

Back in England, WSM wrote his friend Churchill to find a spot for him in the war. While he was waiting to hear from Churchill, WSM heard about an ambulance corp forming to serve in France. Maugham joined as an interpreter. He later learned to drive and also served as an ambulance driver[46]. In France, the forty-year-old WSM met the love of his life, Gerald Haxton. Haxton was twenty-two, a pockmarked, gregarious, energetic, adventurous, devil-make-care, thoroughly unscrupulous, alcoholic, promiscuous homosexual. Shortly after Maugham met him, Haxton was tried in England on multiple counts of gross indecency under a section of the same law as Oscar Wilde. When Haxton tried to return to England after the

---

46. It is interesting that Maugham never attempted to use his medical training in France, and there is no indication that the unit even knew he was a physician.

war he was denied admission as an undesirable alien. WSM knew all this, but as in his school boy crushes he fell for someone who was everything he was not.

Some time circa 1913-1914, WSM must have started writing *Of Human Bondage*, because in 1915 it was published both in the United States and in England. It got poor reviews in England, but a rave review by Theodore Drieser in the United States saved it, and it became a runaway best seller. It eventually caught on in England as well and has stayed in print to this day.

That same year, on September 1, Maugham's daughter Liza was born. Syrie and Wellcome were still married. The birth of Liza prompted Wellcome to sue for divorce. WSM was named as correspondent. As might be expected, the divorce case generated headlines in the tabloids and was detailed in even the most conservative of London's newspapers. Syrie didn't defend herself against the charges of adultery, and on February 14, 1916, Wellcome was granted a divorce and awarded custody of the couple's son[47].

In the meantime, through Syrie, WSM met Sir John Wallinger an

---

47. It is unclear which parent had custody of the boy prior to the divorce.

officer in British Intelligence. Because of Maugham's skill with languages Wallinger thought Maugham could be an asset to the Intelligence Service. WSM was known in Europe as a writer and traveler and that persona was perfect cover. WSM went to Switzerland for British Intelligence. Syrie joined him there, but didn't like Switzerland or the Swiss. She returned to London. Maugham used the time in Switzerland to write, as well as to do intelligence work. In 1916 his play, *Caroline,* opened in London to rave reviews.

Suddenly in August of 1916, he left his post in Switzerland, and sailed for New York. Gerald Haxton either sailed with him or had preceded him, for they were together in New York. Syrie and Liza arrived shortly thereafter. However, in November, Maugham announced he was leaving Syrie and Liza and sailing to Tahiti with Haxton. WSM's purported purpose was to go to Tahiti to research the life of Gauguin. Maugham's frequent travels to third world destinations undoubtedly did supply him with invaluable material for his writing, but he was equally motivated by Haxton's ability to provide him with a never ending supply of young boys as sexual partners without the fear of arrest or notoriety.

Maugham and Haxton traveled to San Francisco and boarded a

cruise ship for Hawaii. On board was a San Francisco Chamber of Commerce group. Maugham met a San Francisco stockbroker and his former showgirl wife, the Bertram Alansons. Alanson came from a German Jewish family that owned coffee plantations in Central America. He had been born in San Francisco but raised in Central America. He returned to San Francisco in 1908 and bought a seat on the San Francisco stock exchange and never looked back. Maugham and Alanson hit it off immediately and, by the time the ship landed, they were fast friends. Maugham, who usually was suspicious of all of humanity, instinctively trusted Alanson, and, by the time they parted, had given him $15,000.00 to invest for him. It turned out to be the smartest move WSM ever made. From that time on, Alanson managed his portfolio, made Maugham a millionaire many times over; saved his fortune from the 1929 crash; and the two remained fast friends until Alanson's death in 1958.

From Hawaii, Maugham and Haxton took a steamer to Samoa. One of their fellow passengers was a prostitute, Sadie Thompson, who the police had forced out of Hawaii. She, of course, became the subject of WSM's most famous short story, *Rain*[48]. From Samoa the two continued to New Zealand and finally Tahiti. Haxton did all the legwork and brought the sources to Maugham. Maugham discovered an original but damaged Gauguin, painted on the door of a native home, and bought it for ₣200[49].

Haxton and Maugham were back in San Francisco by mid-April 1917. Maugham returned to England, leaving Haxton in the States[50]. Syrie's divorce was now final and on May 26, 1917, WSM finally married Syrie Wellcome. By this time, Maugham certainly knew, in detail, of Syrie's many previous lovers, and Syrie certainly knew of his homosexuality. Nonetheless, they seem to have entered the marriage willingly, even though for different reasons. From all reports, Syrie was sexually attracted to Maugham and genuinely loved him. Maugham thought the gentlemanly thing to do was to give his daughter his name, and that having an attractive wife and child was a great shield for his homosexuality.

In the late summer or early fall of 1917, British Intelligence sent

---

48. Probably written in Pago Pago where it rained continuously during his stay.

49. In 1962 it brought $37,400.00 at auction.

50. Haxton was either drafted or enlisted in the U.S. Army and spent most of the War as a German POW.

WSM to Russia on a mission to keep Russia in the war. Maugham got little cooperation from the British Consulate but, through personal sources. made contact with Krensky. In mid-October WSM returned to England with a report that Russia could not stay in the war without substantial Allied support. The British Government did not act on WSM's report, and the matter became moot when Krensky was overthrown on November 7, 1917. WSM claimed later that if he had been sent to Russia earlier, he could have kept Russia in the war and prevented the Bolshevik take over.

WSM was coughing and having night sweats when he returned from Russia. His physicians diagnosed tuberculosis and sent him to a sanatorium in the North of Scotland. Maugham quickly improved and was discharged in the spring of 1918. He was joined by Syrie and Liza and they rented a house in Surrey, where Maugham worked on *The Moon and Sixpence.* In November 1918, WSM was sent back to the sanatorium and remained there until the Spring of 1919. While confined, he wrote the play *Caeser's Wife.* It was produced in London almost immediately and had a successful run of 247 performances. *The Moon and Sixpence* was also published in 1919 with an initial run of 6000 copies. It became an immediate best seller in both England and the United States.

Almost immediately, WSM took off for the homosexual colony on Capri without Syrie or Liza. Syrie was disgusted and used no restraint in letting Maugham know. WSM reacted in typical passive aggressive style. He went to New York; picked up Gerald Haxton; traveled across the United States; then to the orient; and then to England via the Suez with a stop on the Riviera. After a brief stop in England, WSM rejoined Haxton and they were off to the Federated Malay States via the United States. WSM traveled to the outposts; stayed with the local English in their homes; absorbed the gossip; picked up the local stories; and made the Malay peninsula his literary territory. He also took side trips to the Dutch East Indies. While traveling, his first book of short stories, *Trembling Leaf*[51], was published. The book was critically and financially successful. WSM was now a successful novelist, playwright and short story author. WSM and Haxton returned to San Francisco in 1922, and then WSM returned to England.

In the fall of 1922, WSM was off with Haxton again. This time to Southeast Asia. At the same time, the play *Rain* opened on Broadway. Although based on WSM's short story, the actual play was written by John

---

51. Included *Rain* and was dedicated to his broker, Bert Alanson.

Culon and Clemence Randolf by agreement with Maugham, who was to receive a percentage of the royalties.[52] It ran for 648 performances and was later sold to the movies, where it was made in several versions over the years. Maugham returned via Vancouver, Seattle, San Francisco[53], Hollywood and New York and arrived in London in June 1923.

Syrie was now busy making a name for herself as a society interior decorator. There appears to have been a temporary truce between the two and Maugham bought a mansion in London that they occupied as a family. *Our Betters*, a play WSM had written in 1915, was produced in London to rave reviews and a 548 performance run. In November 1924, *The Camel's Back* opened on Broadway. It was a flop. After extensive rewrites it opened in London where it was only slightly more successful.

In 1924 WSM and Haxton traveled to Mexico, the West Indies, and Central America, then back to the Malay Peninsula. By the time Maugham had returned from Malay in 1925, Syrie had had enough. She rented the London house and moved into quarters of her own with Liza. WSM had to

---

52. Eventually WSM's share of the play's royalties came to over $1,000,000.00.

53. While in San Francisco, WSM had Alanson set up a trust fund for Gerald Haxton.

go house hunting. Because Haxton was banned from entering England, and because Maugham felt the warmer climate of southern France might be better for his lungs, he concentrated on the Riviera. He finally found exactly what he wanted -- the priest's house on the former estate of King Leopold II of Belgium on Cap Ferat, between Nice and Monte Carlo. WSM made an offer which was rejected, but, after months of haggling, he finally secured the property. WSM named the property Mauresque and made arrangements for modernizing and repairing it[54]. He finalized his separation arrangements with Syrie and left for the United States. *The Constant Wife* opened in Cleveland with Ethel Barrymore in the lead. It was another hit, running on Broadway for two years and another year on the road. By early 1927, Maugham had another successful play, *The Letter,* open and Maugham and Haxton had moved into Mauresque. WSM was to live there for the rest of his life, excepting four years during WWII.

In July 1927, Syrie came to lunch at Mauresque and asked WSM for a divorce. They quickly came to terms. Syrie held the winning hand. If Syrie sued for divorce in England, she would name Haxton as correspondent.

---

54. He made sure that his father's Moorish symbol adorned the property prominently.

WSM's homosexuality would be exposed to the public. A French decree was finally entered in May 1929. Syrie got the London house and furnishings, the Rolls Royce, and £2400 per year. Liza got £600 per year. WSM was extremely bitter. He hated parting with the alimony and child support, and he blamed Syrie for depriving him of his cover of a wife and child. When Maugham found out it was common knowledge in Syrie's circle that Haxton was the reason for the divorce, WSM's hatred for Syrie knew no bounds. His relationship with Liza was almost too distant to be called a relationship[55].

WSM now fell into a routine while at Mauresque that was, for practical purposes, unbreakable. He would have breakfast in bed, served by one of the thirteen servants he employed; bathe; write for three hours; at 12:45 he would have a single dry martini; then lunch; nap; then a walk, tennis or golf; dinner at 8:00: bridge or conversation with guests; bed before midnight. His house had a an almost unbroken stream of literary, political, artistic, and theatrical greats as house guests, the Winston Churchills and the Duke and Duchess of Windsor among others. Accompanied by Haxton, he

---

55. Liza later stated that between 1927 and 1936 she saw her father once a year when he took her to lunch at Claridge's.

continued to travel widely, spending months on the road.

In 1928, *Ashenden,* the novel based on his experiences as a secret agent, was published. Exactly when it was written is not clear. WSM gave several conflicting dates, some of which predate publication considerably. His play, *The Sacred Flame,* opened on Broadway the same year. It failed miserably in New York, but its condemnation by religious leaders gave it tremendous publicity and it had a successful run in London the following year. 1928 was also significant in that WSM met Alan Searle, an ingratiating, handsome, young homosexual who yearned to travel. Maugham immediately considered him as a likely replacement for Gerald Haxton whose drinking and improprieties were beginning to bother him.

Thanks to Bert Alanson, WSM was not affected by the 1929 stock market crash or the following depression. His routine continued unaltered. In 1930, *Cakes and Ale* and *The Gentleman in the Parlour* were published and his comedy, *The Breadwinner,* produced. 1931 was a lean year. *Six Stories in the First Person Singular* was released to poor reviews and worse sales. With the failure of the play *For Services Rendered*, 1932 appeared to be a repeat of 1931, but then in November 1932, *The Narrow Corner* was published and became a runaway best seller. It was sold to the movies the following year.

By this time, WSM's brother Frederick had become an outstanding lawyer and was a rising politician[56]. The brothers' relationship was ambivalent to say the least. Frederick detested WSM's lifestyle and blatant homosexuality, but was proud of his literary accomplishments. WSM voiced his hatred of Frederick to his intimates regularly, but was extremely proud when Frederick was made Chief Justice in 1933, and defended his political positions against all outsiders. After WSM's sudden contact with Charles after Harry's death, Charles appears to have never entered his life again. Frederick's son, Robin[57], and one of Frederick's two daughters appear to be the only other members of his family he had any regular contact with.

1933 also marked the publication of another book of short stories, *Ah King*. Although his writing was highly successful with the public, and he

---

56. Frederick was a staunch supporter and intimate of Neville Chamberlain, and continued to support him even after his appeasement policy with Germany became such a political disaster leading to WWII. WSM in turn continued to defend Frederick to outsiders. WSM himself recognized the danger posed by the Fascists early on and made his anti-Franco, Hitler, and Il Duce feelings well known. He helped refugee writers he liked, but spitefully rejected help to critics.

57. Robin wrote a book about his famous uncle, but it differs in many areas from what might be called more objective accounts.

had conquered the novel, the play, and the short story, WSM became increasingly sensitive to the fact that he was not considered one of England's "great" writers. The realization came at a time when the facade of a happy heterosexual man-about-town was beginning to fade, and his contacts began to see his true personality -- a severe, cold, bitter, pessimistic, paranoid, vindictive, spiteful, dysfunctional homosexual and pederast. He still traveled extensively with Haxton, but seemed to be joyless with both the travel and Haxton. He fought with the tax authorities incessantly, and distrusted both his agents and publishers.

Late in 1934, WSM re-met Eddie Marsh. He had met Marsh years earlier when he was Winston Churchill's personal secretary. Now Marsh was acting as Churchill's personal editor and correcting the manuscript of *History of the English Speaking World*. Marsh agreed to act in the same capacity for WSM. He edited *Don Fernando* for WSM, and submitted pages of corrections and revisions. When *Don Fernando* was released in 1935, it received critical acclaim and Maugham was elated. From that time on, Marsh edited everything WSM wrote until Marsh died in 1953.

In May 1936, WSM was in London for Liza's wedding to Vincent Paravicini, son of the Swiss Ambassador to England. Syrie did not approve of the marriage, which made WSM take a new interest in Liza and, of course, approve of the match. He gave the couple a house at Henley-on-the-Thames and some stock certificates. In the future, for tax purposes, WSM would buy his art in Liza's name and send her the receipts indicating that the art was hers, but would hang in Mauresque until he died or Mauresque was sold.

By 1937, Haxton's alcoholism had made him a semi-invalid and WSM's romantic attachment was over. He took the management of Mauresque away from Haxton, but couldn't manage a total separation and still traveled with him. A trip to India with Haxton, in December 1937 became the inspiration for the *Razor's Edge*. WSM's interest in Liza continued, and he seemed genuinely thrilled when his grandson, Nicholas Somerset Paravicini, was born.

In 1938, *Summing Up* was published and WSM began his visits to Swiss cellular therapy clinics in continued attempts to increase his virility and prevent aging. Significantly, his companion on these jaunts was not Gerald Haxton, but the man WSM had already chosen as Haxton's replacement, Alan Searle.

When WWII broke out, WSM had a terrible time getting out of

France. He finally made it back to England on a coal barge[58]. Haxton closed up the holdings in France and secreted away the art work. Paravicini entered the British army, and Liza, pregnant with their second child, went to New York. Syrie soon joined her. WSM was recruited to go to the United States to write and speak on behalf of Britain. He left England on October 2, 1940. He flew to Lisbon and took the Clipper from Lisbon to New York, his first transatlantic flight. He spoke all across the U.S., urging America to come to the aid of Britain. When America entered the war after December 7, 1941, Maugham retired to a house publisher Doubleday had built for him on his plantation in North Carolina. He began writing *The Razor's Edge*. Redbook serialized *Up at the Villa*[59] as *The Villa on the Hill*. Critics hated it, but WSM sold the film rights to Warner Brothers for $30,000.00. He also wrote a propaganda novel for the British War ministry called *The Hour Before*

---

58. WSM was reportedly so upset by this problem, that from that time on he carried huge quantities of cash whenever he traveled to cover bribes or other costs of emergency transportation.

59. Written several years earlier and not published before. Generally considered his weakest work.

Dawn. WSM disliked it[60], but magazine and movie sales netted him $90,000.00. Liza, Nicholas, and his new granddaughter, Camilla, moved in with him, probably because Liza refused to live with Syrie. In August of 1943, Maugham finished *The Razor's Edge*. It was finally published in April 1944. The first edition ran 375,000 copies. The critics' reviews were mixed, but the book sold over 500,000 copies the first month after publication. WSM immediately sold the movie rights for $50,000.00.

In November of 1944, Gerald Haxton died. The death of his lover of thirty years seems to have raised a feeling of relief rather than grief in Maugham. Maugham immediately hired Alan Searle as his new companion, secretary and lover. Searle was no more capable of a monogamous relationship than Haxton, but was shy and sweet-appearing in contrast to the bold, outrageously wild, and alcoholic Haxton. However, appearances aside, he was a hypochondriac; pornographer; and a petty, jealous sneak who loved to spread malicious gossip without regard to the truth.

1945 marked the end of WWII. Liza, Nicholas and Camilla returned to England where Liza began divorce proceedings against Vincent

---

60. Rumor has it that he was so embarrassed by it that he would never let it be published in England.

Paravicini. Maugham appears to have feared for the grandchildren's future and asked Alanson to set up a trust for them. WSM went to Hollywood where he began the screenplay[61] for *The Razor's Edge*. In May 1946, *Then and Now* was published to poor reviews. However, it was a Literary Guild selection and sold 750,000 copies in the United States alone[62]. WSM was a bridge fanatic, and his bridge bible was *Goren's Better Bridge for Better Players*, therefore, he was thrilled when Goren asked him to write the introduction to Goren's *Standard Book of Bidding*. His price: Goren had to come to dinner and play bridge. Shortly after the release of *Then and Now*, WSM and Searle left for France via the liner *Columbia*. Before he left, Maugham donated the manuscript of *Of Human Bondage* to the Library of Congress.

Mauresque had been occupied by Italian and German troops and was in poor shape on Maugham's return. However, his secreted art had survived unharmed. Nonetheless, by November 1946, WSM and Searle were back in the repaired and restored Mauresque. The principal difference was that the

---

61. In actuality the film's screenplay was done by Lamar Trott. The studio did not like WSM's version which he had done gratis. WSM received a Pissaro landscape as a present from the studio.

62. Under its projected sales and printing, it ended up on remainder counters.

household was now run by five servants instead of the former thirteen. Maugham settled back into his former routine, which became even more rigid. With his return to France, all his former traits seemed to become stronger and his patience and tolerance become weaker. His hatred of Syrie became more strident, his rudeness and meanness seemed to increase in yearly increments, and his dependence on Allan Searle deepened by equal increments. Soon after they moved back to Mauresque, WSM established a trust for Searle.

In 1947, Liza and the grandchildren came to visit and Searle was obviously jealous and resentful of them. The grandchildren later visited alone and supposedly Searle was openly hostile. The same year WSM established the £500 Somerset Maugham prize, to be administered by the Society of Authors, to allow young novelists to travel abroad. His last book of short stories, *Creatures of Circumstances*, was published shortly thereafter.

In 1948, Liza became engaged to Lord John Hope, the son of Lord Linlithgow whom WSM hated[63]. Surprisingly, WSM seemed elated. He may

---

63. When WSM and Gerald Haxton had traveled in India, Lord Linlithgow was Governor General of India, and had refused to receive them because of Haxton's

have felt Liza's financial future was secure, but, in any case, he was charming to John, settled £20,000 on Liza and paid for the wedding reception at Claridge's. 1948 also marked the publication of WSM's last novel, *Catalina,* and a book of reviews. Although *Catalina* had scathing reviews, it was saved financially by becoming a co-selection by the Book of the Month club and its serialization in a periodical. *Great Novelists and Their Novels* made no great waves, but was later revived and republished.

In 1949, WSM sat for the now famous Sutherland portrait. Although it could hardly be called flattering, Maugham claimed he liked it and bought it for $35,000.00 and gave it to Liza[64]. WSM became a grandfather for the third time when Liza gave birth to a son. The boy was christened in the House of Commons as Julian John Somerset with Anthony Eden as godfather and Mrs. Paul Mellon as godmother. WSM seemed pleased, although Liza's fourth pregnancy four years later infuriated him for some reason.

Over the ensuing years he continued traveling, but spent

---

status as an undesirable alien.

64. WSM retained the copyright and received a royalty on every reproduction made. Liza donated the portrait to the Tate Gallery in 1957.

considerable time in the United States. He read papers at major universities, libraries and other institutions[65]; played bridge with political, literary and theatrical greats; shopped for food specialties unavailable in France; fought unending battles with tax authorities; donated manuscripts and art to various institutions; and received his Doctor of Letters Degree. On his 80th birthday, the Garrick Club gave him a birthday party, an honor only extended to Dickens, Thackery and Trollope before. Finally in 1954, he was named Companion of Honor by the Queen[66].

Thanks to Alanson and the popularity of his stories, he was a multimillionaire, but he worried incessantly about money and taxes. He put Mauresque in Liza's name to avoid death taxes, but immediately began to have second thoughts. He had always been somewhat paranoid, but now his paranoia, fueled by false rumors circulated by Searle and his advancing age, took over.[67] Even his oldest two grandchildren became suspect, and he

---

65. Including the Royal Academy Dinner where the other speakers included Winston Churchill and Clement Atlee.

66. WSM had hoped for the Order of Merit, but the Queen refused to consider him for it because of his blatant homosexuality.

67. Schneck suggests that WSM had Capgras Syndrome, but a look at the man's basic personality shows a man who was always cold, bitter, pessimistic,

became convinced Liza and John were going to have him declared incompetent and take control of him and Mauresque. It is hard to underestimate the role Searle played in this estrangement from Liza and the grandchildren. He had always considered them rivals, and used every means possible to insure Maugham would consider him indispensable and make him his one and only heir[68].

WSM was failing mentally slowly but surely, but physically he was doing remarkably well. He continued to get periodic cellular therapy in Swiss clinics and was still sexually active and seeking young boys. He seemed able to travel to places that catered to his sexual tastes although he seemed to have increasing episodes of confusion and had some sort of syncope episode in Bangkok. His paranoia and confusion was increasing noticeably, and Searle overtly prevented the family from contacting him. Liza, the grandchildren and Frederick's children all realized that WSM suffered from senile dementia, but short of declaring him incompetent in

---

paranoid, vindictive, spiteful rigid, and incapable of maintaining functional family relationships, therefore, it is hard to invoke anything more complicated than senile dementia as the reason for his behavior during his final days.

68. In the meantime Searle spent his spare time collecting pornography and picking up sailors in Villefrache.

court there was no way of removing him from Searle's care[69] and influence.

Under Searle's influence WSM signed all royalties from his writing which were supposed to go to Liza to Searle. Searle then arranged to publish WSM's autobiography *"Looking Back"* as a serial in a London tabloid. The volume contained many lies about Syrie and his regular publisher had refused to print it when it was first written. WSM had given Liza his word he would never attempt to publish it again. The publication devastated Liza and essentially broke all Maugham's social connections in England.

WSM then put his paintings up for auction. He evidently feared that they would be stolen. Many of the paintings had been purchased in Liza's name and she had receipts and letters telling her they were hers. Liza fully aware that WSM was under the undue influence of Searle brought suit for $648,000.00 of the amount realized for her paintings. WSM was now obsessed that Liza would declare him incompetent and throw him out of Mauresque. Urged on by Searle, he now began a weird battle in French Courts to disown Liza and adopt Alan Searle as his only child. Liza challenged him in open court. The newspapers had a field day at the expense

---

69. To Searle's credit, he did take good physical care of Maugham. Maugham was always clean, well fed, and protected when irrational.

of all parties. WSM's senility was amply displayed for the entire world to see. It was a pitiful public ending to a brilliant career. Liza won her suit in the French courts, WSM could not adopt Alan Searle and Liza was his legitimate heir. Searle was enraged, and brought an appeal in WSM's name. The appeal was denied and Searle began a vicious rain of hateful lies against the family.

By this time, WSM was so demented, Liza could not bring herself to force him to come to court in London, or to go through another bout of humiliating newspaper coverage. On January 22, 1964, she let WSM settle the painting claims for $250,000.00 and her legal expenses. Liza received less than half of what she undoubtedly would have received had the case gone to trial.

Over the next year WSM's body began to deteriorate as well. He had bouts of pneumonia and began to fall. By the winter of 1965 he was falling frequently. On the morning of December 12, 1965 he was found unconscious on his bathroom floor. He was taken to the American Hospital in Nice, where he died on December 15, 1965. Alan Searle took him home, and announced he had died on December 16, 1965, at home. Searle did not inform Liza of either the hospitalization or death until the public announcement was made. Despite demands by the family, Searle kept WSM's body in his (WSM's) bedroom until December 20th when he was finally cremated and the ashes sent to London. His ashes were buried at the foot of the Maugham Library wall, Kings School on December 22, 1965. Liza, Lady Glendevon, in attendance.

JOSEPH IGNACE GUILLOTIN

> THERE ARE UNFORTUNATE MEN: COLUMBUS COULD NOT ATTACH HIS NAME TO HIS DISCOVERY, AND GUILLOTIN COULD NOT DETATCH HIS FROM HIS INVENTION. ONLY IT WAS NOT EVEN HIS INVENTION!
> *Victor Hugo*[70]

---

70. As quoted in Garland.

Joseph Ignace Guillotin is included in this volume for numerous reasons. This conservative physician, politician, philantropist, libertarian, Jesuit, Freemason humanitarian was such a study of contradictions, and played such an important role in the French Revolution his story cried out for the telling. As indicated above, Joseph Ignace Guillotin did not invent, design, operate or lose his head to the guillotine[71]. What attached his name to the instrument of the "Great Terror" of the French Revolution was his attempted reform of the French criminal justice system.

Joseph Ignace Guillotin was born on May 29[72], 1738, at Saintes, France. The ninth of twelve children, but only the second son of Joseph Alexandre Guillotin, a prosperous and influentual lawyer, and his wife the former Catherine Agatha Martin. According to some accounts, it was a preterm birth. A popular French story has held that his mother's preterm labor was brought on by stumbling on the scene of a criminal being broken on the wheel. However, little detail is known of Guillotin's

---

71. AKA the French national razor, the patriotic shortener, and St. Guillotine.

72. May 28th in some accounts.

early life and there is no real evidence to confirm the story. He was educated in local Jesuit schools, and proved to be a brilliant student. He was actively recruited by his Jesuit instructors and joined the order in his youth. In 1761 he received his master of arts degree at Rheims.

Guillotin left the Jesuit order sometime in the Spring of 1763 and turned his attention to the study of medicine. He first moved to Paris, where he spent five years as a medical student. He then moved to Rheims, where he finished his studies more economically than was possible in Paris. He returned to Paris in 1870 and was awarded his official doctorate in medicine. His thesis was titled *How to Prevent the Effects of Rabies*. Almost immediately, he was appointed *docteur-regent,* the highest faculty rank of the school of medicine, and became a popular professor. Although these professors held a monopoly on medical education, their courses were entirely theoretical and, for the most part, based on obsolete and often ancient texts. There was a great call from the public for an enlightened medical faculty, but Guillotin was known as a strict traditionalist and an extremely conservative professor until after he became active in politics.

Despite his strong Jesuit ties, Guillotin became a Freemason and was extremely active in his lodge, La Concorde Fraternelle.[73] He eventually became its Master. He also found a patron in the person of the Duke of Montmoency-Luxembourg. Whether because of his patron or his masonic activity, Guillotin soon found himself a highly popular and successful practitioner. His new found success evidently gave him enough courage to marry for the first time in 1787, although details about his bride are lacking and he had no known children.

In 1784, Louis XVI named Guillotin to a commission to investigate Franz Antoine Mesmer's therapeutic claims. Mesmer (1734-1815) emigrated from Switzerland, and had graduated from the prestegious Vienna Medical School. For several years he had operated a magnetic clinic with the Jesuit professor of astronomy. Their theory, simply put, was that a magnetic field ran from the stars to every living thing and that all disease was due to an obstruction of the magnetic flow to the diseased. At some point, Mesmer decided that he was able to manipulate the magnetic fields without the use of magnets. A theory he described as animal magnetism. His theory was rejected by Vienna's medical community and, following an investigation by Maria Theresa's

---

73. From Ober. Donegan lists his lodge as the Masonic Lodge of the Nine Sisters.

court in 1778, Mesmer was forced to leave Vienna. He moved to a Paris with a growing appitite for new ideas. He quickly published his book, *Memoire sur la decouverte du magnetisme animal*. Through strength of character, elaborate staging, strong suggestion[74] and a willing audience, Mesmer developed a following of enthusiastic proponents and soon was the talk of the town. His popularity soon made him a very rich man with a list of patients that included Marie Antoinette. His views were rejected out-of-hand by the Society of Medicine, but he managed to convert one of the Faculty of Medicine who also happened to be the physician to the King's brother.

By 1884, Mesmer's popularity in France was beginning to become an embarassment. Considered a fraud and a charlatan throughout Europe, Mesmer's popularity in supposedly enlightened France, was considered an ironic jest. Louis XVI was convinced to name a commission to investigate Mesmer's therapeutic claims.

In actuality there were two commissions. Guillotin headed a commission of five prominent physicians. Benjamin Franklin headed a commission of five members of the Accademy of Sciences including Antoine Lavoisier, the father of modern chemistry; Sylvian Bailly,

---

74. What we would call hypnotism today.

Europe's leading astronomer; and Antoine-Laurent de Jussieu, a noted naturalist. The commissions' report was quite accurate. It dubbed Mesmer's cures with magnetic water as frauds and credited his successes as suggestions to receptive audiences whose immaginations did the rest. Mesmer was eventually forced to leave Paris.

His commission's report was well received and encouraged Guillotin to take a stand on other public issues, especially within his Masonic Lodge. The French monarchy was nearly bankrupt; had a corrupt and indifferent nobility; and the general population, the Third Estate, had little or no voice in government and wanted a constitution. Popular novels not withstanding, the poverty of the populace probably played a much more minor role in the revolution than did the lack of representation. In the Estates General, the Nobles, the First Estate, had 300 representatives; the Clergy, the Second Estate, had 300 representatives; but the Third Estate, the French population as a whole, had only 300 representatives. Guillotin viewed this as a basic flaw in the governmental process. Under the sponsorship of six Paris guilds he prepared a *Petition From the Citizens of Paris Demanding Double Representation for the Third Estate in Government.* 6000 of the petitions were printed and widely distributed. Guillotin was arraigned in court because of the petition, but the mob of Parisians supporting him was so threatening, he was aquitted of all charges.

Now a popular hero in Paris, he was elected to the National Assembly in the spring of 1789. He worked hard within the National Assembly, first, improving the meeting facilities and, then, when the delegates were locked out of their meeting hall, it was Guillotin who suggested the tennis court in Rue du Vieux Versailles as a meeting place. Here the delegates took an oath not to be dissolved until an equitable constitution was adopted. Guillotin also served on the Poverty Committee under the social reformer Duc de la Rochefoucald-Liancourt and recommended reforms in the country's hospitals, orphanges and homes for the aged. Guillotin proposed and managed the establishment of a Health Committee, becoming its first chair. He championed public health measures. His committee drafted the "Bill for Medical Reform" which, when finally implemented in 1794, became the basis for modern French medical training and marked a complete reversal of his traditional stance. Despite all of these accomplishments, it is his efforts at penal reform that have made him famous or infamous.

An explanation of the French Penal Code in regard to capital punishment is needed to fully comprehend Guillotin's efforts. Prior to Louis XVI, torture, with amputation of limbs or burns with molten lead or boiling oil, prior to execution was common place. Louis XVI had formally abolished "torture" but there was little doubt that it still took place out of sight of the public. However, there was still a diversity of official methods of execution some of which certainly could be considered torture,

Magicians, sorcerers and heretics were burned at the stake. Highwaymen and assasins were broken on the wheel. Any one convicted of attacks on the Monarch or his family, or of treason, would be executed by quartering.[75] Anybody else convicted of one of the 157 capital crimes of the time would be hanged. That is, anybody else but the nobility. The nobility were executed by decapitation by the executioner's sword or axe.

Guillotin was basically a very conservative man, and his proposals for reform were not earth shaking. He made no plea for the

---

75. A horse was attached to each limb and the man literally torn apart. If the horses proved unequal to the task, the executioner would apply his knife to the joints to make it easier for the horses.

abolition of the death penalty or a reduction in the number of capital crimes. He presented his bill of six articles to the National Assembly on the 10th of October 1789. Proposals 1, 2, and 6 were obviously grounded in his personal humanitarian and egalitarian ideas. Proposals 3, 4, and 5, read in today's world, hardly sound revolutionary, but were obviously taken from the clause against bills of attainder in the United States Constitution and were new to Europe[76].

> 1. Offenses of the same kind will be punished by the same kind of penalty whatsoever the rank and station of the guilty party.
>
> 2. In all cases in which the law imposes the death penalty on an accused person, the punishment will be the same, whatever the nature of the offense of which he is guilty; the prisoner will be decapitated; this will be done solely by a simple mechanism.
>
> 3. In view of the personal character of crime, no punishment of a guilty person shall involve any discredit

---

[76]. The numbering used here is from Kershaw. There is obviously disagreement on Guillotin's numbering and at least three different numberings can be found in the literature.

to his family. The honor of those belonging to him shall be in no way soiled, and they shall continue to be no less admissable to any kind of profession, employment, and public function.

4. No one shall reproach a citizen with any punishment imposed on one of his relatives. Whosoever ventures to do so shall be publicly reprimanded by the judge. The sentence imposed upon him shall be written up on the offender's door. Moreover, it shall be written on the pillory and remain there for a period of three months.

5. Confiscation of the condemned person's property shall in no case be imposed.

6. The corpse of an executed man shall be handed over to his family on their request. In every case, he shall be allowed normal burial, and no reference shall be made on the register to the nature of his death.

The phrase, "the prisoner will be decapitated; this will be done solely by a simple mechanism." forever joined the name of Joseph Ignace Guillotin with the device that bears his name and has connected him through the ages with the Great Terror of the French Revolution[77]. In fact, the simple mechanism suggested by Dr. Guillotin had been in use in various forms since at least 1307.[78] Guillotin's role in the guillotine's development, beyond this suggestion of its use, is contoversial. Most historical commentators believe this was his sole role. However, the National Assembly did not adopt Guillotin's bill until 23 months after its presentation. It has been claimed that during the intervening period, Guillotin colaborated with Dr. Antoine Louis, the Surgical Society Secretary, on a series of experiments decapitating corpses with existing decapitating machines. During these experiments, Dr. Louis developed the angled blade that became standard. Whether Guillotin colaborated or not, it was Dr. Antoine Louis who submitted the design for the Guillotine to the National Assembly, where it was approved on March 17, 1792. And it was Dr. Antoine Louis who suggested the National Assembly

---

77. It has been suggested that Guillotin probably submitted a sketch of a machine that had been in use in France since early in the 17th century.

78. Woodcuts and contemporary accounts confirm its use in Ireland on April 1, 1307, and other accounts suggest its use elsewhere even earlier.

commission Tobias Schmidt[79] to make the first working model that was purchased by the National Assembly on March 20, 1792, for 960 Francs. Louis's name was attached to the machine briefly, as "Louison" and "Louisette." Each had a brief vogue before Guillotin's name became linked to it forever. The machine was first used for the execution of a highwayman named Pelletier on April 25, 1792.

Guillotin had no further relationship with the decapitating machine after its adoption. As the National Assembly was racked by battles between ever more radical elements, Guillotin was forced out. He left Paris during the reign of terror and moved to Arras. After the Austro-German forces invaded, Guillotin served a year with the French Army, resisting the invaders. When he left the army he returned to Paris. Citizen Guillotin was arrested on October 3, 1794, on orders of the Committee for National Safety, accused of writing illegal pamphlets. He was released five weeks later. Now 57 years old and a political nonentitiy, he re-established his medical practice and once again became

---

79. Tobias Schmidt is variously described as a Swiss or German harpsichord maker, a piano maker, a watchmaker, a cabinetmaker, a mechanic, and an alcoholic handy man. Despite the variety of his titles, it is obvious he was a skilled craftsman from one of the Paris guilds who had invented a variety of machines, at least one of which was an advanced harpsichord.

a prominent member of the medical community. He founded the Academy of Medicine, and was one of the few French physicians who recognized the value of Jenner's work on vaccination. He was active in its introduction in France, serving as Chairman of the Central Vaccination Committee. He died at 77 on March 27, 1814, supposidly of massive carbuncle of his left shoulder[80].

---

80. Described in one account as an "anthrax of the left shoulder."

THOMAS DOVER

Take opium one Ounce, Salt-Petre and Tarter Virolated, each four Ounces, Ipocacuana one Ounce, Liquorish one Ounce. Put the Tarter and Salt-Petre into a red-hot Mortar, stirring them with a spoon till they have done flaming. Then powder them very fine; after that slice in your Opium; grind these to a Powder, and then mix the other Powders with these. Dose from forty to sixty or seventy Grains in a Glass of White Wine Posset going to Bed.

Thomas Dover's one lasting contribution to medicine was the above formula for the well known Dover's Powder which was used as a diphoretic, analgesic, soporific and general "cure-all" for over 250[81] years. The formula was found in his self-agrandizing home medical volume.[82] Because he was an egotistical, opinionated,

---

81. Dover combined the powder with bed rest, heat and hydration. The powder was used widely in Europe right up to the beginning of WWII, frequently combined with asprin.

82. Dover, *The Ancient Physician's Legacy to his Country,* Bettesworth & Hitch 1732. The book went through at least 7 editions and stayed in print throughout the 18th Century. It was most likely the first home medical care book

agressive, but charismatic, personality who practiced continually on the edge of quackery[83], his medical career, as such, does not bear repeating here. However, the life of Captain Thomas Dover needs to be told.

Thomas Dover was born on Shirley Farm at Barton on the Heath, near Moreton-in-Marsh, England in 1662, the seventh of eight children.[84] His father was a gentleman farmer, a retired Captain of the Horse. His early schooling is generally unknown, but Dewhurst states he attended Chipping Camden Grammar School. In any case, in 1680 he entered Magdalen Hall, Oxford as a commoner. We know nothing of his years at Oxford except that he was awarded his BA in 1684.

After leaving Oxford, Dover precepted with Dr. Thomas Sydenham, one of the most prominent physicians of the day. While still a preceptor and living in Sydenham's home, he contracted smallpox. Dr.

---

ever written in English.

83. Dover was an advocate of using raw (metallic) mercury as a panacea for asthma, worms, colic, sterility, gout, tuberculosis, and several other diseases. His usual dose was one ounce, but for intestinal obstruction he prescribed a pound. This obsession with mercury earned him the title of "Dr. Quicksilver" and forever linked his name to the legions of false medical messiahs.

84. 1660 in some accounts. The area is commonly known as the Cotswolds.

Sydenham treated him with his "cooling treatment,[85]" and Dover recovered. After his two year preceptorship with Sydenham, Dover enrolled in Cambridge and received his BM in 1687. He then moved back to his home and shortly thereafter married[86].

His father died circa 1690, and left the family estates to Thomas. In 1691, Thomas moved to Bristol, then England's second largest city. Bristol was probably the most posperous city in England as well. England's maritime trade with America and the West Indies was based in Bristol, and, when London's monopoly was broken, it became the center of England's slave trade. Dover became one of the few trained physicians in Bristol and his practice flourished. He was the first physician in Bristol to offer free care to the poor and he became a popular hero. By 1701, he had gained enough financial capital to begin a career in the slave trade.

He started as part-owner of ships and sailing as the ship's doctor. As his sail and navigational skills developed, he took on

---

85. Open windows, patient covered to the waist only, massive hydration (beer), only token bleeding and no blistering.

86. We know nothing about his wife except that her name was Joanna and she died on April 27, 1727.

increasing roles as ship's officer. His finances increased proportionally as his shares as part-owner and increasing rank rose. Finally he ended up as captain of his own ship. Exactly how many trips he took between 1701 and 1707 remains unknown, but he was well known as Captain Thomas Dover by 1707, and his financial success was common knowledge among the merchants of Bristol. As best as we can determine today, profits were poured into his estates and, in 1708, into the outfitting of two privateers, the *Duke* and the *Duchess*. The *Duke* was a 320 ton ship, mounting thirty guns and carrying a crew of 180 men. The *Duchess* was a 260 ton ship, mounting twenty-six guns and carrying a crew of 150 men.

The Crown had passed a new Prize Act that allowed privateers to keep all the prize money they won[87]. This was no act of altruism on the part of the Crown. By allowing merchants to outfit privateers for expected profit, the Crown essentially had passed the cost of a navy on to commercial interests. Dover had joined a syndicate of Bristol merchants/slavers, and town officials in putting up the £15,000 necessary to outfit the privateers. Thomas Dover was the second largest individual

---

87. Previously the Crown had taken one-third of the prizes. Two-thirds of the value of the prizes was to go to the owners and one-third to the crew.

contributor to the syndicate, with an investment of £3000, and, because the largest contributor was a Quaker with no sea experience, Captain Dover was appointed Owner's representative or supercargo and third in command of the expedition. The commander of the expedition, Woodes Rogers, held a commission from the Lord High Admiral of Great Britain and Ireland to cruise in the South Seas against the French and the Spaniards[88].

Plain Thomas Dover, MD, was egotistical, opinionated, and confrontational enough to alienate most of his fellow physicians. Captain Thomas Dover, relegated to third in command at sea, was almost immediately on a collision course with Woodes Rogers. Fortunately, shortly after they left the West Coast of Ireland, there was an attempted mutiny by the crew. The officers were, by force, banded together, and although Woodes Rogers notes in the log that Dover was egotistical, opinionated, agressive, and confrontaional, there was no irreparable break between the two crossing the Atlantic.

The privateers took one small ship prior to reaching the Canaries and then ransomed it without difficulty. The *Duke* and the *Duchess* were

---

88. Woodes Rogers would also act as Captain of the *Duke* with Dover second in command and Captain of the marines. Captain Courtney would act as Captain of the *Duchess*. Captain Dampier was the expedition pilot.

resupplied in the Canary Islands, and then sailed across the South Atlantic without incident. They approached Cape Horn via the Falkland Islands and then battered their way around the Cape. As they made their way up the West Coast of South America, scurvy began showing up in the crew. This was a disease Dover was very familiar with and he insisted that the ship obtain a supply of fresh fruit and vegetables as soon as possible. The expedition's Navigator, Captain William Dampier brought them to Ma's a Tierra, one of the Jaun Fernandez Islands off the coast of Peru. Thomas Dover commanded the longboat that rowed ashore first. In addition to the fresh water, fruit and vegetables[89] that he was seeking, he found a wild looking man clad in goat skins.

The man turned out to be Alexander Selkirk, from Ayrshire, Scotland, who had been stranded alone on the island four years before. The exact circumstances of his being left on the island are debatable. Selkirk had his clothes, books, bedding, and firearms with him. The most neutral account is that he was a petty officer on his ship, the *Cinque-Ports,* and had a disagreement over the condition of the ship with his

---

89. The only supplies noted in detail were goat meat, pimentos, turnips and turnip greens and water cress.

captain. The captain considered the disagreement mutiny and left him on the island in lieu of a death sentence. However, Selkirk always maintained that he was left on the island by choice rather than continue sailing on what he considered an unseaworthy ship[90]. Selkirk had sailed with the pilot, Dampier, previously, and, upon Dampier's recommendation, was taken aboard as a sailing master.

The privateers were overhauled and restocked in the Jaun Fernandez Islands. They immediately began taking prizes along the coast of Peru and Chile. Their fleet increased to eight ships with over 300 prisoners. It was then decided to attack the town of Guayquil, at that time, a town of about 2000 with a garrison of about 500 soldiers. It was Peru's largest ship building port. Dover commanded the attack force. After failing to agree with the town officials on the amount to be paid to call off the attack, Dover took the town, looted it of its flour, sugar, oil, arms and jewelry, and then ransomed the town back for 30,000 pieces-of-eight. However, the English paid a stiff price for their victory. Plague hit

---

90. The account of Selkirk's rescue, of course, became the basis of Daniel Defoe's *Robinson Crusoe*. The first edition of *Robinson Crusoe* was published in 1719, some eight years after the privateers return to England and Woodes Roger's account of the voyage.

the men of the landing party after they left the coast and they lost ten men despite Dover's best efforts. They took several rich prizes, and a badly wounded Woodes Rogers and Dover came into conflict over who would command their largest prize, the *Batchelor*[91]. Despite Woodes Rogers strong opposition, Dover eventually prevailed and commanded the *Batchelor* home via Guam and Batavia. In Guam, the privateers resupplied and careened the hulls of their ships.

On the trip home, the privateers came under the scrutiny of the East India Company. Dover, as owner's representative, feared the East India Company would make claim on the privateers' prizes. Dover had made fast friends with an East India Company captain, Captain John Opie commander of the frigate, *Oley*. He made arrangements for one of the prize ships, the *Marquis*, to be sold to Opie for the bargain-basement price of 575 Dutch dollars. The sale was made on the provision that Opie sail his frigate directly to Bristol and warn the owner's syndicate to

---

91. The privateers' richest prize, the 400 ton treasure ship, *Nostra Seniora de la Incarnacion de Singano*, mounting 40 guns. They had attacked the even larger Manila Treasure ship, but it fought them off.

prepare to fight the East India Company. Opie did just that[92]. The privateers spent more than three months in Cape Town waiting for the annual Dutch convey home. The slow Dutch convoy they finally joined consisted of 16 Dutch and nine English ships and offered ample protection. They reached England on October 14.,1711. They had been at sea almost exactly three years[93].

The privateer holds were laden with treasure. It is estimated that their plunder was valued at between £120,000 and £170,000 the richest haul by privateers in English maritime history. The East India Company did make a claim, charging the privateers of trading in waters in which the East India Company held a monopoly. In a final settlement, reportedly negotiated by Dover, the Bristol owners paid the East India Company £6,000. Dover's share of the profits was reported as £6,067, plus £423 as physician, £100 as storm money, £24 as plunder money, and £35 as captain of the *Batchelor,* for a total of £6,689.

In September, 1711, Robert Harley, leader of the Tory

---

92. Besides becoming Thomas Dover's best friend and fellow South Seas Company employee, Opie married Dover's daughter, Elizabeth.

93. Reports vary with some taking the time at sea from when the privateers left Bristol and some from the time they left Cork.

government, pushed through a bill in Parliament setting up a company of merchants to trade in the South Seas and South America, The South Seas Company. Besides gaining the privilege of acting as a national bank, it had a monopoly on the lucrative slave, hide, tallow, quinine and mineral trade with South America. It is a matter of record that Dover had been recommended to Harley, but Dover's almost immediate investment of £6,000[94] in the company certainly made him a conspicuous choice for a role in the company. Nothing much happened with South American trade immediately, but in March, 1713, the Asiento Treaty signed in Madrid transferred the assets of the French Guinea Company to the British South Seas Company. That gave the South Seas Company trading posts, or "factories," and any slaves remaining at the factories, at Buenos Aires, Vera Cruz and Carthagena. Under the terms of the treaty, 4000 slaves per year could be brought into South America by the British, 1200 of whom were to be processed through the Buenos Aires factory. The British were limited to two trading vessels to bring goods to the factories.

Captain Thomas Dover was named President of the Buenos Aires

---

94. Dover reportedly had to mortgage the family estate to buy the stock. This would seem extremely unlikely in view of his recent share of the privateer venture and his years in the slave trade.

factory at a salary of slightly over £1,000 per year, which was to be paid to his daughter Elizabeth, his attorney-in-fact, in quarterly payments. In September of 1714, the 53 year old Dover and his five factors were assigned to *H.M.S. Warwick*, under the command of Captain Henry Partington. Partington was short tempered, jealous of his command and a strict disciplinarian[95]. It was inevitable that he would clash with Dover. Dover and his Assistant Martin almost immediately had a quarrel with Partington, and complained to the South Seas Company Directors of his "ill usage and general lack of cooperation[96]." The Directors contacted the Admiralty who sent a letter of reprimand to Partington. Partington bitterly fought Dover and Martin's charges and brought counter charges of his own[97]. The result was Partington and Dover became bitter enemies.

Even before they left port, Dover also clashed with the South Seas Company Directors. Their first clash came over medical supplies.

---

95. A later incident involving two young boys taken as servants suggested that Partington was a pederast. However, the charges were dismissed on testimony of the ship's chaplain.

96. Dewhurst at 112.

97. Despite the fact that only the factors were supposed to be transported, it appears that Dover attempted to transport maids, secretaries and his mistress.

Dover was a commercial employee and had not been appointed surgeon. The directors quite pointedly told him medical supplies were beyond his domain and rejected his list of medical supplies.

The *Warwick* finally was loaded and sailed from Plymouth on February 17, 1715. They had an uneventful voyage to the river Plate via Maderia, arriving on June 12, 1715. The ship anchored in Castillos Bay and an armed longboat was sent ashore, reportedly with Dover in charge. Ashore, he found water and killed several of the cattle found wandering in the area. Restocked with water and meat they started up the river and arrived at Montevedeo on June 23, 1715. Partington had trouble navagating the river and ran ashore at least once. As a result, Dover and his factors did not arrive in Buenos Aires until mid August and the *Warwick* did not reach Buenos Aires until September 11, 1715.

Dover immediately established a good relationship with the Spanish government and church authorities. With their help, and seemingly in violation of his instructions, he took over the French post, with a few hides and twenty-two slaves, and greatly expanded the post. By the end of 1715, Dover was processing West African slaves and shipping hides and tallow. There is no doubt that Dover and the South

Seas Company were secretly exceeding the terms of the treaty from the time they took over the post. It also appears that Dover was doing some major trading on his own[98], an unforgivable sin in the eyes of the South Seas Company, and perhaps was taking a commission on the hides and tallow he was buying for the South Seas Company, another unforgivable sin. Because his surgeon was also being investigated, there is speculation that the medical bills for slaves were also being inflated. In any case, the South Seas Company began getting disturbing reports from the returning merchant ships. On April 30, a letter from Partington, most likely critical of Dover was discussed by the directors. To get a better idea of the situation in Buenos Aires, the directors spoke with the former President of the French factory there. They also set up a committee to study the Buenos Aires factory. On July 18, 1716, Dover was dismissed from the South Seas Company for breach of his instructions and neglect of duty.

It took several months for the news to reach Dover and even longer for his replacement to arrive. He was finally relieved on February 24, 1717. He immediately returned to England and set up a small medical

---

98. It appears this trading was in partnership with his son-in-law, John Opie who was also employed by the South Seas Company.

practice in London. He was barely making anything over expenses. Meanwhile, Dover's fortune was still tied up in the South Seas Company, and the Company was heading slowly but surely into bankruptcy. The South Seas Company bubble finally burst in 1720. Dover lost everything he had invested.

His practice and income was temporarily saved by a London smallpox epidemic. His cooling treatment made more sense than any of the prevailing treatments, and his patients survived in greater numbers than those of his competitors. It brought him some short lived prominence, but his criticism of and refusal to consult with fellow physicians brought him before a disciplinary committee of the Royal College of Physicians. Rumors about his competency began to circulate. His practice began to dwindle away.

In 1726, Dover left London and returned to the family estate with his wife. By this time he was heavily in debt. Shortly after moving back to the Cotswolds, his wife died and Dover was forced to sell the estate. Widowed, almost bankrupt and homeless, Dover went to live with a cousin, Robert Tracey. Some six years later, at the age of seventy, Dover published the first edition of his home medical book which contained the formula for his popular powder and earned him the title of Dr. Quicksilver for its constant advice to take crude or raw (metallic) mercury. The book temporarily revived his medical practice and he kept practicing medicine until 1742 when he returned to the Traceys. He died on April 27[99], 1742 and was buried in the Tracey vault at Stanway Church.

---

99. Some reports have his date of death as April 20, 1742 and give the April 27th date as the date of his burial.

ERNESTO GUEVARA de la SERNA

Ernesto Guevara de la Serna, better known to the world as Che Guevara, was born into an aristocratic Argentine family on June 14, 1928 in Misiones Provence, Argentina according to his birth certificate. However, family records show his actual date of birth to have been on May 14, 1928. The later date of birth was courtesy of an obliging physician and records clerk who helped his parents obscure the fact that his mother was three months pregnant when she married his father.

Ernesto's father, Ernesto Guevara Lynch, was the handsome offspring of an aristocratic but impoverished Argentine family. He had gone to state schools and probably had never attended college. He worked as a surveyor and whatever family money he had inherited was tied up in the family boat building business. His ambition was to become a planter and raise *Yerba Mate,* the basis of the Agentine national drink.

Ernesto's mother, Celia de la Serna, was a rich blueblood, but plagued with allergies and asthma. Her father was a famous law professor, a former congressman, and ambassador, who had died when she was a child. She was raised by a religous aunt who had not only preserved, but increased, her fortune. She had been educated at the Sacre Coeur, an exclusive girls' school.

Exactly how they met and how Lynch managed to seduce the naive Celia is not known. Her family had been dead set against her seeing Lynch from the start. Nonetheless, at age twenty, Celia found herself three months pregnant. The two finally married at the home of Celia's older sister, Edelmira Moore de la Serna on November 10, 1927. The couple quickly fled 1200 miles up the Parana River to Misiones Provence, where they bought a 500 acre plantation in Peurto Caraguatai with Celia's money.

The new baby developed bronchial pneumonia shortly after birth, and by age two, little Ernesto was diagnosed with severe chronic asthma. His paternal grandmother and spinster aunt, Beatriz, showered the sickly toddler with attention. Because of financial problems with the boat building business and Ernesto's asthma the family moved to Buenos Aires circa 1929-30. The boat business burned and, with little or no insurance, what was left of Ernesto Lynch's fortune was gone. Although he gave lip service to being a planter, Ernesto Lynch never really worked the land, and, for practical purposes, Celia's fortune supported the family from that time on. Both parents were poor money managers and lived a lavish lifestyle which belied their limited investment income.

In 1932, the family, which now included two siblings besides Ernesto, moved to Alta Gracia in the foothills of the Sierra Chica mountains where the climate was supposed to be better for Ernesto's asthma. In 1934, Ernesto's sister Ana Maria was born. She rapidly became the center of his attention, and by far the closest of his four siblings.

Alta Gracia was a heaven for the young Enesto. his asthma became better. When free of asthma, he played tennis, soccer, and golf; he shot, rode horseback, swam and hiked. Even at this young age he loved to court danger and was naturally rebellious and opinionated. His parents held him out of school, and he roamed alone much of the day as he became more and more wild and undisciplined[100].

When the school authorities finally caught up with him, he could already read and write. He was almost immediately spotted as a bright student, but a showoff and a classroom discipline problem.

Ernesto's first real political exposure probably came with the Spanish Civil War of 1936-1939. Refugees from Republican Spain began showing up in Alta Gracia. Among them was the Gonzales-Aguilar family. The father was the former Spanish Minister of Health, and their children were the same age as Ernesto and his siblings. The two families became fast friends. In addition, it was during this period that Celia's sister Carmen and her two children moved in with the family while her husband, the communist poet Polico Cardova-Iturburu, covered the war as a foreign correspondent.

Ernesto Lynch formed a support group, Accion Argentina, for the Republican refugees and helped them get settled in Alta Gracia. The same organization became a strong support group for the allies during WWII.

---

100. Harper claims that at age seven he broke street lights to support an electrical worker's strike. The evidence seems to show he was guilty of numerous acts of aimless vandalism and that any street lights he broke were without political motive.

In 1942, Ernesto, age fourteen started high school in Cordoba necessitating a twenty-three mile bus ride each way. The family soon moved to Cordoba, both because of the schools and because Ernesto Lynch finally had a job constructing and selling houses. Unfortunately, he contributed little to the family. The money disappeared on women and entertaining. Celia became estranged, but Ernesto Lynch talked her into a reconciliation and their fifth child was conceived.

Ernesto became friends with a bigger, huskier classmate, Tomas Grando. Tomas played rugby on a team coached by his elder brother Alberto, a first year university student majoring in biochemistry. Influenced by Tomas, Ernesto tried out for the rugby team. Despite his relatively small size and his asthma Ernesto charged so furiously and so recklessly, that Alberto, the coach, began calling him "Fuser." Despite the relative age difference, Alberto Grando, not Tomas, became Ernesto's best friend. In November of 1943, Alberto was arrested during a student demonstration against dictator Pedro Ramirez. Town students organized a demonstration calling for his release, but Ernesto would not participate[101]. However, he and Tomas visited Alberto in prison and brought him food.

Begining circa 1942-1943, Ernesto began having sex on a more or less regular basis with servant girls and other poor girls he either paid or coerced. His one romantic affair was reportedly with his young cousin, Carmen Cordova Iturburu de la Serna. He, like his father, would remain a womanizer for the rest of his life.

In 1945, at age seventeen, and after a school career marked by discipline problems, he suddenly became a serious student. He started a ten-volume philosophical dictionary, and became a serious reader. Celia always had a salon of intellectuals on call and now Ernesto, handsome, self-assured, and with contempt for formality, joined them. His combative intellectualism and his love for the shocking, fit right in with his mother's salon,

At age eighteen, Ernesto graduated from high school and took a job in the local Public Works office as a soil specialist. He expected to become an engineer, and thought the job would be good experience and

---

101. He told the organizers that they would not accomplish anything and "get the shit knocked out of them."

money for school. While he was working, his parents formally separated, and his mother and siblings moved back to Buenos Aires. In 1948, his paternal grandmother suffered a stroke and became seriously ill. Ernesto was summoned to Buenos Aires and arrived seven days before her death. She had smothered him with attention, and he was grief stricken.

He suddenly decided he would study medicine instead of engineering. The decision, coming on the heels of his grandmother's death, has prompted the family to claim that was the reason for the change of vocations. However, many observers believe it was his obsession with his asthma that made him seek a medical degree. He wanted a cure for the ailment that had plagued him all his life. He applied for admission to the Faculty of Medicine at the University of Buenos Aires. He worked at a local allergy clinic to help pay the bills. Shortly after he began his freshman year in the medical school, he was called up for the Argentine military draft. His severe chronic asthma made him unfit for duty. He studied and ate at his aunt Beatriz's apartment, and, according to some of the family, he felt closer to her than to Celia. To get away from the books and studying, he began taking hitchhiking trips on the weekends.

Because Ernesto Lynch was perpetually broke and, even when he worked, contributed nothing, the siblings all worked to help support the family. They finally managed to sell the long dormant plantation and used the funds to buy a house in Buenos Aries.

It is interesting to note that by most accounts Ernesto joined no political groups and had no political activity while in medical school. This is particularly noteworthy because the university was ripe with anti-Peron activity at this time. However, many remember him remarking that he thought South America's twin problems were United States intervention in South America's politics and the South American oligarchies. Ernesto is remembered fondly by most of his classmates as an attractive eccentric and an unrelenting womanizer. Despite this reported interest in women, Ernesto never could learn to dance and was extremely careless of his dress and personal hygiene.

On January 1, 1950, Ernesto began a 4000 kilometer motorcycle trip with his best friend, Alberto Grando. The trip was supposed to go first to Cordoba and then north to San Francisco del Chanar where Grando was to work in the Jose Puente Leprosarium, but Ernesto continued on to Jujuy, Argenina's northern most city. Ernesto began a diary of the trip, a habit he would continue until he was killed.

During his fourth year of the medical school course, Ernesto fell madly in love with Cinchina Ferreyra, the sixteen year old daughter of the oldest and richest family in Cordoba. The family barely tolerated Ernesto, and after he proposed to Cinchina, their oposition became open and strong. Cinchina evidently felt too young for marraige and put Ernesto off without making him feel she was rejecting him totally or forever.

When the fourth year ended, Ernesto shipped out as the doctor[102] on a coastal freighter, and visited numerous South American ports. When school resumed, Ernesto's interest in medicine seemed to wane considerably, and when, at the end of his fifth year, Aberto Grando suggested a trip on his vintage, 500cc Norton motorcycle from one end of South America to the other, Ernesto readily agreed. On January 4, 1952, the two set out on what was to be a year long trip. The details of this trip, taken from Ernesto's journals, have been published elsewhere and will not be repeated here.[103] However, the trip reportedly resulted in

---

102. Some sources say his title was nurse.

103. The reader is referred to Guevara, *The Motorcycle Diaries.*

Ernesto believing that all of Latin America was one, and cemented his theory that Latin America's twin problems were United States intervention and national oligarchies. While Ernesto was on this trip, Cinchina Ferreyra finally put a definite end to their romance.

Ernesto returned to medical school for his final year and passed his final examinations on April 11, 1953[104]. In June of 1953 he left Argentina with his friend Calica Ferrer with the aim of joining Aberto Grando at the leprosarium he was working at in Venezuala. Their first stop was LaPaz, Bolivia where the Movimento Nationlista Revolucianaro (MNR) had just taken over. The MNR had disbanded the army and nationalized the mines. The country was in chaos. Peasants were attacking plantaion owners, militias roamed the streets and the MNR was fragmented and unable to establish any sort of order. If Ernesto was there to view a socialist revolution, he was certainly disenchanted. The two travelers left La Paz as soon as they could obtain the necessary visas from the Argentine Embassy.

---

104. There is no evidence for the frequent claims that Ernesto: (1) graduated from medical school in half the required time; (2) did not complete his final university examinations. However, the critics seem to be correct in that there is no evidence that he was ever licensed to practice medicine in any jurisdiction.

Their next stop was Peru and then Ecuador. In Ecuador, the two friends parted, with Ferrer continuing on as planned to Venezuala and Ernesto deciding to continue north all the way to Guatemala. At this point, Ernesto Guevara announced to his family that he had decided to abandon medicine and become a professional adventurer. He proceeded in to Panama where he seems to have run out of money and also had a problem in getting entry into Costa Rica. He wrote a couple of travel articles and a fiercely anti-United States article in which he accused the United States of looting Machu Picchu. He now declared to all who would listen that the United States was his mortal enemy. He finally ended up on a United Fruit boat and legally or illegally gained entry to Costa Rica, where he met up with the communist leader, Manuel Mara Valverde, and had some contact with the paramilitary organization, the Carribean Legion. From Panama he made his way to Nicaragua, Honduras, El Salvador and finally Guatemala.

In 1952, Jacobo Arbenz had taken control of the government, instituted land reform, and nationalized the United Fruit Company properties. By the time Ernesto arrived in 1953, problems between Guatemala and Washington had escalated to just short of "sending in the

Marines." The United Fruit Company, with CIA help, organized and armed a force training in Nicaraugua to overthrow Arbenz. It seems to have been in this environment that Ernesto became an authentic revolutionary. He totally identified with Arbenz's cause. He felt the only way a people's government could survive in South America was by confronting the United States head on.

It was here he met a wide variety of leftists, including Hilda Gadea, the rather unattractive exiled leader of Peru's leftist youth group, and several of Raul and Fidel Castro's followers[105]. It was this group of Cubans who gave Ernesto the nickname "Che" from the Argentine custom of using "che" as "hey you."

As his stay in Guatemala lengthened, Ernesto/Che became increasingly close to Hilda Gadea. Hilda mothered him through asthma attacks and offered him a job with the communist youth group. Ernesto refused. Hilda also introduced him to the writings of Mao, and she became a regular resource for Ernesto's sex and cash. Not that he was monogomous by any means. Che became enamored with Mao and if one

---

105. Raul and Fidel Castro had attempted an unsuccessful coup in Cuba about six months before Ernesto arrived in Guatemala. Both were imprisoned on the Isle of Pines, but several of his co-conspirators had made it to Mexico and Guatemala.

insists on classifying his political philosophy, he became a Maoist.

However, the other foreign leftists and communists could see the handwriting on the wall and began to leave Guatemala. Ernesto stayed on. With Hilda's help he began writing a book, *"The Role of the Doctor in Latin America."* The gist of the book was that the Latin American physician should not limit himself to medical problems, but devote himself to the social, economic and political problems plaguing the people as well.

On June 18, 1954, after a Swedish ship arrived in Guatemala with Soviet arms, the CIA/United Fruit Company troops, with Washington's approval, invaded Guatemala and captured the capital of the Provence of Salama. Ernesto, now answering only to Che, enlisted in an emergency medical brigade. Hilda formed a women's brigade. The regular army was either incapable of or unintersted in ousting the invaders. Ernesto couldn't understand why Arbenz wouldn't arm the populace. He was sure a "people's army" could prevail over the United States and the United Fruit Company. The United States effectively prevented any United Nations effort to intervene and sent in fighter bombers to support the invasion. By July 3,1954, Arbenz was seeking asylum in the Mexican Embassy and a U.S. backed puppet was in power. Che fled to the Argentine Embassy, but Hilda was arrested and held several days.

In August, Che finally left the Embassy, found Hilda, and by September had left Hilda and entered Mexico. By this time, his hatred of the United States bordered on obsession. In Mexico City, he quickly fell in with a group of twelve to fourteen Cuban exiles who were followers of the Castro brothers. Che was unable to find regular medical work, but worked part time at a local allergy clinic. Sometime in the winter of 1954, Hilda rejoined him.

In the spring of 1955, Che presented a paper at a medical meeting in Leon. As a result of that paper, he was offered an internship at Mexico City's General Hospital. However, before the internship could begin, in May 1955, Raul and Fidel Castro were released from prison. Shortly thereafter, Raul showed up in Mexico City. Che and Raul became almost instantaneous friends. Their philosophies meshed on almost every plane. Raul became a frequent guest at Che and Hilda's apartment. Raul introduced Che to Nikolai Lenov, who held a junior post in the Soviet Embassy. Raul had met Lenov some years earlier at a European Youth

Festival.

On July 7, 1955, Fidel Castro arrived in Mexico City. About two days later, Raul brought Fidel to dinner at Che and Hilda's apartment. Almost immediately Fidel invited Che to join his guerilla organization as its medical member. Che accepted readily.

At almost the same moment, Hilda Gadea announced to Che that she was pregnant. Che married Hilda on August 18, 1955. Raul stood up for Che and Fidel was at the post-wedding party. Che immediately broke the news of his marriage to his family.

Fidel Castro had begun a pamphlet campaign in Cuba to pave the way for popular support of his upcoming guerilla campaign. He decided to launch his guerilla campaign in the Sierra Maestra Mountains. It was Fidel's home region and he knew the country well. Marti had launched the revolution against the Spanish from the same region, and it was close to Cuba's second largest city, Santiago. Fidel hoped Santiago could be a source of recruits, funding, intelligence and weapons.

Fidel recruited Spanish Civil War General Alberto Bago to train his guerilla band[106] while he went on a very successful fund raising trip to the United States. Che took the training seriously. He climbed mountains and did whatever he could to get himself conditioned. Che turned out to be a crack shot, was well conditioned despite his asthma, showed great leadership and was soon the standout of the movement.

On February 15, 1956, Hilda gave birth to Che's first child. A daughter, Hilda (Hildita) Beatriz.

By May, 1956, Castro had about forty Cubans in Mexico and moved the lot to Rancho San Miguell for training in guerilla warfare. Despite some grumbling by the Cubans, Che became General Bago's second in command. On June 20, 1956, Fidel Castro was arrested. Che got word of the arrest in time to hide all the weapons before the ranch was raided. Che claimed he was just the physician for the group, but the press named Che as the ringleader and his Latin American notoriety began. Most of the Cubans were released by early July, but Che, Fidel Castro and Calixto Garcia continued to be held.

Che was free with his press interviews and stated that he was a

---

106. Numbering in the neighborhood of thirty-four men by January 1956. Castro labeled the guerilla movement 7/26.

communist and supported armed rebellion throughout Latin America. Fidel was furious. He was still hoping for support from the United States and didn't want any hint of a communist connection to his movement. Fidel was released from the Mexican jail by the end of July, but Che and Calixto were not released until the authorities were bribed and the two swore to leave Mexico immediately. The two went underground in Mexico.

Finally on November 23, 1955, Che and Calixto joined the Castro invasion force at Pozo Rico, Mexico and on November 24th the force departed for Cuba aboard the thirty-eight-foot *Grenada*. Some of the force of 82 was left behind because of lack of space. The boat took seven days to make the trip, and was spotted by a Cuban Coast Guard cutter. The group's navigation was faulty and they landed at the wrong beach without any support from their group based in Cuba. The group almost immediately ran into an army ambush. Che was wounded, but managed to escape. He eventually collected a group of seven or eight survivors and led them to Castro. Only twenty-two of the original landing party managed to regroup in the mountains.

The press reported the invasion force had been wiped out. Hilda and Hildita left Mexico and returned to her family's home in Peru. Che's family was also in the dark for about a month until Che managed to have word sent to them that he was alive.

By the first of the year, Fidel had made contact with local mountain residents and secured some local help. He also received reinforcements from the Cuban branch of his movement. He moved from a defensive camp to one from which he could move offensively and then on January 19, 1956, raided a small garrison at La Plata on the coast. The captured garrison supplied them with guns, ammunition and much needed food. They set up a deadly ambush for the pursuing army troops and got away without problems.

Che thoroughly enjoyed the life of a guerilla, but as a guerilla fighter, not as a medic. Despite the fact he suffered from his asthma, sporadic diarrhea, and, by some accounts, malaria, he was considered a brave, aggressive, guerilla fighter. The Cubans continued to grumble about his strict discipline and harsh dealing with infractions, but admired his courage and readily followed him. Che's asthma laid him low periodically. On several occasions he had to be left behind well-hidden when the guerillas were forced to retreat.

Soon the effects of the guerilla force began to be felt throughout Cuba. At a February 15, 1956, meeting with his National Directorate, Fidel Castro lobbied to have his guerillas be the top priority of the national movement. When the National Directorate did not immediately agree, a rift between Castro's mountain guerillas and the middle class urban Directorate began to grow. Castro and his band made good press and the New York Times began running a series on them. When Che stepped in to deliver a shot to the head of the first traitor executed by the guerillas, his reputation as a cold blooded killer was born.

Throughout 1956, the guerilla force was barely surviving. But the press painted them as a much larger force than they really were, and by early 1957 they were finally gaining strength through new recruits. Che was in charge of conditioning and training the new recruits. Castro now felt he had enough men to divide them into three commands. By April of 1957, the guerillas had an effective supply system in place and Che was given command of one of the three commands.

On May 28, 1957, Castro attacked and took the coastal garrison at El Uvero. Many consider this the turning point in the guerilla war. Che was left behind in charge of the wounded and a small rear guard. This unit continued to act independently for about six weeks before rejoining Castro. Castro was impressed with how well the independent units functioned and gave Che command of a group of seventy-five men to act independently. But combat was not Che's only accomplishment. He laid the basis for agrarian reform while still in the Sierra Maestra; built an arms factory; invented a bazooka like weapon and a tin can hand grenade; built a bakery to supply bread to the guerrillas; a hospital and school for both the guerrillas and the local peasants; and started the rebel newspaper.

Che's column was very successful in setting up ambushes, and, at the end of July, 1957, successfully attacked the garrison at Bueycito. With the increasing strength and success of the guerillas, Castro's disgust with the lack of support from National Directorate was becoming more open. Raul Castro and Che encouraged a complete break, but Fidel still wanted the mainstream identification provided by the national organization.

Finally, in 1958, the guerillas were strong enough to come out of the mountains and attack on the plains[107]. Prior to decending onto the plains, Castro set up a radio station and began broadcasting his propaganda message throughout Cuba. He now felt strong enough to reject a cease fire negotiated by the Catholic Church and to complete the break with the mainstream National Directorate. Che was now put in charge of the rebel military school at Mino del Frio. Che's students were thoroughly indoctrinated with an anti-Yankee hatred and secondarily with a lefitist philosophy as well as guerilla tactics. During this period, Che's principal mistress was an attractive single mother, Zoila Rodrigues.

After the National Directorate called for a general strike, but would not let the Cuban Communist Party participate, Castro endorsed the Communist Party position and effectively joined the Communist Party to his guerilla movement. There was an immediate influx of communist recruits who were welcomed by Raul Castro and Che. Fidel Castro announced that the only National Directorate of the 7/26 movement was located with him and his guerilla forces. With the

---

107. The rebels had received at least one plane load of weapons and ammunition from Costa Rica. Where the financing came from or what the original source of the weapons was is speculative at best.

alignment with the Communists, Che took an increasing role in controlling the armed forces and increasing influence with Fidel.[108]

In late May 1958, the Cuban army began an all out assualt against the guerilla forces. Che was put in charge of a flying column and acted as the trouble-shooter as hot spots developed. Raul and a column were sent to start an offense in the Sierra Cristal to take the pressure off Fidel's forces. By July 20, 1958, the tide began to turn in favor of Fidel's guerillas. Several other rebel movements now joined Fidel's movement, and by August 5th, the regular army troops began to retreat. By the end of August, Fidel's forces were back on the plains and Che was sent with an expeditionary force to the Escambray Mountains in Central Cuba.

If nothing else, Che was a charasmatic leader. His forces were extremely loyal to him and he gathered new recruits readily. Sometime in early November, 1958, Che met Aleida March, the beautiful emissary from the Los Villas rebel underground. The two were mutually attracted and, at some time shortly after they met, began an affair. Throughout the fall, Che's command gathered strength.

In December of 1958, the army attacked Che's column in

---

108. Raul appears to have supported Che's role.

strength. Che beat back the army attack and felt strong enough to go on the offensive. They captured town after town, essentially cutting Cuba in half. They then marched on Santa Clara, Cuba's fourth largest city, guarded by 3500 of Batista's most loyal troops. Che's attacking force numbered about 340 men, but they were joined by numerous city dwellers. The garrison finally surrendered on January 2, 1959 after hearing that Batista and 40 of his cronies had fled to the Dominican Republic late on New Year's Eve 1958.

After Che's column had accepted the surrender of the garrison, it was immediately dispatched to Havana where Che was placed in command of the Fortress La Cabana. Originally one of the principal fortresses defending Havana, it was now used mainly as a military prison. It certainly was not a prestigious assignment for someone who had distinguished himself in the revolution the way Che had. Commentators speculate that a political savvy Fidel wanted Che, a known Maoist, out of the lime light while he sought international recognition for his new government. In addition, Che was already known as a ruthless prosecutor of traitors, and putting him in charge of La Cabana would put the onus of purging the military and prosecuting Batista war criminals on his head and not either of the Castros. Raul Castro too was conspicuously absent from any important post. Fidel Castro named himself Commander in Chief of the Armed Forces and placed a puppet, Urrutria, in the presidency. Urrutria and his cabinet appeared safe to the U.S. and by January 10, 1959, the U.S., Venezuela and the U.S.S.R had recognized the Castro government.

Che arrived at La Cabana early on the morning of January third, 1959 and installed himself and Aleida March in the Commander's house. One of Che's first actions was to arrange for mass weddings to formalize the unions formed during the revolution. Che's reputation as a ruthless prosecutor is probably overdone in his biographies. It is true that he was the prosecutor and judge of the majority of the Batista party members tried, but his reported death sentence rate was less than 6% compared to almost double that rate in courts Raul Castro presided over outside of Havana.

In addition to his court duties, Che was named Chief of the Department of Military Training and started a military education program at La Cabana. Besides the regular military courses, there were programs promoting literacy, and there was a strong political orientation with communist party members as instructors[109]. He also had a secret assignment from Fidel to start a State Security and Intelligence department.

Some time in January 1959, Che's Argentine family arrived in Havana for a visit, and Hilda and three-year-old Hildita also arrived from Peru. Exactly what transpired between Che and Hilda at this point is debatable. The various versions differ badly. In any case, they finally agreed on a divorce and Hilda and Hildita agreed to stay on in Cuba. The one fact everyone is in agreement on is that Hilda Gadea and Aleida March were enemies from the moment they met. From all accounts it appears that Che did try to establish a father-daughter relationship with Hildita. The divorce became final on May 22, 1959, and Che married Aleida March on June 2, 1959.

In February 1959, the Cuban government approved a new constitiution. It contained a clause that made Che a Cuban native citizen. With approval of the new constitution, Fidel took over as prime minister and named Che to a committee to draft a comprhensive agrarian reform

---

109. There is some evidence that as early as 1959, guerillas from other South American countries were being trained at La Cabana.

bill. Che's Maoist outlook put him at odds with the traditional communists[110], but his views on agrarian reform prevailed. The bill was finally signed by Fidel in May.

In March, Che developed a severe respitatory infection and moved out of La Cabana. It was during this time that he began his book on guerilla warfare, quoting Mao extensively. Raul Castro and Che continuously pushed a more middle-of-the-road Fidel to the left. Their position was reinforced when, on a trip to the U.S., Fidel was patronized badly by Nixon. The CIA now considered Che the most dangerous man in Cuba and claimed that the Cuban Armed Forces would follow him and not his credo. The Russians attempted to send an agent to contact Che. Fidel attempted to get Che out of the limelight by sending him on an international good will tour.

When Che returned to Cuba he was made head of the Department of Industrialization. The Russian Agent, a Spanish Civil War veteran, Alexandr Alexiev, finally made contact with Che in Cuba. Che did not think the revolution could survive without help from the Soviets.

---

110. Che advocated that the army should be the agent of change and not the peasants or workers.

Che brought Fidel Castro together with Alexiev. Fidel and Alexiev set up trade relations but agreed to postpone formal diplomatic and cultural relations until the population was more indoctrinated. They arranged for a Soviet trade show to come to Havana. In February 1960, U.S.S.R. Deputy Premier Mikoyan arrived with the trade show. Accompanying him was Nikoli Lenov, Raul and Che's friend from Mexico. He immediately contacted Che and presented him with a Russian pistol. Fidel now named Che to head the Cuban National Bank. Che signed the new Cuban Bank Notes "Che."

Che was sent on a trip through the Eastern Bloc. The U.S. State Department's assessment of Che's trip was summed up in a March 23rd secret memo:

> By the end of the visit, Cuba had trade and payments agreements and cultural ties with every country in the bloc, diplomatic relations with every country except East Germany, and scientific and technical assistance accords with all but Albania.[111]

Che's description of the "new man," a concept that would

---

111. From Anderson, at 497.

become synonymous with him, was spelled out in his July 26, 1960 Oriente speech[112]:

> How does one reconcile individual effort with the needs of society? We again have to recall what each of our lives was like, what each of us did and thought, as a doctor or in any other public health function, prior to the revolution. We have to do so with profound critical enthusiasm. And we will then conclude that almost everything we felt and thought in that past epoch should be filed away, and that a new type of human being should be created. And if each one of us is his own architect of that new human type, then creating that new human being - who will be the representative of the new Cuba - will be much easier.[113]

Also in 1960, Alieda became pregnant with their first child, Che's second, and Che's book on guerilla warfare was published. His

---

112. One must take in consideration that by this time there were Soviet arms and advisors in Cuba, and from Che's perspective the Cuban revolution was safe despite a CIA led counter revolutionary armed revolt.

113. From Anderson at 479.

main points were that people's forces can win against organized armies, that such forces need not wait for the time to be ripe, and that in South America the armed struggle should be fought in rural areas, not the cities. Che also pushed the American oil companies out and seized their refineries. By the end of 1960, he had seized all of the hated Americans' property. In late 1960, Che traveled to both Russia and China. He developed firm ties to China and sold the Chinese over one million tons of sugar.

By 1961, Che's siezures of American property and the obvious Cuban ties to the U.S.S.R and China had caused the U.S. to sever all diplomatic ties to Cuba. On February 24, 1961, there was a failed attempt on Che's life[114]. From that point on, Che became very security minded. He usually had a cortege of teenaged bodyguards and is reported to have carried a cigar box of hand grenades with him continuously. We know he never drove anywhere by the same route two days in a row.

Even through the Cuban Missle Crisis of 1962, Che continued to make Cuba the center of guerilla training and arms for the whole of Latin America and Africa. But following the crisis and the Soviet withdrawl

---

114. While it is popularly believed that the attempt was CIA inspired, the evidence points to it being inspired by local discontent.

from Cuba, Che's obvious enchantment with Chinese communism gradually alienated him from the Russians. His unrelenting hatred of the United States and his strong opposition to any rapprochement with the United States or Western Europe also slowly eroded his relationship with Fidel Castro.

Despite his ties with Cuba, the fact that four of his five children were born there and all of them lived there, and his many years of residence, Che never really adopted Cuban culture or habits. He never socialized widely or partied, a Cuban passion; he never swam at Cuba's glorious beaches although he reportedly was a strong swimmer and loved to swim; he didn't drink local rum or Cuban coffee but continued drinking *yerba mate,* a traditional Argentine herb tea; and never engaged in the lewd, irreverent social interchange that is so common between Cuban men. He was also out of step with most of the Cuban population. Few could understand Che's message or example of his all consuming spiritual, economic, and self-sacrificing dedication to revolution. He preached austerity and sacrifice to the Cuban people, who valued creature comforts and fun above all else. Che himself completely failed to understand why the Latin Americans he depended on always failed to live up to his passion and self-sacrifice. His inability to understand these human personality differences probably was his greatest weakness and did more than anything else to undermine his position and place in Fidel Castro's Cuba, and the world at large.

By 1964, Che's industrialization program was a complete failure and the emphasis was back on agriculture. His monetary program was out of step with the rest of the government and opposed by the Soviets. His support for guerilla forces in Latin America was opposed by Moscow and the local communist parties who wanted to be legitimate political parties and win election victories. Even Raul Castro was taking steps to distance himself from Che. When Che refused to attend the Communist Party Congress in Havana, the handwriting was on the wall. Che would have to leave Cuba to pursue his revolution. He turned his attention to the Congo, where, in his eyes, the imperialist mercenaries were opposing the local people's forces.

In December 1964, he left Cuba to fly to New York as the Cuban representative to the UN General Assembly. He spoke sharply to the UN about its policy in the Congo. When he left the UN, he did not return to Cuba. He flew first to Algiers, then to several spots in Africa and finally to China. His exact purpose is unknown, but it is commonly thought that he was getting Chinese approval for a move into the Congo. From China he flew back to Africa and contacted Congo rebel leaders with offers of Cuban military advisors[115] and arms. He was not received with open arms by most of the rebel leaders, and, in Cairo and Algiers, he was warned that the Congo forces were not like South American forces and that as a caucasian he would not be accepted by black troops. Along the way, Che made speeches criticising the Soviets in the increasing schism between the Russians and Chinese.

When he returned to Havana, his reception was cold. It is reported that Fidel Castro told him to leave Cuba with his Congo force as soon as possible or that he would have to take action against him to placate the Soviets. In any case, on March 22, 1985, Che made the public announcement that he was going to the fields to cut sugar cane and disappeared from sight. He left Cuba about the first of April, 1965, disguised as the clean-shaven, glasses-wearing Ramon Benitez. He took a circuitous route and arrived on the shores of Lake Tanganyika on or

---

115. Che evidently had about 30 Cubans lined up to go to the Congo with him at this time.

about April 24, 1965. The rebel forces were even worse than Che had been led to believe. Not only were they undisciplined and poorly led, but they were much more interested in exploiting the native civilian population than they were in fighting. For the most part, the Cubans remained unoccupied while their force was decimated by disease. On the few occasions when there was an actual battle, the Cubans fought and the rebels fled. The Cubans became furious. If the rebels wouldn't fight for their cause, they saw no sense in the Cuban force remaining in the Congo. Che's force began to desert. By mid November, the situation had deteriorated to the point that they were evacuated on Fidel's orders. The main body of the force returned to Havana.

Che and his loyal bodyguards did not return. They holed up in the Cuban Embassy in Tanzania. Whether it was his pride and Che didn't want to return to Havana in defeat, or if he felt the climate in Havana was still not warm enough is not known. After his presence in the Congo became known, he had become one of the most wanted and hunted men on Earth. He definitely did not want to show his face in public anywhere outside of Cuba. He began dictating his account of the Congo campaign and Alieda visited him in the embassy. In March 1966, Che moved to a safe house in Prague. A disguised Alieda visited him again in Prague and brought word that he would be welcomed back in Cuba. His friends and advisors all urged him to return.

Che remained convinced that his idea of Latin American revolution would work. He thought about joining the guerilla movements in Peru or Bolivia. When the guerilla movement in Peru collapsed, he decided on Bolivia. The Bolivian Communist Party was not interested in having Che as a guerilla, but agreed he could transit through on his way to Argentina. By August 1966, Bolivian Communists had established a base camp about 150 miles from Santa Cruz and an equal distance from the Argentine border. They expected Che to mount his guerilla attack in Argentina from there. Che arrived at the base camp in November 1966. Che's force consisted of nine Bolivians[116] and fifteen Cubans. Much as he wanted more Bolivians, the the Bolivian Communist Party wanted nothing to do with Che or an armed uprising and effectively cut him off from supplies or recruits.[117] Che remained undisturbed and expected to

---

116. It would seem the only Bolivians in Che's force were Maoists who had broken with the traditional communist party.

117. It is popularly believed in Cuba that the Bolivian Communist Party leaders betrayed Che's force to the army. The confilcting account is that two Bolivian

get Argentine recruits. The recruits never arrived, and on March 23, 1967, Che, with the force he had, ambushed an army patrol, killing seven soldiers and taking twenty-one and all their weapons prisoner. Che's band continued functioning effectively well into April, setting up ambushes and escaping pursuing troops. By April 10, 1967, U.S. counter-insurgency advisors and CIA agents were on the scene.

Che divided his men into two columns and then lost radio contact between the columns and with any outside help. He began losing men to the pursuing army forces. By August the situation was becoming desperate. Food was in short supply because the rebels had no rapport with the locals. Many of the remaining twenty-four men, including Che, were ill. Having lost his outside contact, Che was unable to obtain refills for all his asthma medications. Unknown to Che, his second column had been massacred by the army within a day's march of reaching him.

Out of desperation, the guerillas headed for Alto Seco. They reached there on September 21, and seized enough food supplies to take care of their immediate needs. The locals were hostile and Che could recruit no guides. They moved out of Alto Seco in the open with no

---

members of the force were captured and told all they knew and identified Che.

guides and no knowledge of the country ahead. On September 26, 1967, they were ambushed by the army at La Higura. Che and the seventeen survivors of the ambush escaped into a canyon as other army units began to surround them. They continued to descend the canyon as the army closed in on them. On October 8, the army found them and opened up with machine gun and mortar fire. Che was wounded and captured by the Bolivian military. He was questioned by the Bolivians and CIA and his documents all analyzed and photographs taken. He was then bound hand and foot and kept on the floor of the La Higura school house for the night. The next day he was shot on the order of the Bolivian military[118]. After his death, both Che's hands were cut off and preserved in formaldehyde to make sure his finger prints were preserved against claims that he had not been killed. He was buried in an unmarked grave somewhere near La Higura.

In death he became the martyred symbol he had hoped to become in life.

As the veteran Cuban intelligence official, "Santiago" observed

---

118. To this day, the CIA agents involved maintain they lobbied to keep Che alive in order to gain more intelligence.

recently:

> "Toward the end, Che knew what was coming, and he prepared himself for an exemplary death. He knew his death would become an example in the cause of Latin American revolution, and he was right. We would have preferred him to remain alive, with us here in Cuba, but the truth is that his death helped us tremendously. It's unlikely we would have had all the revolutionary solidarity we have had over the years if it weren't for Che dying the way he did."[119]

Graffiti many times reflects the nature of a time or of a nation in a way no other media can. In the case of Latin America the scrawled message sometimes found beside "Yankee Go Home" on white-washed walls, "Che - Alive like they never wanted you to be!" probably sums up the nature of Ernesto "Che" Guevara's Latin American legacy better than this or any other writer could.

Over fifty years of U.S. newspaper coverage has left a legacy that is quite different in the United States.

---

119. Anderson at 753.

HUGH MERCER 1726-1777
OUR FORGOTTEN HERO

Hugh Mercer was born near Rosehearty, Aberdeenshire, Scotland on January 17, 1726. His father, William Mercer, was the Presbyterian Minister of the Pitsligo Parish Church. His mother was Ann Monro. Little is known of his early life or education, but at the age of fifteen he entered the University of Aberdeen, Marischal College, and completed the medical course[120].

Reportedly, he practiced medicine in his father's parish until the

---

120. Hill and Waterman both claim he never received his degree. They state that while Mercer was a fourth year student, he forsook his degree and left to join Charles' forces. Most historians state he received his degree and practiced medicine for a short time before joining the Stuart army.

return of Charles Edward Stuart (Bonnie Prince Charles) in 1745. Charles found Scotland impoverished and resentful of its exploitation by the English crown, the Hanoverian King George II. The Scots saw Charles as the savior of Scotland and readily joined his campaign for the English throne. Most of the English army was fighting in France and the rebels made early victories, gaining strength as they moved south[121]. Even though Hugh Mercer's grandfather, Sir Robert Munro[122], was a regimental commander in the British army, he joined the rebel army as an assistant surgeon.

Once the Stuart forces reached England, they gained few, if any, recruits. While Prince Charles moved south, the English were bringing their troops home from France. Faced with the superior English force, and expecting French aid, Charles retreated back to Scotland. French aid never arrived, and an English force of 9000-12000 men invaded Scotland. The two forces met at Culloden Moor near Inverness on April

---

121. Charles' forces probably numbered about 6000 by the time he left Scotland.

122. Sir Robert Munro was killed in a clash with the Stuart forces.

16, 1746. In the ensuing battle, Charles' army was slaughtered[123]. Hugh Mercer survived the battle and escaped. The English were not satisfied with the victory on the field, but pursued the survivors[124]. Hugh Mercer remained at large by hiding on a relative's farm. After almost a year as a fugitive in Scotland, a friendly fisherman smuggled him onto the docks in Edinburgh. There, he finally found passage on a ship to America in March 1747[125].

Hugh Mercer landed in Philadelphia in May 1747. The British presence in Philadelphia made Mercer uneasy and he drifted west. Mercer finally found refuge in a small Scottish settlement[126] in the Cumberland Valley on the Pennsylvania frontier. He practiced medicine there for eight years. In June, 1755, General Braddock's army, trying to use continental tactics, was cut down by French and Indian forces using

---

123. The Duke of Cumberland had given a "no quarter" order to the English forces. The Scots charged with swords against muskets and artillery.

124. Even the noncombatants like surgeons and drummer-boys were imprisoned or executed.

125. Brody gives the date as the fall of 1746, but the 1747 date appears to be the accurate one.

126. One of the Conccocheague settlements now named Mercerburg.

frontier tactics[127]. There were over 400 wounded British and colonial troops. Mercer volunteered his services to the British medical officer in command. He treated the wounded and attached himself to the colonial troops.

When the British troops retreated to Philadelphia, Hugh Mercer abandoned his medical duties and took up arms. By 1756, he was commissioned a captain in a Pennsylvania regiment and put in command of Fort Shirley, the most remote of the frontier posts. In July 1756, he took part in an attack on Fort Du Quesne. In September of that same year, he took part in the definitive battle of the frontier, the Battle of Kittanning. The Indian village of Kittanning was the headquarters for the Indian war parties. Colonel John Armstrong led the party that raided and destroyed the village. During that battle Mercer was shot in his right arm, breaking the bone. On the trip back from the raid, Mercer's column was ambushed by the Indians and in the chaos he became separated from his unit. He had to make his way alone, injured, without arms or supplies, through hostile territory for over 100 miles before he reached the safety

---

127. General Braddock himself was killed.

of a frontier fort[128]. He was awarded a medal by the City of Philadelphia for his exploits.

Mercer rose rapidly through the ranks and soon was a colonel in the colonial forces.[129] During this time he developed a close and lasting friendship with a fellow colonel, George Washington. On January 15, 1761, Hugh Mercer was mustered out of the service[130]. Washington and some of his fellow Virginia officers persuaded Mercer to move to Fredericksburg, Virginia. Fredericksburg was a predominately Scottish community of about 3000 and the commercial center of northern Virginia.

Mercer resumed his medical and surgical practice in Fredericksburg[131] and soon opened an apothecary shop as well. His

---

128. Mercer survived on berries, the meat of a large rattle snake he killed, and some wild plums.

129. He was the first commander of Fort Pitt (the renamed Fort DuQuesne) and thus the first American leader of what was to become Pittsburgh.

130. For practical purposes, the French and Indian war was over.

131. Washington helped him get started by introducing him to leading citizens and arranging for Mercer to be appointed physician for the local militia.

practice[132] and the shop thrived and Mercer became a leading citizen of the community[133]. Mercer invested almost every cent he earned from his practice and shop in land. Mercer married a local woman, Isabella Gordon[134], the daughter of a Scottish tavern owner. He fathered five children, Ann Mercer Patton[135], John Mercer, William Mercer[136], George Weedom Mercer, and Hugh Tennant Mercer[137]. Although raised a Presbyterian, in Fredericksburg he joined the Anglican Church.

In 1767, Mercer joined the Fredericksburg Masonic Lodge and

---

132. Mary Washington, George Washington's mother was one of his patients as were Patsy Custis Washington, George Washington, James Monroe, John Marshall and many other political figures of the day.

133. George Washington kept a desk in the shop and conducted his business in Fredericksburg from there.

134. The sister-in-law of George Weedon, a friend of Hugh Mercer and George Washington and also a future Revolutionary War general.

135. General George Patton is a direct descendent of Hugh Mercer.

136. William was born deaf and dumb. He became a well known painter of his day.

137. Other famous descendants are the Confederate General Hugh Weedon Mercer, and song writer Johnny Mercer.

later became its master.[138] In that same year he became a corresponding member of the Philadelphia Medical Society.

In 1774, Mercer bought the Ferry Farm[139] from George Washington for £2000, and settled his growing family on it.[140] When the Royal Governor of Virginia sent marines to remove the gunpowder from a local armory in 1775, Mercer became a member of the Fredericksburg Committee of Safety, the local revolutionary group. For reasons that are unclear, he was excluded from command of the first regiment formed by the Virginia Convention, but later was elected colonel of the Minutemen of several Virginia counties. On January 11, 1776, Mercer was appointed Colonel of the 3rd Virginia Regiment of the Virginia Line. John Monroe, a future president, and John Marshall, a future Chief Justice of the Supreme Court, served under him. In June 1776, Mercer was appointed

---

138. George Washington and James Monroe, two future presidents, were also members of this lodge, and at least eight Revolutionary generals were also members.

139. This was Washington's childhood home and the property he inherited from his father. Mount Vernon (Probably named after English Admiral Vernon) was actually his brother's larger farm that Washington inherited upon his brother's death.

140. By one account he never actually occupied the farm.

Brigadier General of the Armies of the United Colonies by the Continental Congress. He was assigned to Washington's New York command.

Mercer's first action was a raid on the British troops on Staten Island. Then Mercer was put in charge of the construction and manning of Fort Lee, the fort on the New Jersey side of the Hudson opposite Fort Washington. In the debacle of Washington's defeat in New York, Fort Lee was abandoned without a fight on November 20, 1776, and Mercer and his troops joined Washington's retreat through New Jersey.

Popular legend has it that Hugh Mercer devised the plan for Washington to cross the Delaware River and attack the Hessians at Trenton on December 26, 1776[141].

In any case, Mercer and his troops played the principal part in the First Battle of Trenton and Mercer reportedly was in charge of the defense of the city in the Second Battle of Trenton on January 2, 1777. The next day, Washington decided to flank the British army, and march against Cornwallis' rear guard at Princeton.

---

141. English implies that Mercer was indeed the man primarily responsible for the attacks.

Mercer led Washington's vanguard of 350 men. In an apple orchard near Princeton, Mercer encountered two regiments of British infantry[142] and a mounted unit of some sort. In the ensuing action, Mercer's troops broke, his horse was shot out from under him, and he was soon engaged in a man-to-man fight with the British infantry. Mercer refused to surrender, and tried to defend himself with his saber. Mercer was clubbed to the ground and bayoneted repeatedly. He was left on the field[143] as the British retreated. Washington rallied Mercer's troops and, with his main army, pushed back the British. When Mercer was found, Major Armstrong carried him to a makeshift field hospital in the nearby home of Thomas Clark[144] at the eastern end of the battlefield. Mercer and the other casualties were cared for by Benjamin Rush[145]. Hugh Mercer

---

142. His Majesty's 17th and 55th Regiments of Foot

143. Legend has it that even though mortally wounded he would not let his men evacuate him, but sat at the base of an oak tree while those around him stood their ground. The so call "Mercer Oak" is featured on the seal of Mercer County, New Jersey

144. Also spelled Clarke in several accounts.

145. While most authorities state Mercer was treated by Benjamin Rush, Ketchum states he was cared for by a British Surgeon's Mate and English states he was cared for by the British staff surgeon in one paragraph and Benjamin

hung on in agony for nine days before dying on January 12, 1777.

An extremely popular hero, he was carried to Philadelphia where his mangled body was displayed in an open casket. His funeral ceremony was attended by a crowd estimated to be over 20,000. His place of burial is questionable. Most historians state that he was buried first in Philadelphia's Christ Church Cemetery, and then, in 1840, moved to Laurel Hill Cemetery of Philadelphia, where there is an imposing monument bearing his name. Others maintain the body is still buried at Philadelphia's Christ Church Cemetery and one version has it buried under the "Mercer Oak."

The inscription on the Laurel Hill Monument reads:

> **General Mercer, Physician Fredrericksburg, Virginia.**
> **Distinguished for his skill and learning, his gentleness**
> **and decision, his refinement and humanity.**

Mercer's efforts in New Jersey are generally credited as being the catalyst that produced Washington's victories at Trenton and Princeton. Following his defeats there, Cornwallis pulled his forces back

---

Rush in another.

to New York. That permitted Washington to winter his troops at Morristown. The victories also stimulated much needed re-enlistments in the continental army, began to erode British public support for the war, and helped the French decide to supply arms.

OLIVER GOLDSMITH

*"in genius lofty, lively, versatile;
in style weighty, clear, engaging"*[146]

Oliver Goldsmith was a failure in every aspect of his life, except one. His writing endures.

Although, the exact year of his birth is uncertain, November 10, 1730 is the usually accepted date.[147] He was born in the small village of Lissoy[148] Westmeath Ireland. His father, Charles, was the vicar and one of a long line of Anglo-Irish gentry tied to the Church of England. Oliver

---

146. Translation of epitaph on Goldsmith's memorial in the Poet's Corner of Westminister Abby.

147. The year is missing from the family bible, and Goldsmith himself made references to his age that would make his year of birth anything from 1728-1731.

148. AKA Auburn.

was the second son of a family of seven children. His older brother, Henry, was everyththing Oliver was not -- tall, handsome, outgoing, a good student. He graduated Trinity College, joined the clergy and eventually took over his father's pulpit. Oliver, on the other hand, was considered ugly, dull, shy, and doomed to obscurity. A bout of smallpox as a child added insult to injury by pockmarking his already unattractive appearance. Small as a child, he eventually did reach the height of 5'8", but was the shortest male in the family.

Little is known of his early schooling, although one school master, Thomas Byrne, was supposed to have given him a background of Irish legends and fairy tales. Despite what he described as an uneven education, Oliver eventually entered Trinity College in Dublin in June 1744. It is generally accepted that he was allowed entry only as a concession to his influential family[149]. His father died while Oliver was still a student. Oliver seems to have enjoyed Dublin if not his studies, and

---

149. Swinton reports he was admitted as a sizar, a menial who lived in a garret and served his more fortunate fellows in return for free education and board.

eventually graduated[150].

For the next three-and-one-half years he skipped from one failure to another. First he dissipated his meager inheritance on his passion for bright, outlandish clothes and high living. His uncle, Thomas Contarine, gave him a horse and £30 pounds to migrate to America. Oliver missed the ship and gambled away the horse and money. Then he was rejected in an attempt to join the clergy.[151] Thomas Contarine then agreed to finance a career in law. Oliver attempted to study law, was unable to complete the course or qualify for the bar. He took a series of jobs as a private tutor or house master at private schools, but lost or left the jobs repeatedly.

Finally, he decided to study medicine in Edinburgh. Somehow he again pursuaded his elderly, kindly uncle, Thomas Contarine, to forgive and forget, to take one more chance on him, and finance his

---

150. There is a great discrepancy between commentators as to how well Goldsmith did at Trinity. Reports vary from him being an award-winning student to being graduated as last in his class. There seems to be no doubt, however, that he did graduate and receive his Bachelor of Arts degree in 1749.

151. One story has it that he appeared for his interview with the Bishop in a scarlet suit.

studies. He actually arrived at Edinbugh in 1752. He studied at Edinburgh for some eighteen months[152], and then left for Leyden. There is a record of Oliver Goldsmith being elected to the Edinburgh Medical Society on January 13, 1753. How long he remained in Leyden and whether he actually took his degree there is uncertain, for he soon began a tour of Europe with a major stop in Padua. Again it it uncertain of exactly how long he stayed there and whether he took his degree there. However, by most accounts he stayed in Padua a minimum of six months, and it appears highly likely that is where he took his degree. At the time of his travels, it was the common practice to take your basic medical studies at Edinburgh and take your degree at Leyden or especially Padua. Despite many claims to the contrary, it appears certain that Goldsmith had obtained his degree and was a bona fide physician. It also appears certain that considering the state of medicine at that time, he was probably little worse than his fellow physicians.

In any case, sometime in early February 1726, a broke and tattered Oliver Goldsmith returned to England. If his date of birth is

---

152. There are no actual records of attendance. At the time, only the professors kept the records and the fees.

correct, he would have been 25 years of age. He lived a hand-to-mouth existence. First. he acted as an assistant to a chemist named Jacob on Fish Street Hill in London. Then, he set up a skimpy medical practice in Bankside, and decided to try his hand at writing for some extra money. Writers in the 1750s were completely dependent on the booksellers for their living. Goldsmith had no such connections, and his writing income was negligible. He was a hack writer for whoever would hire him[153]. In desperation, he applied for a job as a surgeon with the East India Company in Madras, India. He also appealed to a classmate, and, as a result, Goldsmith became an "usher" at a boy's school in Pecham owned by the classmate.

For a change, Oliver seemed to be suited to the job of usher[154], and appreciated by his classmate. Through the classmate, Oliver met Ralph Griffiths, owner-publisher of the *Monthly Review.* Griffiths reviewed some of Oliver's writing and hired him to do book reviews for

---

153. There is some evidence that he wrote children's stories for John Newbury and may be the creator of *Goody Two-shoes.*

154. There is no exact account of Goldsmith's duties at the school. Some accounts state he was a tutor, while others say he was a house master.

Monthly Review. He was given board and room above Griffiths' bookshop and £100 per year. Oliver started writing the book reviews in April of 1757 and continued writing them until September of 1757. His exposure in *Monthly Review*[155] gained him some prominence within the English literary society and his work was considered excellent. Exactly what happened between Griffiths and Goldsmith to sever the relationship is unknown, but after September 1757, Oliver was writing on his own.

Because of problems with the French in India, the East India Company had been delaying taking action on Oliver's deployment to Madras. However, in December of 1757, Oliver was ordered to Surgeon's Hall to take the surgeon's examination[156]. Oliver failed the examination. All hope of a post in India disappeared. Oliver Goldsmith had been spending on the basis of his future with the East India

---

155. Goldsmith wrote some 19 full length reviews and 37 shorter notices,

156. There is some question about this examination. By most accounts, it was ordered by the East India Company. However, another version has it that Goldsmith was attempting to become a ship's surgeon and the examination was for that position. Still another version has him applying as a "hospital mate." In any case, it resulted in the East India Company rejecting him for a post in India.

Company. He owed everyone he knew. He translated two popular French novels for enough money to pay off his debts.

The two translations plus his work at *Monthly Review* brought him to the attention of the publisher of Smolletts' *Critical Review,* the chief competitor of *Monthly Review.* Oliver Goldsmith became the book reviewer for *Critical Review.* While he was working for *Critical Review*, Oliver Goldsmith wrote *An Enquiry into the Present State of the Polite Learning in Europe,* an analysis of the taste of the European reading public. *An Enquiry into the Present State of the Polite Learning in Europe* was published by Dodsley's circa 1759. At about the same time, John Wilkie, a London bookseller, began a new magazine, the *Bee,* with Oliver as editor. The *Bee* ran for eight editions before failing.

Beginning in 1760, Goldsmith published a series of essays titled *Chinese Letters* in the *Public Ledger.* While his work to this point had made his name known to English literary circles, *Chinese Letters* made him known to English readers and brought him popular fame. The series also brought him into Dr. Samuel Johnson's circle and friendship. The *Chinese Letters* essays were compiled into a book titled *The Citizen of the World,* and published in 1762[157].

From that time on, Oliver Goldsmith's career as a writer was golden. He was probably the most successful writer of his day. His long verse, *The Traveller* was published in 1764. *The Vicar of Wakefield*[158], his strongest novel and one which has survived until this day, was published in 1766[159], and *The Deserted Village* in 1770. His two great comedy plays, *The Good-natured Man* and *She Stoops to Conquer*[160] were published in 1768 and 1773, respectively.

Goldsmith was a spendthrift throughout his career. He continued to sport garish, outlandish clothes throughout his life. His manner was coarse and vulgar. His love of gambling and drink were legend.

---

157. If one counts the essays from the *Bee, Chinese Letter, Lloyd's Evening Post, Weekly Magazine, British, Royal Magazine,* and *Lady's Magazine*, Oliver Goldsmith probably published over 200 essays in his early career.

158. It really attained its great popularity after Goldsmith's death and was more popular in the 19th and 20th century than it was in the 18th.

159. It is reported that Dr. Johnson found Goldsmith being evicted from his lodgings and arrested for payment of rent and took *The Vicar of Wakefield* to a bookseller and received £60 for it.

160. Goldsmith reportedly beat the publisher of the *London Packet* for unfavorable comments following the rave reviews at the opening of *She Stoops to Conquer*. Goldsmith was charged with assault and forced to pay a £50 fine. Goldsmith published a rebuttal in the *Daily Advertiser*.

Nonetheless, he was a founding member of the Literary Club and a personal friend of Boswell, Samuel Johnson, Garrick, and Joshua Reynolds.

On March 25, 1774, Oliver Goldsmith became ill with a headache and fever. He called two fellow physicians, Drs. Fordyce and Turton. He told them he had "fever and kidney trouble." Goldsmith was self-medicating himself with a wine of Ipecac and James Powder, a mix of Antimony oxide and Potassium tartrate. Antimony was known to produce perspiration, nausea and vomiting and, because of this, was thought to be curative in some way. The apothecary warned Oliver that Antimony was toxic, but Oliver insisted that his prescription be filled. Each James Powder contained about 66 mg of Antimony. Therefore, Oliver Goldsmith received about 198 mg of Antimony per day. A toxic dose. Even though his physicians pleaded with him not to take the drug, he persisted and died April 4, 1774.

Jousha Reynolds and Dr. William Hawes took charge of Goldsmith's affairs after his death. They originally expected to bury him in Westminister Abbey, but after determining his financial status (At the time of his death he owed in excess of £2000), they auctioned his belongings and paid for a simple funeral at the Temple Burying Grounds. Eventually, a memorial sculpted by Joshua Reynolds with the epitaph written by Samuel Johnson was erected in the Poet's Corner of Westminister Abbey.

Samuel Johnson perhaps summed up Oliver Goldsmith's life most succinctly when he wrote: "No man was more foolish when he had not a pen in his hand, or more wise when he had."[161]

---

161. From Swinton at 1081.

EMIN PASHA

Few men in history have so dominated the world's attention in their day, nor faded so rapidly from the public's memory as has Emin Pasha. Emin Pasha was born Eduard Schnitzer on March 28, 1840 in the small Prussian Town of Oppin[162]. However, his family is reported to have later moved to Niesse in an area that is now Poland but has been alternatively German. His background is hazy. His birth father is said to have been Jewish, but his mother, a Lutheran, divorced the birth father while Eduard was an infant. His mother remarried when Eduard was five and her new husband was also Lutheran. Eduard knew his stepfather as his father, and Moorhead, usually considered a reliable historical source, reports he was Lutheran.

Eduard reportedly suffered from bouts of depression as a youth,

---

162. Oppin can no longer be located on a modern map.

but was an excellent student and excelled in the natural sciences. Even as a child he was noted for his collections of birds, insects and animals. Foreign languages were absorbed almost like magic and he was supposedly fluent in German, French, Polish, Russian, Greek, Italian and eventually in Turkish, Arabic, Farsi, and Swahili. He was an accomplished musician and played the piano at a professional level. He studied medicine in Breslau, Konigsberg and Berlin and is remembered as a brilliant student who took honors in his botany and zoology courses. He received his MD at age twenty-four from the University of Berlin.

Exactly what happened immediately after his degree is uncertain. By one account, he had volunteered to become a surgeon with Maxmillian's troops in Mexico and did not think it was necessary to take the state examination. When his appointment was cancelled, he was left without the necessary license to practice in Germany. Another version has it that in applying for his license, he found out that his birth father was Jewish. When his medical fraternity found out he had a Jewish father, it expelled him. Eduard felt disgraced and he failed to take the State Qualifying Examinations and thus was barred from practicing in

Germany. Another account states that, as a Jew, he was forbidden to take the state examinations. Still another account has him starting a practice and finding it impossible to make a living because of the oversupply of physicians in Berlin and suggests he found economic opportunities outside of Germany more appealing than those within Germany. A final version has him interested in converting to the Moslem religion and wanting to live in an Islamic country.

In any case, shortly after graduation, and financed by an uncle, Schnitzer emigrated first to Trieste, and then, in April 1864, to Antivari, a port in Northern Albania, then under Turkish rule. En route, Eduard had acquired a patron, Ismail Hakki Pasha, the Albanian governor and an important national political figure in Turkey[163]. Schnitzer spent six years in Antivari, practicing medicine and later as the Turkish Quarantine Officer[164]. He had converted to the Moslem faith, changed his name to

---

163. One account has Eduard traveling on the same boat as Ismail Hakki Pasha, and Ismail Hakki Pasha being completely captivated by Eduard's piano concerts.

164. The title is really misleading; it would seem Schnitzer's administrative duties involved much more than just his medical duties. He was a minor central government administrative and political functionary for the city.

Hairouallah Effendi, and soaked up and practiced Turkish manners, dress, and way of life[165]. When the Albanians revolted, Hairouallah Effendi stayed loyal to the Turks. He armed himself, continued with his duties and fought his way out of several armed attacks.

As his reputation grew among the Turks, his patron, Ismail Hakki Pasha, wanted him by his side. Ismail Hakki Pasha invited Hairouallah Effendi to become his personal physician in Trebizond, the capital. Hairouallah Effendi accepted and became the palace physician and tutor to the harem children.. Once in Ismail Hakki Pasha's palace, Hairouallah Effendi became infatuated by Emila, one of Ismail Hakki Pasha's wives. She was a legendary beauty and slightly older than Hairouallah Effendi. They soon became secret lovers. After Ismail Hakki Pasha died, Hairouallah Effendi moved to Janina with Emila and her children by Ismail Hakki Pasha.

In 1875, Hairouallah Effendi, now calling himself Eduard Schnitzer again and using his German passport, took Emila and her children first to Italy and then to the family home in Niesse. He

---

165. Throughout the rest of his life, Schnitzer attended the Mosque every Friday and said his daily prayers.

introduced Emila as his wife, although there is no indication that they ever married. The conservative family was shocked by the religion, the dress, the language, the exotic wife, who was now pregnant, and the children by another man. They fled to a spa and left the house to Eduard, Emila and their brood. Emila and Eduard's daughter, Pauline, was born in Niesse. Shortly after Pauline was born, Eduard Schnitzer left Emila and the children stranded in Germany and disappeared.

A little historical background is now necessary. Egypt and its vassal state Sudan were originally in the sphere of the Ottoman (Turkish) empire. Ever since the defeat of Napoleon's fleet in Egypt, the British had been expanding their influence in Egypt and the Sudan. With the completion of the Suez Canal in 1869, the British and French had established a permanent physical presence in Egypt. However, the French presence was merely financial, while the British had both a financial and a vital strategic interest in the Canal. It was their life line to India and their Asian territories. Even though most of the administrative posts were still held by Egyptians and Turks, the French and English really governed through the puppet ruler, the Khedive[166]. The key Egyptian Army generals were British. The British influence extended to the Sudan. The British persuaded the Khedive to appoint General Gordon Governor of Equatoria, the Southern most Sudanese Provence. Gordon was a great administrator and made his presence felt almost immediately. He fought the Arab slavers, established civil rights, limited the authority of the Arab clergy, and set up a communication system. It was a refreshing rebirth of a Provence that had been suffering under the corrupt and oppressive Egyptian/Turkish rule.

Exactly when Eduard Schnitzer showed up in Egypt is unknown, but the likely date is sometime in 1876. He was still traveling under his German passport, but calling himself Hairouallah Hakim. He applied for a job as a medical officer with the British/Egyptian administration. The physician assigned to Gordon, Emin Pasha, either had not appeared or had to be replaced for some reason[167], and Eduard Schnitzer/Hairouallah

---

166. The Khedive was overthrown by a popular uprising in 1881. Using violence against Europeans as an excuse, the British invaded Egypt in 1882 and took possession of the Suez Canal and then the entire country.

167. He may have been the victim of a debilitating fever.

Hakim was assigned as Gordon's Surgeon. When Eduard Schnitzer/Hairouallah Hakim showed up in Equatroria he now called himself Emin Pasha, the name of the physician he was replacing. Again Emin Pasha showed that he was more than a competent physician. Gordon recognized Emin Pasha as one of the finest minds then in Africa and persuaded him to join his administrative staff. Emin Pasha turned most of his medical practice over to Vita Hassan[168], and began what was to be one of the most able colonial administrations in the history of Africa. In addition to being an able administrator, he was a fearless and aggressive fighter against the slavers.

By 1877, the British had, for practical purposes, wrested control of Egypt and Sudan from the Turks. General Gordon was called to Cairo and appointed Governor General of Sudan. Gordon traveled down the Red Sea to Massawa, and then overland to the Nile by Camel. He traveled up (south) the Nile to Khartoum, and arrived there May 4, 1877. One of his first acts as Governor General was to appoint Emin Pasha Governor of Equatoria. As Governor, Emin Pasha carried on Gordon's

---

168. Variously described as an Arab or Turkish physician or apothecary.

programs with even more vigor than Gordon. Emin Pasha was fearless, a great tactician, and had the best trained troops in the Sudan. He started a campaign against elephant poachers and seized tusks worth over £60,000. Equatoria became the best governed Provence in Sudan. The Arab slavers and poachers hated Emin Pasha even more than they hated Gordon.

Emin Pasha was an accomplished botanist, ornithologist, and zoologist. In addition to his full time devotion to his office, he collected thousands of specimens, and wrote numerous reports on the natural history of the specimens he sent; the migratory patterns of birds; the geography and weather of the upper Nile; tribal customs; and even details on winds and rainfall. His work was impressive and much of it ended up in European and British universities and museums. His troops could not understand his interest in nature, and mocked him and his collecting obsession.

He arose every morning at 6:00 and made medical rounds with Vita Hassan before going to the Governor's office. He tried to introduce improved agricultural methods and new industry to Equatoria.

Emin Pasha became enamored with an Abyssinian girl, Safaran, he had freed from Arab slavers. He married Safaran, a formality he had never observed with Emila. Almost exactly one year after Emin Pasha freed Safaran, their daughter Ferida was born. Emin Pasha was a devoted husband to Safaran and father to Ferida.

In July 1882, the British Army invaded Egypt in response to the overthrow of the puppet Egyptian Government. By mid-September they had defeated the Egyptian Army and occupied the whole of Egypt, but not Sudan. Sudan rose in a jihad, a religious war, organized around Mahdi Mohammed Ahmed Ibn el-Sayyid. The Mahdi hated the Egyptians as much as the Europeans. On November, 5, 1883, the Mahdi's forces massacred a British column trying to regain control of the Sudan and every Provence fell to his forces except for Equatoria, where Emin Pasha kept control and continued to hold out. Gordon was sent back to Khartoum to lead the Egyptian troops out. By March 1884, the Mahdi had isolated Gordon in Khartoum and was laying siege to his garrison. The British finally decided to try to relieve Gordon in August 1884, but there was no action against the Mahdi until January 1885. The British didn't reach Khartoum until two days after Gordon and his garrison had been massacred. The British retreated down the Nile and withdrew from Sudan. Emin Pasha, still holding out in Equatoria, was forgotten.

In 1888, the Mahdi's son-in-law and successor set out on a campaign to crush Emin Pasha. Emin Pasha was even more isolated than Gordon had been, and the world didn't even know he was still holding out. As his supplies ran out[169] local honey was substituted for sugar, and beeswax was used for candles. Emin Pasha started a local soap works, making the soap from animal fat and potash. As Emin Pasha's position became more isolated, his Egyptian troops began to mock his impotence, but refused to attempt to make contact with Cairo. Emin Pasha finally got word out with a German-Russian explorer, Dr. Junker.

When word of Emin Pasha's plight reached Europe, the press was full of the news of his scientific contributions and the fact that he alone had held out in the Sudan. Overnight, the name, Emin Pasha, became one of the best known names in the world. Germany now claimed him as a national hero, despite the fact that he worked for the

---

169. The last supplies Emin Pasha received from the British/Egyptian government was a small shipment smuggled in sometime in 1886.

British and claimed Turkish citizenship. The British Government, on the other hand, appeared to ignore his plight. The Prime Minister, Lord Salisbury, rejected sending in any sort of relief column and took no alternative action, despite public pressure. Into this breach stepped William Mackinon.

Mackinon, a wealthy Scottish shipping magnate and member of the Royal Scottish Geographic Society, saw Emin Pasha's plight as a rare opportunity to combine philanthropy with a potential business opportunity. In return for rescuing Emin Pasha, Mackinon expected to receive trading rights in Equatoria and Uganda. Operating through the Royal Scottish Geographic Society, Mackinon formed the Emin Pasha Relief Committee and raised money by public subscription. The Emin Pasha Relief Committee, financed by Mackinon and the public contributions, offered Henry Morton Stanley, of Dr. Livingstone fame, the opportunity to lead the expedition. Stanley was lecturing in the United States when he received the offer. He readily accepted.

Henry Morton Stanley was born John Rowlands in Denbigh Wales. The family was impoverished and close to starvation during his childhood. At age fifteen he ran away from home and became a cabin boy on a ship bound for New Orleans. He deserted ship in New Orleans and worked at a variety of jobs until the outbreak of the Civil War. He served in the Confederate Army, later as a seaman on merchant ships, and finally in the U.S. Navy. When he left the Navy he became the foreign correspondent for the *Missouri Democrat* covering the Indian Wars for that paper. He moved to the *New York Herald* and covered the British Campaign in Ethiopia. His next assignment for the *Herald* was his historic quest for Livingstone. Despite the popular view that Stanley was the premier African explorer of his day, his exploratory data was shoddy and inaccurate to say the least. Neither his data nor his integrity could be trusted. There appears to be no doubt that during his previous stint in Africa he became an agent of King Leopold of Belgium who then controlled the Congo. There also appears to be evidence that he was a willing accomplice to and in the pay of Arab slavers and elephant poachers. Stanley's route and principal purpose in undertaking the rescue mission appears to have been extending Leopold's influence in Uganda and Equatoria. In fact, he carried a personal message from Leopold to

Emin Pasha, offering Emin Pasha a Belgian post with the purpose of annexing Equatoria into the Congo. In retrospect, it appears Stanley's only personal interest in Emin Pasha, if indeed he had any at all, was to get his hands on the £60,000 worth of ivory Emin Pasha had wrested from the Arab elephant poachers.

Mackinon knew Stanley would use the trip to write dispatches to newspapers and to write a book, but had no idea of Stanley's allegiance to and secret orders from King Leopold. He expected Stanley to persuade Emin Pasha to establish British trading posts from Equatoria and Uganda to the coast. Thanks to Mackinon and the Emin Pasha Relief Committee, Stanley was outfitted with the very best and latest in equipment, including a Maxim machine gun. He had a multinational force of nine gentleman volunteers. It was only after the expedition had been outfitted that Stanley revealed his convoluted route for the rescue force. Rather than heading inland from the east coast of Africa, opposite Zanzibar, Stanley was going to sail to Zanzibar, pick up 100 to 150 porters there, and then sail around the Cape of Good Hope and enter Africa up the Congo River and then through the Congo rain forest to

Equatoria and Emin Pasha and then continue east to the coast. Although the route made no sense without knowing Stanley's political agenda, his reputation was such that it prevented anyone from ordering him to enter from the east coast.

In the meantime, Emin Pasha did not want to be rescued. He wanted a relief column with heavy arms and unlimited ammunition. He was determined to stay and continue Gordon's work. He envisioned the British retaking the Sudan by moving north from Equatoria, simultaneously with a movement south from Egypt. It would seem he considered himself Gordon's logical successor to bring an able administration to the Sudan. While waiting for this expected relief column, Emin Pasha suffered a personal blow. His beloved wife, Safaran, died. His daughter Ferida, now became the center of his personal life. For a man who had deserted his first daughter almost at birth, his devotion to his second daughter is both extraordinary and impossible to explain. However, every observer, including Stanley, who knew Emin Pasha during this period, makes note of his passionate devotion to Ferida.

Stanley's route was a disaster. Not only was it longer than the logical route, but it was more difficult than he had ever imagined. There was strife with his volunteer force almost from the start. He was extremely harsh with his porters and had desertions almost continually. He contracted with Arab slavers for replacements, and then lost equipment when the porters were coerced back to their Arab owners. He finally established a base camp in the Congo and left half his party and supplies there while he pushed on with the remainder. The rain forest, raids by pygmies, and disease wiped out over 50% of his party. When he finally reached Emin Pasha, Stanley was in rags. The five-foot-six-inch Emin Pasha greeted the towering Stanley wearing an immaculate white suit and was in no immediate distress or danger. Stanley had nothing but a token supply of ammunition to give him, and it was Stanley, not Emin Pasha, who needed rescuing. There was no way Stanley could get Emin Pasha and the Egyptian garrison with their women and children to the coast with his current party. After recuperating with Emin Pasha for a while, Stanley decided to retrieve the rest of his men and supplies from the Congo, and began an arduous retracing of his route.

When Stanley left, the Egyptian troops revolted and took Emin

Pasha prisoner. When Khaifa Abdullah's troops renewed their attack, the Egyptian troops realized they could not survive without Emin Pasha's leadership and released him. However, in the interim, Equatoria was penetrated. It was no longer an intact state with a coherent government. When Stanley returned, Emin Pasha had no alternative but to add himself, Ferida, and his Egyptian troops, with all their camp followers, to Stanley's column and accompany him on the arduous trip to the east coast of Africa. Emin Pasha and Stanley hated each other from their initial encounter, and the trip to the Zanzibar Coast did nothing to improve their relationship.

Stanley was forced to put down a second revolt by the Egyptian troops and Stanley deserted a large number of Emin Pasha's troops en route, but finally rounded the Southern tip of Lake Victoria and reached a planned relief column. The column rested for three weeks and then proceeded east. The Germans intercepted the column as it neared the coast and provided much needed relief. Finally, on December 4, 1889, some two years and ten months after Stanley reached the mouth of the Congo River, Stanley and Emin Pasha reached the port of Bagamyo in

German East Africa.

Emin Pasha was greeted as a German hero. There were German battleships in the harbor, as well as a single British ship. There was a cable from the Kaiser awaiting Emin Pasha and he was awarded the Order of the Crown 2nd Class with a Star by the German government. There was no such acknowledgment from the British government.

The German garrison threw a Champagne supper for Emin Pasha and Stanley. Emin Pasha evidently had too much to drink, for he fell from his bungalow's porch when returning from the dinner. He fractured his skull and it took over four months for him to recover[170]. Emin Pasha was left with difficulty swallowing and deaf in the left ear.

Overwhelmed by the German reception, dismayed by Britain's lack of recognition, and thoroughly disgusted by Stanley, Emin Pasha now reclaimed his German identity[171]. He bought an estate in or near Bagamyo, and settled Ferida there with a German housekeeper and

---

170. Stanley sailed for Zanzibar the day after Emin Pasha fell and while Emin Pasha was still unconscious.

171. Actually, he had maintained his German passport throughout his Turkish and British/Egyptian service.

German tutor. He began a new inland expedition on behalf of Germany to secure the lands south of and along the shores of Lake Victoria up to Lake Albert. It was a blatant attempt to seize Uganda from the British. He was accompanied by three German officers and the German zoologist, Franz Stuhlman, and 700 African troops and porters.

After Emin Pasha's column had started west, Germany conceded Uganda to the British, and Emin Pasha was directed to go to Lake Tanganyika. Emin Pasha ignored the change of plans and continued on his original route. It is uncertain exactly what he was planning. It is speculated that he either wanted to retrieve his troops deserted by Stanley or to attempt to set up an independent Equatoria. Emin Pasha set up a town, Bukoba, on the West shore of Lake Victoria and then pushed North. In 1891, he reached the deserted Egyptian soldiers. They had gone wild and joined local tribes. They no longer had any loyalty to Emin Pasha or to the British/Egyptian government. Emin Pasha, reluctantly left them and finally moved south into the Congo. By this time, the Germans and their troops had deserted him. But Emin Pasha and Stuhlman pushed on alone collecting specimens and with the general idea of getting to the west coast. When smallpox broke out in the Congo, Emin Pasha decided to stay and help. He sent Stuhlman out with their specimens.

In 1892, about eighty miles South of the Congo's Stanley Falls, Arab slavers rushed Emin Pasha's tent and cut his throat. He was fifty-two years old. The world did not learn of his death for a full year. He left an estate of £5200 to his daughter Ferida. Ferida was brought to Germany and cared for by Emin Pasha's relatives.

Alan Moorehead probably writes the most apt epitaph for Emin Pasha/Hairouallah Effendi/ Eduard Schnitzer:

> Emin's certainly was the most intelligent brain in Cental Africa since Burton's time. Harry Johnston arriving in Uganda as British Administrator some years later, rated him as one of the greatest African explorers in the sense that he tried to understand Africa and the teeming life he found there, rather than treat the country as a blank space to be 'discovered' and delineated on a map.[172]

---

172. Moorehead at 329.

SIR LEANDER STARR JAMESON

Leander Starr Jameson was born on February 9, 1853 at Stranraer on the west coast of Scotland. He was the twelfth child born to Robert William Jameson and Christian Pringle Jameson, the daughter of Major General Pringle of Symington. His name supposedly is derived from the fact that Robert William Jameson was awaiting his son's arrival by taking a walk during which he fell into a body of water. He was rescued by a visiting American, Leonard Starr. Leonard Starr immediately became the baby's godfather and the baby named after him.

Robert William Jameson started his career in Edinburgh as a

lawyer and writer to the Signet.[173] He soon became a successful playwright, poet and editor of *Wigstownshire Free Press*. As his fame as a writer grew, Robert William moved the family to London. Leander was sent to the Godolphin School in Hammersmith. He was reportedly an excellent student and excelled in sports. In January 1870, he was admitted to University College Hospital as a medical student. Again he proved to be an excellent student and took the Gold Medal in Materia Medica. After completing his studies, he was made Resident Medical Officer at University College Hospital. He became a member of the Royal College of Surgeons in 1875 and was awarded his MD in 1877.

---

173. An exclusive legal society in Scotland made up of solicitors who previously were authorized to use the seal of the King of Scotland.

He served as house physician, house surgeon, and demonstrator in anatomy at University College Hospital until 1878. It was generally expected that Leander would assume a highly successful practice in London.

Instead, in 1878, Leander Starr Jameson sailed for South Africa and opened up practice in Kimberly. Most biographers state that his health broke down from overwork at University College Hospital and he went to South Africa to recover. However, the lack of details and the suddenness of the decision indicate that there must be more factors involved than overwork.

Nonetheless, his practice in Kimberly and his reputation grew. He became known throughout South Africa as "Doctor Jim". President Kruger, Cecil Rhodes and Lobengula, Chief of the Matabele Tribe,[174] were his patients. His friendships with Cecil Rhodes and Lobengula became close. He became one of Rhodes' confidantes and Lobengula made him a commanding officer (Induna) of one of his favorite

---

174. Lobengula had been suffering terribly from gout and Jameson treated it successfully.

regiments[175]. It is probable that Rhodes used Jameson's influence with Lobengula to help him get the concessions of 1888 that led to the founding of the British South Africa Company. From that time on Jameson's life was tied to Rhodes, Rhodes' ideas of a unified South Africa[176], and the dealings of the British South Africa Company.

In 1890, when the British South Africa Company opened up the Mashonland territory, Jameson abandoned his medical practice and joined the occupying column. Immediately after the pioneer column had occupied Mashonland, Jameson, F.C. Selous and A.R. Colquhoun moved east to Manicaland and were instrumental in securing that territory for the British South Africa Company. By 1891, Jameson had succeeded Colquhoun as Administrator of Rhodesia.

The discovery of gold in the Boer ruled Transvaal had brought a large number of foreigners[177] and industry to what had been a close knit

---

175. Jameson reportedly underwent all the native initiation ceremonies required by one assuming the rank of commander.

176. Victoria's Britain was still site of world power in Rhodes era, and his expansionist ideas were part and parcel of those of the British Government.

177. Mainly English and Irish miners.

Boer agricultural society. The Boers called the newcomers "Uitlanders" and made it plain that they were not welcome. The Uitlanders pressed for political recognition and economic security for their investments. Their efforts came to naught. Many dissident groups founded rifle clubs and threatened military action if the Boers continued to view them as interlopers without rights. Jameson was well aware of the crisis in the Transvaal and, like Rhodes[178] and the British Colonial Office, highly sympathetic to the plight of the Uitlanders.

In November 1895, a piece of Bechuanaland Protectorate bordering the Transvaal was ceded to the British South Africa Company by the British Colonial Office. The purpose of the land transfer was, at least for public consumption, to protect the rail line running through it. In reality it was a move by Rhodes, the British South Africa Company, and the British Colonial Office to encourage the resistance of the Uitlanders and to pressure the Boers. Rhodes considered the Transvaal to be an essential part of his consolidated South Africa. He expected the British South Africa Company troops to invade the Transvaal as soon as

---

178. Now Prime Minister of the Cape Colony.

the Uitlanders began their uprising.[179] The British Colonial Office was well aware of Rhodes' plans, and Joseph Chamberlain, the British Colonial Minister[180], had plainly been consulted and given his approval of the invasion in response to the uprising.

Jameson was in command of one of the British South Africa Company's units at the Transvaal border. Whether from some order from above, or because of his own impatience, on December 29, 1895, Jameson and 470[181] men invaded invaded the Transvaal prior to any uprising in the Transvaal. He thought it would take at least two weeks for the Boer militia units to organize and that the spontaneous uprising of the Uitlanders would lead to an easy defeat of the Boers. Jameson pushed to within twenty miles of Johannesburg before the well-organized and well-armed[182] Boer forces forced him to surrender at Doornkop on January 2,

---

179. The uprising was expected to begin on Boxing Day (December 26th).

180. Not the Chamberlain of WWII appeasement policy.

181. From the many reports it is hard to tell if he started with 468 or 478 men. 470 men seems a good compromise.

182. The German Kaiser sent Kruger a congratulatory cable on Jameson's defeat and it seems likely that the vast store of arms possessed by the Boers was

1896.

Chamberlain first heard of Jameson's premature raid on December 31, 1895, and rushed to the Colonial Office to cable the Governor General of the Cape Colony to repudiate the raid and try to recall Jameson. Chamberlain also warned Rhodes that he would lose his office if his role in the whole affair was ever revealed. Throughout the aftermath of the raid, Chamberlain continued to deny any role in suggesting, planning or carrying out the raid.

After the captured members of the raiding party were released by the Boer Government in Pretoria, Jameson and five of his officers were extradited to London to stand trial for an illegal raid into a friendly foreign country. Jameson took sole responsibility for the raid and refused to implicate Rhodes, the Colonial Office or Chamberlain[183]. The Liberal Party described the raid as "a disaster and a disgrace" and the conservatives sought to distance themselves from the raid in every way possible. The popular press was well aware of the role played by these

---

German in origin.

183. Despite his attorney's urging, Jameson failed to produce cablegrams implicating the others in his defense.

others and Jameson was idolized by the English public[184] as a martyr to the expansion of the Victorian empire. Jameson and his officers were sentenced to fifteen months in Holloway Prison, but Jameson was pardoned in less than a year. Many historians credit the raid as being the turning point in Anglo/Afrikaner relations that eventually led to the disastrous Boer War.

Upon his release, Jameson returned to South Africa where he first worked with Rhodes on the Cape Town-to-Cairo telegraph project. Still an advocate for Rhodes' unified South Africa he became active in Cape Colony politics and was elected to the Cape Colony parliament in 1900. He was appointed prime minister in 1904, and served in that capacity until 1908. He was made a Baronet in 1911 and rose to President of the British South Africa Company in 1913. To his dying day, he maintained that had his raid succeeded he not only would have been forgiven, but would have obtained the status in England of another Nelson or the Iron Duke.

---

184. Most authorities state that Rudyard Kipling's famous poem *If-* was written to celebrate Jameson's personal behavior following the raid. England's Poet Laureate, Alfred Austin, described Jameson as an Englishman gallantly going down to defeat in a rightous cause in his 1896 poem.

Leander Starr Jameson died on November 26, 1917. Jameson is buried at Malindidzimu Hill, a granite hill in Southwestern Zimbabwe (Formerly Rhodesia) about twenty-five miles south of Blawayo. It was designated by Cecil Rhodes as a final resting place for those who served Britain well in Africa. Rhodes lies nearby.

THOMAS CLARK DURANT

Today, few remember the name of Dr. Thomas Clark Durant, but he was undoubtedly one of the most important personalities of the 19th century. Many one-word descriptions have been appended to the Durant name, most of them pejorative, but the man's complex personality, accomplishments, and failings defy assigning him to a simple category or appellation.

Durant was born in Lee, Massachusetts in 1820 to an old, established, New England family. The family did not claim to have been one of the original Massachusetts settlers, but definitely reached America from England before 1660. Little is known of Durant's early education or life; however, he graduated from Albany Medical College in 1840. Hochschild states that he practiced surgery "for a few years" but offers no details. Ambrose and Klein are silent about his practice of medicine, and wonder if he, indeed, ever practiced medicine at all. Nonetheless, he used his title of "Doctor" for the rest of his life.

In 1847 he married an English woman, Heloise Hannah Trimbel. Two children were born to this union, Heloise, and William West Durant. By the time of his marriage, Durant had become a partner in his uncle's Albany export firm of Durant, Lathrop and Company. The firm exported flour and grain. Durant opened a New York City office for the firm. From the first, he had a flare for the export business, and rapidly expanded the firm and its scope. He also rapidly became an accomplished and rather ruthless stock market speculator. In addition, he seemed embroiled in commodity speculations especially in cotton[185]. However, during these early years, his business affairs remained

---

185. Following the Civil War, there were accusations that Durant had dealt in contraband Southern cotton during the war. George Francis Train and General Grenville Dodge were often accused of being co-conspirators in the cotton transactions, but the accusations seem to have remained nothing more than accusations.

relatively private.

Thomas Clark Durant burst upon the public scene in 1851. He joined Henry Farnam, a well known engineer and railroad pioneer, as a minor partner in building the Michigan Southern Railroad and part of the Chicago and Rock Island Railroad. Maury Klein describes Durant at this time in his life as follows:

> Tall, lean, slightly stooped, with sharp features and penetrating eyes, his mouth covered by drooping mustache and straggly goatee, Durant looked the part of the river boat gambler some thought he was. In 1852 he was only thirty-two years old, bristling with nervous energy and filled with grandiose and often contradictory ambitions. A close associate noted perceptively that "his mainspring seems to be not love of money for itself or notoriety in any sense, but a love for large operations - a restless desire to be swinging great enterprises and doing every thing on a magnificent scale."

When Farnam wanted to push the Mississippi and Missouri

Railroad across Iowa in 1853, his former backers withdrew their support, and Durant stepped in as a full partner. Their surveys laid the path of their rails to Council Bluff, crossed the Missouri and into the Platte River Valley. Their rails reached Iowa City by the end of 1855, but their funds were exhausted at that point and they could proceed no further. They received some additional funding in 1856 and had barely begun extending their rails when the panic of 1857 threw the incomplete railroad into receivership. Farnam and Durant had a bitter falling out when it was revealed that Durant had used the Mississippi and Missouri Railroad assets as security for some of his stock speculations. As Hochschild rightfully points out, ". . . Dr. Durant was not troubled with moral considerations in his dealings with the public." Farnam was the first, but not the last, to find out Durant was also not troubled with moral considerations in dealing with his business associates. The partnership was dissolved, but both Farnam and Durant remained on the Board of the now-dormant Mississippi and Missouri Railroad.

Prior to its demise, the Mississippi and Missouri Railroad had hired Grenville M. Dodge to survey a possible route beyond the Missouri

River, west of Omaha.[186] Dodge became convinced that the route west for any proposed railroad was along the Platte River Valley. This was already the wagon road west and produced an almost invisible climb to the Rockies. This confirmed Council Bluffs as the logical terminus for the Mississippi and Missouri Railroad if the funds could be found to restart construction and its great advantage should the often proposed transcontinental railroad ever come to pass. Dodge reported his findings to the Mississippi and Missouri Railroad Board of Directors, but most of the directors were uninterested. Farnam and Durant were the only directors to grasp the significance of Dodge's report. Durant in particular became fixated on the idea of a transcontinental railroad.

As important as Dodge's report to the Mississippi and Missouri Railroad was, his conversation with the Mississippi and Missouri Railroad consul, Abraham Lincoln[187], was even more important. Lincoln

---

186. Omaha is located at the junction of the Platte River with the Missouri River directly across the Missouri River from Council Bluffs, the proposed terminus of the Mississippi and Missouri Railroad.

187. For all the myths about Lincoln being a homespun country lawyer, Abraham Lincoln was a high powered, big business attorney. He represented railroads and major businesses. He was considered the nation's authority on business bankruptcy and railroad litigation.

had adopted the political philosophy of a transcontinental railroad as the means to tie the country together. His conversation with Dodge was probably the first indication he had received that such a project was practical. As a result of his conversation with Dodge, Lincoln made sure that a transcontinental railroad was part of the Republican Party platform in the elections of 1860. The outbreak of the Civil War delayed congressional action on the transcontinental railroad, but in 1862 the Pacific Railroad Act passed congress.

The Mississippi and Missouri Railroad was still at a standstill. However, in June of 1863, Farnam yielded control to Durant and retired. Durant was now convinced that the future was in the transcontinental railroad and the Mississippi and Missouri Railroad's only significance would be if it could connect with that railroad to the Pacific. He immediately assumed the title of "Mr. Transcontinental Railroad". He made the rounds of Wall Street and pressured the Directors of the Mississippi and Missouri Railroad and quickly had enough subscribers to form a Transcontinental Railroad Company.

That company, the Union Pacific, was incorporated on October

29, 1863. The dignified and reliable John A. Dix was named president while Durant was nominally only vice president. Dix rapidly became a figurehead and the Board of Directors was too large and disorganized to assume any real authority. Both Dix and the Board were completely dependent on Durant for information and day-to-day administration and management. Therefore, Durant wielded the real power. He was, in fact, and in his mind, the Union Pacific.

In 1863, with the Union Pacific still an idea in progress, Durant formed the Adirondack Company with a group of English investors. The plan was for a railroad from Saratoga, New York to the central Adirondacks. Durant envisioned the line eventually as a link to Canada. Work started on the road in 1865 and about sixty miles of track was eventually laid[188]. The railroad was never profitable and went into receivership by 1875[189]. Eventually the road to nowhere was acquired by the Delaware and Hudson Railroad. However, Durant, his son, and his

---

188. This is the line that carried Teddy Roosevelt on his emergency run from his climb on Mt. Marcy when he received word that President McKinley was dying (September 14, 1901)

189. By some sort of manipulation, Durant was appointed as Receiver.

associates made out well on their land speculations along the route.

Dodge was now a well respected general in the Union Army and was known to have close ties to President Lincoln. Durant realized he needed help in Washington to make sure that Omaha was designated the eastern terminus of the transcontinental railroad and to modify the Pacific Railroad Act of 1862 to make it easier to raise capital to build the railroad. He hired a myriad of lobbyists, but because Dodge supported both these ideas, Durant knew that Dodge was the key to the success of the Union Pacific. Dodge became Washington's strongest engineering proponent and lobbyist for the Union Pacific. Whether Durant paid Dodge[190] or whether Dodge did so out of his own strong convictions that a transcontinental railroad was the key to the west and that the Platte River Valley was the only practical route for such a road are still matters of debate. Dodge had strong congressional support from the Iowa delegation who saw the Mississippi and Missouri Railroad's position

---

190. The exact amount Durant spent on lobbyists and outright congressional bribes has never been completely calculated. Later investigations were able to verify $437,754.00, but most observers feel that amount is only the tip of the iceberg. Payments from other entities, participation in Durant's numerous other ventures, and complicated stock and money transfers have come to light at various times over the years.

bringing prosperity to Iowa.

Dodge's efforts bore fruit almost immediately. On November 5, 1863, Lincoln issued a presidential order that the transcontinental railroad should start west from Omaha. The Union Pacific broke ground in Omaha on November 30, 1863. Nonetheless, Durant was still juggling different schemes and could not seem to make up his mind how to proceed to his, not the Union Pacific's, advantage. He changed orders several times a day. He put his own henchmen into the key positions. He even bought an interest in a competing railroad that was promoting an altogether different route. It appears clear that from the day it was formed, the Union Pacific was mismanaged.

However, in Washington, Durant's efforts were clear and directed. The Pacific Railroad Act of 1864 gave Durant almost everything he asked for. It allowed the Union Pacific to issue its own first mortgage bonds for every twenty miles of track laid, and made the U.S. Government second mortgage holder. The 1864 Act also doubled the land grant and gave the railroad mineral rights along its route.

Even with these concessions, the Union Pacific was still a risky investment. All equipment would have to be manufactured elsewhere and transferred to Omaha by barge up the Missouri. Transport alone was going to be one of the greatest business expenses of all time. The route was going into wilderness. There was no ready-made market for passenger or freight traffic along its proposed route. Durant figured, quite rightfully, it would be years before the Union Pacific made money from its operations. But Durant had already factored all that into his plans. When it became evident that the 1864 Act was going to give the Union Pacific what Durant wanted, Durant and George Francis Train, a frequent participant in Durant's financial deals, bought an inactive Pennsylvania railroad credit agency, Pennsylvania Fiscal Agency. Pennsylvania Fiscal Agency had broad powers in relation to railroads. Train and Durant became its only directors, and changed the company's name to Credit Mobilier of America. Then, by the use of a transfer through straw men, Durant arranged to have the contract for the construction of the Union Pacific Railroad rest with Credit Mobilier of America. Even if the Union Pacific never made a cent, Durant would make a fortune constructing the railroad.

Durant couldn't or wouldn't stop using every angle he could to keep the odds in his favor. Even though the Union Pacific had already broken ground in Omaha, he kept threatening to move the terminus in order to get concessions from Omaha, where his brother was busy buying property. He inserted Silas Seymour, an engineer he had used on previous railroad projects and a man who served Durant's interests as his own, as the Union Pacific consultant engineer. Seymour's job was to continually advise new routes, and added miles, to any agreed upon route. Almost immediately Durant added a twenty-mile loop to the line, known as the Oxbow, for the sole purpose of keeping the connecting line from the east in doubt. He manipulated and micromanaged each and every decision. Klein estimates that Durant's ploys during this early period delayed the Union Pacific by at least ten months and cost the Union Pacific about $500,000.00.

Even more important than the time and money lost by the Union Pacific was the fact that Durant was so intent on keeping control of all aspects of the transcontinental railroad, that he set up no organization for controlling the logistics, engineering and construction. He was constitutionally unable to delegate authority; too insensitive, imperious, and insulting to establish good relations with associates or suppliers; too reluctant to meet payroll obligations to establish a loyal work force; and he ran through money faster than it could be raised. The result was that the Union Pacific was always short of cash, supplies and laborers.

Stock in the Union Pacific was too risky for most big money investors, but, in 1865, Durant managed to interest the Ames brothers, Oakes and Oliver, in both the railroad and especially Credit Mobilier. The Ames brothers had made a fortune in the gold rush, manufacturing picks and shovels. Now they saw a chance to make another fortune supplying picks and shovels for the railroad construction. The brothers invested $1,000,000.00 of their own money and raised another $1,500,000.00 for Durant[191]. Oakes Ames was a congressman and, through his efforts, several key congressmen received blocks of Union Pacific stock. In the investigations that followed construction, these shares caused a major scandal.

With the increasing number of shareholders in both companies;

---

191. Much of this additional money was in the form of lines of credit with various financial institutions with the pick and shovel company as cosigner.

the influx of knowledgeable business men like the Ames brothers; and pressure from the press, public and congress; Durant's power began to dilute. Suddenly, he began construction in earnest. However, his aforementioned failures made the task tremendously difficult. Durant had known for some time that the one man who could actually build the railroad was Grenville Dodge. But, Dodge had been in the Union Army during the Civil War, and would not resign his general's commission to work for Durant. Now that the war was over Durant offered Dodge the job of Union Pacific Chief Engineer. General Dodge agreed, provided he was given complete control of construction. Durant needed Dodge and the Ames brothers were insisting he meet Dodge's terms; therefore, he reluctantly gave lip service to honoring Dodge's insistence on control.

Dodge soon brought some organization to the entire construction process. Construction of the railroad began to progress in a measured way. Despite his deal with Dodge, Durant continued to act unilaterally. He considered himself to be Union Pacific and Credit Mobilier, and able to make or renew contracts, purchase mineral rights or make deals without consultation or approval of anyone. In Dodge's absence, Durant would authorize Seymour to change the route to his advantage. He reportedly skimmed money from both corporations and would hoard important or hard-to-find materials until the price increased and then pocket the difference. By November of 1867, the Union Pacific Board finally had enough and elected Oliver Ames President of the Union Pacific. Further, Durant was forbidden to act without Board approval. Credit Mobilier Directors removed Durant as President in May, 1868. However Durant still controlled the records and the administrative offices of both corporations. He fought all attempts to oust him from either the Union Pacific or Credit Mobilier. He tied up both organizations by withholding information and records necessary to conduct business and in court litigation. It is more than likely that he also threatened to reveal all the illegal operations of both corporations. The Board struggled, but found they could not control Durant without ruining themselves. Durant stayed on.

The battles between Dodge and Durant became legend, but despite the infighting, Durant managed to keep the supplies and the money coming and Dodge kept the line advancing. On January 9, 1869, the line reached a point 1000 miles west of Omaha. The Central Pacific and Union Pacific set the meeting of the roads at Promontory Summit for May 8, 1869. However, the Union Pacific had a washout on its line and the Union Pacific officials were delayed until May 10. A hole was drilled for the golden spike that marked the joining of the two lines, and telegraph wires attached to the spike and the sledge-hammer, but there was an immediate impasse as to who was to drive the golden spike. A compromise provided that Durant give the spike its first tap and Stanford of the Central Pacific the second.

The Union Pacific was still in financial trouble. Durant and contractors had diverted an appreciable amount of material the Union Pacific was liable for. The Mormon laborers who had done most of the work on the grade through Utah had never been paid. Shortly after the meeting of the rails, Durant was finally forced off the Union Pacific Board. It appears that he went without a fight. Construction was done. There was no cash in the Union Pacific coffers. The challenge and profit were gone. The Ames Brothers and their allies finally took control. A compromise was worked out with Brigham Young. The Mormons accepted rails, spikes, bolts and rolling stock valued at roughly $600,000.00 in lieu of cash. Young intended to build a spur from Ogden to Salt Lake City.

Durant's health broke down shortly after he left the Union Pacific, although no details are given in any of the sources. It appears he retired to his mansion at North Creek in the Adirondacks. His retirement did not stop him from bringing periodic suits against the Union Pacific.

Durant was lost to the national scene only temporarily. He reappeared again as a sinister player in the scandal that broke after the details of the Union Pacific construction arose in congress and the press in 1872. Despite Durant's dominant role in Credit Mobilier, the target of most of congressional and public anger, Durant was able to maneuver a settlement that put money in his now empty[192] pocket and failed to require him to relinquish any of his ill-gotten gains.

Thomas Clark Durant died in his home in North Creek[193], New York in 1885. After Durant's death his estate was deluged with claims,

---

192. Ambrose claims Durant lost his fortune in the financial panic of 1873.

193. The terminus of his Adirondack line.

most dating back to the Union Pacific and Credit Mobilier. There are reports of single judgments of over $20,000,000.00 against the estate. Nonetheless, several years later, litigation between Durant's son, William, and daughter, Heloise, revealed Durant's estate to still be valued at $1,278,000.00.

There is no doubt Thomas Clark Durant was, judged by present-day eyes, at best, a robber baron of the worst sort. However, without his foresight, drive, ambition, and stamina, a transcontinental railroad would probably not have even been in the planning stages until after the end of the Civil War. Without his lobbying and bribery, it is highly unlikely that Congress would have passed the type of legislation needed to make the line to the Pacific a practical reality until late in the 19th Century or early in the 20th Century. He worked hard on the transcontinental railroad from 1862 to 1869, and is the person primarily responsible for its early completion. He clearly entered the project to make money – not to become famous or infamous, nor as a matter of national unity, nor for any altruistic reason; nonetheless, the railroad was built. It opened the west, tied the west coast to the east coast and changed our concept of time and transportation forever. Like him or not, you must give the devil his due. Dr. Thomas Clark Durant is the man responsible for the Union Pacific and the transcontinental railroad. Most historians concede he did deserve to give that golden spike its first tap.

WILLIAM HENRY HARRISON

"He was not a great man, but he lived in a great time, and he had been a leader in great things."

William Henry Harrison occupies a unique place in American history. The ninth American President, at 68 when elected, he was the oldest man to be elected president until the election of Ronald Reagan, 140 years later in 1980; he gave the longest inaugural speech of any American President (one-hour-forty-five minutes in a raging snow storm); served the shortest time in office (32 days, 12 hours and 30 minutes) of any American President; was the only president with a grandson who was also president; and was the first American President to die in office. However, the reason we tell his story here is because he was also the only American President to have studied medicine.

William Henry Harrison ("Harrison" hereinafter) was born at

Berkeley Plantation[194], Charles County, Virginia on February 9, 1773. He was the youngest of seven children and the third boy born to Benjamin Harrison V and Elizabeth Basset. Benjamin Harrison was a close friend of George Washington, and served as a Virginia Delegate to the Continental Congress from 1774 to 1777[195]. While in Philadelphia he and Peyton Randolf shared rooms with Washington. Washington was a frequent dinner guest at Berkeley before and after the revolution, and both Lafayette and Washington dined at Berkeley during the siege of Yorktown. Benjamin Harrison V signed the Declaration of Independence in 1776. After leaving the Continental Congress, Benjamin Harrison was speaker of the Virginia House of Burgesses from 1777 to 1782; served as Governor of Virginia from 1781 to 1784; and, in 1788, served in the Virginia Convention formed to ratify the Federal Constitution[196].

William Henry Harrison never attended a primary school. He was tutored at home in the classics. He was whisked into hiding when the

---

194. His father's tobacco plantation.

195. Benjamin Harrison V and John Hancock were both candidates for the office of Speaker in the Continental Congress of 1775.

196. Benjamin Harrison opposed the Federal Constitution and voted against ratification.

British, under Benedict Arnold, sacked and burned Berkeley Plantation in 1782. The incident made an indelible impression on the child. Reportedly Harrison was a brilliant student and was admitted to Hampden-Sydney College at age fourteen[197]. He studied classics and history there for one to three years before Benjamin Harrison made arrangements for him to go to Philadelphia to study medicine with his old friend Benjamin Rush[198]. Robert Morris acted as his guardian while Harrison was in Philadelphia. Details of his training are sketchy, but it is likely he took two 16 week courses at the Philadelphia College of Physicians and Surgeons and a preceptorship with Dr. Rush.

Benjamin Harrison V died in 1791. Most commentators use his death and a lack of funds as the reason for Harrison's sudden shift from the study of medicine to seeking a commission in the regular army. However, this explanation jumps at some unlikely conclusions. First, Benjamin Harrison's death did not materially effect the extensive assets

---

197. The dates and time spent in college and in the study of medicine found in Harrison's biographies are in wild disagreement and none of them compute. The author has used the most likely educational sequence.

198. Contrary to most historical authorities, the White House official biography of Harrison notes that his medical training occurred in Richmond.

of the family. Second, both Rush and Morris were personal friends of the family and would hardly have severed their relationship for financial reasons. Third, at this stage of Harrison's training, he was probably able to earn his own way in the practice of medicine.

A far more logical explanation is that with his father's death, Harrison wished to pursue a political career like that of his father. This was a political family. His brother, Carter Basset Harrison, served in the United States House of Representatives from Virginia. The social status of a military officer was higher than that of a physician, and a military career, especially a distinguished one, was a better background for obtaining political office than a career as a medical practitioner. The fact that Harrison's commission was obtained for him by Richard Henry Lee[199] adds weight to the conclusion he was being groomed for political office.

In any case, Harrison accepted a commission as an ensign in the

---

199. Richard Henry Lee and his brother, Francis Lightfoot Lee, served in the Continental Congress and with their brother, Arthur Lee, were described by John Adams as follows: ". . .that band of brothers, intrepid and unchangeable, who, like the Greeks at Thermopylae, stood in the gap, and in the defense of their country, from the first glimmering of the revolution in the horizon, through all its rising light, to its perfect day."

regular army and was assigned to the 10th Regiment stationed at Fort Washington. With less than a year of service, he was promoted to lieutenant and assigned to the Northwest Territory. As further evidence of his political influence and grooming, he was immediately assigned to be aide-de-camp to General "Mad Anthony" Wayne. It was in this capacity that he served at the American victory in the Battle of Fallen Timbers in 1794 that brought the Northwest Indian wars to a successful conclusion. General Wayne cited Harrison for bravery in that battle. Lieutenant Harrison was one of the signers of the Treaty of Greenville that opened up what is now Ohio to settlers in 1795. 1795 also marked the date of Harrison's marriage to Anna Tuthill Symmes, the daughter of Judge John Cleves Symmes, a wealthy land speculator[200].

In 1798, Harrison resigned from the army to become Secretary of the Northwest Territory[201]. In 1799, he was nominated by the Jeffersonian Party and was elected the first representative of the Territory to the sixth United States Congress. Harrison was active in the

---

200. The marriage produced ten children and their grandson, Benjamin Harrison became the 23rd president of the United States.

201. An appointment promoted by another family friend, Congressman Robert Harper of South Carolina.

congress and introduced the Harrison Land Act that aided settlers obtain title to land in the Territory and influenced all future land grants in newly opened territories. In 1800, Harrison resigned from Congress to accept John Adams' appointment as the first governor of the newly formed Indiana Territory. He served in that capacity until 1813.

Harrison was primarily responsible for securing title of native held lands. He had sponsored legislation promoting more equitable treatment of the Indians and laws preventing the sale of liquor to the Indians. Harrison was accepted by many chiefs and seemed to be well suited to the task of purchasing land. He negotiated many treaties that secured the bulk of what is now Indiana from the tribes. However, in 1809, he created great tension within the tribes by the massive purchase of over 2,500,000 acres secured in the Treaty of Fort Wayne. Indian resistance, fostered by the British, centered around Tecumsch[202], the Shawnee Chief, and his brother, Tenskwatawa ("The Prophet"). Tecumsch immediately began to gain allies from neighboring tribes and formed a tribal confederation. With his increased strength, Tecumsch called on Harrison to nullify the Treaty of Fort Wayne, and threatened

---

202. Also spelled Tecumseh in some sources.

war on any settlers who came onto the disputed land. Harrison organized a militia force and marched against Tecumsch and his Indian confederation. He won an impressive victory against the Indians at the Tippecanoe River on November 7, 1811[203]. He was known for this victory for the remainder of his life.

After the ignominious defeat of the American forces at Detroit during the War of 1812, President James Madison gave Harrison command of the United States forces in the Northwest Territory. Harrison immediately assumed command and won impressive victories in Ohio and Indiana. Following these victories, Harrison led a force in the invasion of Canada and crushed the combined British and Indian forces at the Battle of the Thames. Tecumsch, who was fighting with the British, did not survive the battle.

Harrison had an ongoing series of personality clashes with the then Secretary of War, John Armstrong. In 1814, when Armstrong gave Harrison no active assignment and bypassed Harrison by giving an order to one of Harrison's subordinates, Harrison resigned his commission and left the Army. Armstrong accepted Harrison's resignation without

---

203. Many historians consider this the first battle of the War of 1812.

consulting the President. The President, James Madison, named Harrison to negotiate a peace treaty with the Northwest Indians. Harrison negotiated two treaties that essentially severed the Indians' ties with the British.

Following his resignation from the army, Harrison served as a congressman from Ohio from 1816 to 1819, when he resigned to run for Governor of Ohio. He was defeated, but promptly won a seat in the Ohio Senate. In 1824, he was elected to the United States Senate, where he served until 1828, when he was named Minister to Columbia. Harrison was recalled from Columbia after a year. He returned to his North Bend, Ohio farm and almost political obscurity. He did manage to secure the lucrative appointment as Clerk of the Court of Common Appeals of Hamilton County Ohio and seemed happy with his rural life.

In 1836, the Northern Whig Party drafted Harrison as their presidential candidate after he had been proposed at mass meetings in Pennsylvania and New York. Harrison lost to Martin Van Buren, but his better-than-expected results at the polls surprised everyone. At the Northern Whig Party convention in 1839, Henry Clay, the real leader of the party, was rejected as a candidate because he was a Mason and the party thought the votes of the old Anti-Masonic party were essential to a successful campaign. The Northern Whig Party ran Harrison again in 1840. This was the first big media campaign in presidential history. Harrison's war record was touted and he was pictured as a common man, living in a log cabin on his farm and drinking hard cider instead of wine. The slogan "Tippecanoe and Tyler Too" became the byword of the campaign and one of the most famous political slogans in history. An economic downturn in Van Buren's term helped Harrison win a landslide victory.

Anna Harrison was too ill to accompany her husband to Washington and Harrison arrived with his daughter-in-law Jane Irwin Harrison. Harrison was inaugurated on March 4, 1841. Washington was in the midst of a cold spell and the wind was whipping the falling snow into the inaugural party. Nonetheless, Harrison stood on the platform without a top coat, and delivered the longest inaugural speech in presidential history[204]. Harrison relied heavily on his classics background in drafting the speech, and it was hardly in keeping with his log cabin

---

204. Reportedly Harrison's initial draft of the speech ran to almost four hours. It was only through the editing efforts of Daniel Webster, Harrison's choice for Secretary of State, that the final speech was reduced to under two hours.

and hard cider image so heavily touted in the campaign.

While his exposure to the elements has been popularly credited with his subsequent illness, there is no doubt that his limited exposure to crowds in rural Ohio made him a likely recipient of a viral infection while facing the crowds of Washington. In any case, Harrison caught a cold soon after arriving in Washington. He tried to rest in the White House, but office-seekers badgered him night and day for appointments. The upper respiratory infection rapidly spread to the lower respiratory system and Harrison developed a full blown pneumonia. His physicians' attempts to treat did more damage than good, and Harrison died on April 4, 1841, reportedly of right lower lobe pneumonia and septicemia[205].

Harrison is buried in Harrison Tomb State Memorial, North Bend, Ohio.

---

205. Harrison's death laid the ground work for a popular myth - The curse of Tecumsch - Every president elected in a year divisible by 20 would die in office: Harrison 1840; Lincoln 1860; Garfield 1880; McKinley 1900; Harding 1920; Roosevelt 1940; Kennedy 1960. Ronald Reagan 1980 and George W. Bush 2000 seemingly broke the curse.

AYMAN MUHAMMAD RABI al-ZAWAHIRI
1951-?

If you go to the FBI's web site[206] listing the most wanted terrorists, you will find the name Ayman al-Zawahiri listed as the second

---

206. <www.fbi.gov/wanted/terrorists/teralzawahiri.htm>

most wanted with a twenty-five-million-dollar ($25,000,000.00) reward offered[207]. Ayman al-Zawahiri is generally considered the intellectual and ideological influence behind Osama bin Laden's Al-Qaeda organization. However, to even begin to understand Dr. Ayman al-Zawahiri, we must start our account a full year before he was born.

In 1950, Sayyid Qutb[208], a professor and writer for the Egyptian Department of Education, returned to Cairo after spending two years at the University of Colorado in Boulder. Before his departure for the United States, Qutb was reportedly an Egyptian nationalist without strong religious ties. However, his two year residence in Colorado convinced Qutb that Americans were devoid of manners, religion, or principles, and lusted only for power, sex and wealth. Qutb returned to Cairo a militant Muslim. He was convinced that Islam must confront the West in bloody jihad, religious war. He and his book, *Under the Koran's Umbrella(Banner)*, became the voice of the Islamic fundamentalist movement.

---

207. It is interesting to note that the FBI site lists al-Zawahiri's languages as Arabic and French. His fluency in English has been noted by several European and Israeli intelligence sources. One wonders why the FBI fails to list it.

208. Also spelled Quib in at least one reference.

Clearly, the primary *salafi*, Islamic fundamentalist, aim in Egypt was to create an Egyptian Islamic theocracy. However, it is also clear from Qutb's writing that the ultimate aim of the *salafi* was to extend that theocracy to the entire middle east and then the entire world. Qutb quite literally projected jihad to confront the West in bloody conversion to Islam. He wanted *Shari'a,* Islamic law, to be the law of the world. All nonbelievers were considered parties of Satan subjects to be destroyed. Democracy was also a despised target. There could be no will of the people, only the will of Allah. There was to be no compromise, negotiation, or modification, only bloody jihad. The world would be ruled by the Prophet's words of the seventh century.

Sayyid Qutb was arrested in 1954 after one of his faithful made a failed assassination attempt on Gamel Nasser's life. Undoubtedly, Qutb suffered extreme torture during his incarceration prior to his trial. He was sentenced to life in prison, but the term was later reduced to a fifteen year sentence because of his failing health. During his prison stay, Qutb continued to write inflammatory tracts that were smuggled out and published under the title *Milestones*[209]. In *Milestones* his basic message became even more extreme. In 1964, the president of Iraq, Arif, persuaded Nasser to grant Qutb parole. However, within a year of his release, Qutb was re-arrested on the charge of conspiracy to overthrow the government. He was found guilty and hanged on August 29, 1966. With his death he became a martyr in the cause of Islamic jihad and the inspiration for numerous cells of Islamic fundamentalism and jihad throughout the Middle East.

Ayman al-Zawahiri and his twin sister, Umnya, were born in the middle class Cairo suburb of Maadi.[210] Maadi, in 1951, was considered one of the more pleasant Cairo suburbs and was home to many of the foreign residents of Cairo. Maadi was also home to a large number of affluent Egyptian Jews. Life in Maadi centered around the Maadi Sporting Club, that was open to all of Maadi's residents. The Zawahiri family was unique for an affluent and influential Egyptian family. in that

---

209. Also interpreted as *Signposts* by Aboul-Enein.

210. Some sources say he was born within Cairo proper and moved to Maadi with his parents at age nine. Nonetheless, his school records would indicate he was in Maadi by the time he started school probably by age five or six. Maadi is probably his birthplace.

they lived on the "wrong side of the tracks," the native section of Maadi, and did not join the Maadi Sporting Club. Ayman's father, Dr. Rabie al-Zawahiri, was professor of pharmacology at Ains Shams University in Cairo. The family was one of the most prominent in Egypt. Of the forty-six members of the extended family, thirty-one were physicians, pharmacists or chemists; among the others were an ambassador, a judge, and a member of parliament. However, the al-Zawahiri name also was connected to Islamic learning. Rabie's uncle had been the Grand Imam of the university and mosque of Al-Azhar, a position akin to Pope in the Roman Catholic church. Rabie's father and grandfather studied at Al-Azhar as well[211]. His mother's family was equally distinguished and considerably wealthier. His maternal grandfather was President of Cairo University and a former ambassador, and his mother's great-uncle was the first Secretary General of the Arab League. Ayman's maternal great-uncle is vice president of the Egyptian Labor Party.

Although Maadi boasted one of the most prestigious private schools in Egypt, Ayman and Umnya attended a public school of limited

---

211. Again, Aboul-Enein gives a different version of Ayman al-Zawahiri's linage. He states Ayman's paternal grandfather was Iman of the Al-Azhar.

quality. Both were devout, bookworms, brilliant students and reportedly led their classes all through school. Qutb was hanged in 1966 while the fifteen-year-old Ayman was still in high school. Ayman immediately set up a secret cell devoted to Egyptian revolution through jihad[212]. Although his younger brother Mohammad was a member of his cell, Umnya evidently was excluded. There were similar cells springing up throughout Egypt. With Israel's stunning victory in 1967's Six Day war, Muslims were devastated. They had believed that God had favored Islam. With the Arab defeat, came a reactionary fervor not seen before. The enemy was not just Israel, but modern secular society. Al-Zawahiri's goal of returning Egypt to the 13th Century and rule by caliphate, the rule of Islamic clerics and *Shari'a,* Islamic law, was no longer confined to his and similar cells -- it became a political force in Egyptian politics. Ayman advanced quite rapidly in the jihad movement and before he

---

212. From the start, Ayman al-Zawahiri made a point of distinguishing between "near jihad" and "far jihad". Near jihad concerned overturning Egypt's secular government with a caliphate. Once the caliphate had been established in Egypt, the rest of the Arab countries would become the target of jihad. Only after the caliphate was established in the Middle East, would far jihad be directed against the western world. Al-Zawahiri would not deviate from this distinction until his Egyptian plans were thwarted following the Afghan war.

graduated from highschool he was marked as a future leader of the movement.

In 1968, after graduating from the Maadi high school, Ayman al-Zawahiri enrolled in the Cairo University Medical School. He was a brilliant student. He received his MD degree (cum laude) in 1974. He then enrolled in the University's surgical program, most likely the equivalent of a residency program in the West. He received his Masters Degree in Surgery in 1978. He began practice at the Muslim Brotherhood clinic[213] in Cairo, and, in late 1978 or early1979, married Issat Ahmad Nuwair, a Cairo University graduate and a devout Muslim. The couple are reported to have had five children. Rumors abound that his wife and children were killed in an American bombing attack on a cave in Afghanistan, but actually there is no reliable information available about the exact number of children or their current status.

Ayman remained in Cairo a very short time. In 1980, he joined the Director of the Muslim Brotherhood Clinic in a trip to Peshawar, Pakistan to care for Afghan refugees. The team of three Arab doctors

---

213. Some sources say he started his own clinic and only worked part time in the Muslim Brotherhood Clinic.

were the first to arrive in Pakistan. Al-Zawahiri spent four months in the refugee clinic.. There are unconfirmed reports that he also crossed the border and viewed the fighting in Afghanistan. In March of 1981, he returned to the clinic in Pakistan but stayed a much shorter time because the political scene in Egypt was heating up.

In the summer of 1981, he was arrested for conspiring in the assassination of Anwar Sadat. Under torture, Ayman named his cell members and betrayed his close friend, Isam al-Quamari. To their disgust, he also testified against them at their trials. Ayman al-Zawahiri spent three years in prison. It appears that he was active in the jihad movement within the prison and that he might even have assumed some sort of leadership role there. In any case, his prison experience furthered his radical philosophy. When he was released in late 1984, he returned to Cairo and essentially disappeared from the public eye. Whether this was because of police surveillance or his almost total elimination from the Islamic Jihad leadership is uncertain[214]. Some time in late 1985 or

---

214. It would seem despite his acceptance by the prisoners, he was viewed with distrust by the Egyptian Islamic Jihad still at large.

early 1986 he left Egypt to serve as a contract physician in Jiddah[215], Saudi Arabia. The decision to leave Egypt probably was also motivated by his guilt over his testimony and his worries about its consequences to his political career. There is absolutely no doubt that despite his bitterness over his lack of a leadership role, he was still a seasoned, committed, determined proponent of jihad.

Osama bin Laden, some six years Ayman's junior, was also based in Jiddah. He was not widely known and functioned mainly as a fund raiser for Arab fighters in Afghanistan[216]. Although Ayman al-Zawahiri probably knew who Osama bin Laden was, there is no evidence that the two actually met while their time in Jiddah overlapped. In any case, al-Zawahiri soon left Saudi Arabia for Peshawar, Pakistan, where he worked as a surgeon in the Kuwaiti Red Crescent Hospital. His wife and children reportedly joined him in Peshawar. His efforts in Afghanistan at this time seemed to be solely medical. He would cross the

---

215. Also Jidda in some sources.

216. By some estimates bin Laden's efforts had raised as much as $250,000,000.00, roughly the same amount that the United States poured into the same channels yearly in support of the mujahideen.

border for three months at a time to treat battle casualties.

Exactly when and how al-Zawahiri met bin Laden is unknown, but the two met in Afghanistan and became friends. Ayman al-Zawahiri became Osama bin Laden's personal physician. With Osama bin Laden's financing, al-Zawahiri opened an Islamic Jihad office in Peshawar. He operated the office as both a gateway for Egyptian Mujahideen[217] to enter Afghanistan and as a recruiting station for the Islamic Jihad. Al-Zawahiri considered the war in Afghanistan a war fought under a strictly Islamic banner, and, therefore, a "holy war." However, al-Zawahiri could not seem to cooperate with other Islamic organizations that were now operating out of Peshawar, and his Egyptian funding effectively dried up. His other funding, including bin Laden's, at its level at the time, would not allow him to be a power player. Ayman al-Zawahiri seemed to realize very early in the game that the future of the Islamic movement rested with bin Laden. He moved from Peshawar to Afghanistan to be close to bin Laden.

His role changed with his move. No longer was he strictly a

---

217. Also spelled Mujahedeen.

medical man. Now he distributed arms to, and arranged training, through bin Laden, for Egyptian Mujahideen. He reportedly took part in the actual battles as well. Above all, he concentrated on getting close to bin Laden. He remained bin Laden's attentive personal physician, confidante, and ideological advisor on jihad. Bin Laden, in turn, began to rely on al-Zawahiri's Egyptian Islamic Jihad members to run his affairs. [218] Ayman al Zawahiri, with little or no funding from Egypt, became fully dependent on Bin Laden's considerable Saudi and Sudanese funds.

In 1989, the Russians finally pulled out of Afghanistan. Many of the Arab Mujahideen returned to their countries of origin. But many, including bin Laden and al-Zawahiri, remained in Afghanistan. Toward the end of 1989, a meeting of the leaders of these remaining Mujahideen was held. An Iraqi, Abu Ayoub, proposed the formation of a new organization to spread jihad outside of Afghanistan. That organization was named Al Qaeda. Because Osama bin Laden still controlled the

---

218. Abu Hafs became head of security; Said Al-Masari became head of finance; Omar Abdul Rahman became head of operations and training; and Midhat Mursi became head of weapons and research.

financing for the Mujahideen, he became the de facto leader of the group. Al-Zawahiri's Egyptian Jihad members became the administrators of the new organization.

Soon after the formation of the new organization, bin Laden returned to Saudi Arabia, supposedly to work in the family business. When Iraq invaded Kuwait the following year, bin Laden offered the Saudi Royal Family his Mujahideen to defend the Saudi oil fields. His offer was refused and the Royal Family accepted the aid offered by the American coalition. When American troops were still present in Saudi Arabia a year after the end of the Gulf War, bin Laden felt betrayed and returned to Afghanistan. Now, the Saudi government became an Al Qaeda target, and bin Laden an enemy of the Saudi Royal Family.

Al-Zawahiri had remained in Afghanistan and eagerly renewed his relationship with bin Laden. However, bin Laden was fearful that the Saudi Royal Family had recruited members of the Mujahideen to kill him, and left Afghanistan for Sudan in 1992. Ayman al-Zawahiri soon joined him there and attempted to reorganize his Egyptian Islamic Jihad movement. However, he still was receiving no support from Egypt, and, despite his friendship with bin Laden, only token amounts from Al

Qaeda. He could not sustain his movement without adequate funding. Al-Zawahiri attempted to raise money in the United States, but American mosques contributed very little. In view of his inability to raise funding of his own, al-Zawahiri and his administrative team began working for bin Laden for wages, but kept their organization a separate entity. Even at this early stage of their collaboration, it seems obvious that al-Zawahiri realized the only way his jihad movement could survive was by an allegiance with Al Qaeda.

With the funding provided by the jihad's wages, al-Zawahiri made two failed attempts on Egyptian officials' lives. In one of these attempts, twenty-one innocent people were injured and a twelve-year-old girl was killed. Egyptian public outrage was intense. Al-Zawahiri's offer of blood money to the girl's parents did nothing to diminish the wave of antiterrorist outrage. Two-hundred-eighty Egyptian Jihad members were arrested and six executed. Among those arrested was the jihad's membership director, with a computer data base containing details on the entire jihad membership in Egypt. Over 1000 members were eventually arrested. Al-Zawahiri had lost his entire Egyptian organization.

Al-Zawahiri then directed his attention elsewhere. He traveled extensively in the Middle East, the Balkans, the Philippines, and South America. He reportedly was a participant in the war in Bosnia. He was instrumental in introducing the suicide bomber and taping the bomber's vows of martyrdom, acts that have come to symbolize a jihad operation. He returned to the Sudan in April of 1995.

With the remnants of his movement in the Sudan, al-Zawahiri planned the assassination of the Egyptian President Mubarak on a state visit to Ethiopia. The assassination attempt resulted in the death of two Ethiopian policemen, but Mubarak was unhurt. The Egyptian government reacted with a brutal crackdown against dissidents within Egypt and increasing pressure on the Sudanese government to arrest al-Zawahiri. Al-Zawahiri responded with the suicide bomber attack on the Egyptian Embassy in Islamabad, Pakistan in November 1995. Sixteen people were killed and sixty wounded. It was the first successful operation of al-Zawahiri's Jihad Movement.

Egyptian and Saudi Secret Services now directed their attention to bin Laden and al-Zawahiri in the Sudan. Several attempts were made to assassinate the two. Al-Zawahiri executed two young boys coerced by the Egyptians into an assassination plot against him, and was brazen enough to make a tape and distribute it of their trial and execution. This incident, combined with the strong international pressure, finally forced the Sudanese government to expel bin Laden and al-Zawahiri along with their followers in May of 1996. Bin Laden flew to Afghanistan with his family and followers. Al-Zawahiri's movements after he left Sudan are more speculative. It would appear he first spent time in Switzerland, then briefly visited Holland, but he is also credited with multiple trips to Yemen, Malaysia, Singapore, and China. At any rate, by December of 1996, al-Zawahiri had set up a headquarters for the Islamic Jihad in Chechnya.

In April 1997, al-Zawahiri was sentenced to six months in prison for entering Russia illegally[219]. However, al-Zawahiri was using false papers and the Russians were unaware of his true identity. This episode elicited a storm of criticism against al-Zawahiri within the Islamic Jihad for his reckless behavior. It would appear bin Laden also was critical. He withheld all but token amounts from the Islamic Jihad during al-Zawahiri's imprisonment. Al-Zawahiri and his Islamic Jihad were now

---

219. By the time of his trial, al-Zawahiri had already served close to five months of his sentence, and was released in late May or early June of 1997.

financially and politically teetering on the edge of bankruptcy. Al-Zawahiri moved to bin Laden's headquarters in Afghanistan.

On February 23, 1998, al-Zawahiri officially allied his Islamic Jihad with bin Laden's Al Qaeda. By this time, Al Qaeda and al-Zawahiri, emboldened by the American pullout from Somalia, had concentrated their actions against America. This did not sit well with the entire jihad movement. Many members of al-Zawahiri's Islamic (Egyptian) Jihad movement and other Islamic groups resented al-Zawahiri's turn from the "near" enemy to the "far" enemy, and all resented his failure to consult the membership about the formal allegiance. Al Zawahiri called a meeting in Afghanistan of the movement's leaders to explain the new combined organization. If the meeting was intended to mend fences, it failed. Many members, including his brother, Mohammad al-Zawahiri, resigned from the organization.

American intelligence sources link the Al Qaeda bombing of the American Destroyer Cole to al-Zawahiri. They place him in Yemen, running Al Qaeda operations there at the time of the attack.

The allegiance of the two organizations resulted in more

European and American action against jihad cells in Europe. After the members of the Albanian Cell were captured by the CIA and turned over to the Egyptians, al-Zawahiri claimed that the American embassies in Kenya and Tanzania were bombed in retaliation[220]. However, it now appears that the bombings had been planned by Al Qaeda well before the CIA action and even before Islamic Jihad's allegiance with Al Qaeda. The bombings triggered the American air strikes against the Al Qaeda training camps in Afghanistan. Neither al-Zawahiri nor bin Laden were injured in the air strike, and the air strike is generally evaluated as having been ineffective.

By this time, internal strife had forced al-Zawahiri to temporarily relinquish control of the Jihad and had reduced his followers to about forty. In June 2001, after al-Zawahiri regained control of the Jihad movement, he formally merged it with Al Qaeda. The name of the new organization, Qaeda al Jihad, reflects the fact that al-Zawahiri's Egyptians still are the administrators of al Qaeda. Even though al-Zawahiri is second to bin Laden in command of Al Qaeda, American

---

220. The embassies were assaulted by suicide bombers. 223 people died and more than 5000 were injured,

Intelligence believes he is equally as dangerous. There is some evidence that it was al-Zawahiri that planned the 9/11 attacks on the World Trade Center and Pentagon[221].

Al-Zawahiri is interested in developing biological and chemical weapons for Al Qaeda. He has done some elementary experiments with nerve gas and hoped to set up facilities in Afghanistan for the production of anthrax. The U.S. invasion stopped work before production could begin. He is rumored to have paid millions to the Chechens for Russian atomic bombs. Among his identified targets are secular Muslim nations; Muslim nations allied with the west; multinational corporations; the United Nations; international news organizations; communications and data exchange systems; international relief agencies, especially those sponsored by non-Muslim religions; Christian missionaries; and all democratic countries. He exhorts his followers and sympathizers with the same rhetoric that has marked his stance from the beginning.

Killing them (Americans and Jews) with a single bullet,

---

221. Both bin Laden and al-Zawahiri fled to the mountains with their staffs on 9/11. Subsequent U.S. bombings of fortified cave positions resulted in the death of some 18 Al Qaeda functionaries and it is rumored that al-Zawahiri's wife and children were killed as well.

a stab, or device made up of a popular mix of explosives or hitting them with an iron rod is not impossible. Burning down their property with Molotov cocktails is not difficult. With available means, small groups could prove to be a frightening horror for the Americans and Jews.[222]

There is no consensus as to whether al-Zawahiri is alive or dead, or if alive, his present location. Some American Intelligence officers reportedly believe al-Zawahiri was killed by Pakistani mercenaries after he was wounded by American bombings. Others believe he is somewhere in the mountainous region between Pakistan and Afghanistan. He also could be in any one of numerous Islamic countries, protected by advocates of Islamic Jihad and/or sympathetic governments. However, that is probably looking at too narrow a range of possibilities. Al-Zawahiri's ability to remain undetected in secular countries in Europe, Asia, and South America is legend, and he could be holed up literally anywhere in the world. A trained physician who has become an

---

222. *Knights Under the Prophet's Banner* from Aboul-Enein at 17.

experienced agent of death.

JEAN PAUL MARAT (1743-1793)

Jean Paul Marat[223] is justly considered one of the great enigmas of modern history[224]. About the only things left- and right-leaning writers can agree upon is: (1) that Jean Paul Marat, almost singlehandedly, is responsible for the reign of terror that developed in the final days of the French Revolution and (2) that he was driven by an insatiable urge for fame. He has become a villain to most Western writers and a hero to the Soviet bloc.

Jean Paul Marat was born May 24, 1743 in Boudry in what is now Switzerland. He was the eldest of six children born to Jean Paul and

---

223. Also spelled Jean-Paul Marat.

224. One of the problems is Marat himself was such an unreliable source. He essentially gave any item of his personal history a self aggrandizing spin that varied with the situation at hand.

Louise Mara[225]. The elder Jean Paul Mara was a shadowy figure from Sardinia who, in 1740, migrated to Neuchatel[226] and converted from Catholicism to Calvinism[227]. He married the daughter of a French wig maker, Louise Cabrol. Mara was well educated, and earned a living as a language teacher and sometime chemist.

The younger Jean Paul was a sickly child, and poor health plagued him his entire life. He was small[228] and had frequent headaches, boils and fevers[229]. In addition, he was physically ugly, repulsively so. Almost all sources agree he was educated at home by his father[230]. He also seems to have been an avid reader and this contributed to his self-

---

225. .Marat added the "t" sometime after leaving Neuchatel, presumably to sound more French.

226. One of the states that now make up modern Switzerland.

227. Some biographers state that he was ordained as a priest in Sardinia and that accounts for his excellent education. Other biographers state he was Jewish. There is no clear evidence to support either contention. His conversion is the only verified fact.

228. He never exceeded five feet.

229. Some writers state that he had skin problems from childhood.

230. Ober states he also attended classes at the local college.

education. All sources also agree that almost from birth, his ambition was overwhelming. He constantly sought attention and glory. Fame was his sole goal.

The Mara family prized education and Jean Paul and his siblings were all offered university educations. At the age of sixteen, Jean Paul left to study at the universities of Toulouse and Bordeaux[231]. Most biographers imply that he studied medicine, but there are really no records of his course of study and it does not appear he ever received a degree of any sort. He later claimed he continued his studies in London and Dublin, but there is nothing to confirm these claims. However, it appears he opened a medical practice in Paris. His appearance and lack of credentials discouraged patients and the practice failed. Marat turned his attention to self-directed experiments in electricity and optics. His experiments were flawed. His theories were largely criticized for lack of evidence, and his writings ignored. Undaunted, he left Paris, hoping for a better reception in both his medical practice and scientific endeavors elsewhere. He went to Holland briefly and then arrived in England

---

231. Murphy states he studied in Paris, not Bordeaux.

sometime between 1765 and 1767. He began an unlicensed practice of medicine and seems to have made living. In1772, he published *An Essay on the Human Soul*, in which he claimed the meninges were the seat of the soul. In 1773, He published *Philosophical Essay on Man*. Neither publication achieved serious consideration. A French translation of *Philosophical Essay on Man* was published in Amsterdam in 1775. However, an extremely critical attack on his thesis by Voltaire killed sales in France although it made his name well known throughout France.

In 1774 he became a Mason[232] and published his first radical essay, *The Chains of Slavery,* urging British voters to reject the King's suggested parliamentary candidates. In 1775, he returned to medical subjects with an article on gonorrhea. On the strength of this article, Marat persuaded Hugh James, MD and William Buchan, MD to recommend him for an M.D. at the University of St Andrews[233]. He also

---

232. July 15, 1774, Freemason of the Grand Lodge of Freemasons of London.

233. Appleyard states all that was needed were recommendations from two doctors. Ober implies that St. Andrews had fallen on hard times and was not above selling a degree. He also indicates the Royal College of Physicians did not accept the Scottish degree.

began applying some of his optical research to diseases of the eye and tried to gain some recognition as an innovative eye physician. Neither the degree, nor his works on the eyes gained him the fame he so desperately needed.

Exactly why and when he left London and returned to France is unclear[234], but, in 1777, he used his new found degree to secure employment as the physician to the guards of the Comte d'Artois[235]. This opened the door to much of the French aristocracy and some moderate success. However, despite his claims of a thriving practice, he had too much time on his hands. He returned to research in the physical sciences. He attempted to show that fire, hot gasses and phlogoston[236] were a fluid. He disputed the value of lightening rods, using speculation rather than evidence to support his theories.

Marat presented his collected works to the French Academy of Sciences for membership, but was turned down. His rejection by the

---

234. There are rumors he was involved in the theft of museum artifacts.

235. The younger brother of the king and later Charles X of France.

236. Lavosier had already blasted the very existence of phlogoston.

Academy hurt his reputation and his practice. It was a crushing blow to his ego, and, though he had always blamed others for his errors, he now became truly paranoid. Many considered him a quack. Marat was terribly embittered and viciously attacked the Academy in his writings for the remainder of his life. Marat always believed that Lavoisier was the member who orchestrated his rejection, and made his hate for the man common knowledge[237]. The leftist biographers describe Marat's rejection by the French Academy of Sciences as an example of the establishment unjustly rejecting the outsider. On the other hand, Ober, Schama and Jackson defend Lavoisier and the Academy, claiming Marat's research was never taken seriously by the scientists of the day, and rightfully so.

In April 1786, Marat resigned his position and began a translation of Newton's *Opticks*. In 1788 he published his twelfth book, *Academic Memoirs or new discoveries about light.* That same year, he left science behind and turned his attention to the French reform movement. His writings, directed to the Estates-General, promoted

---

237. Jackson considers Marat the individual primarily responsible for Lavoisier's execution.

control by the third estate and a constitutional government.

In 1788, he also began an affair with Simone Evard, the twenty-seven year old sister-in-law of one of his printers. Simone Evard eventually became his common law wife[238].

Also some time in 1788 he developed a crippling, pruritic, chronic, skin disease. The lesions started in the perineal and scrotal areas and then progressed over the rest of the body. It is unclear if the onset of the rash was coincident with a severe respiratory infection Marat suffered about this time. The unrelenting pruritus resulted in scratching that left him with weeping, open sores. The doctors at the time diagnosed his skin disease as scrofula[239]. Since then, the malady has been considered as everything from atopic dermatitis, to leprosy, to arthritic psoriasis, and even diabetic dermatopathy[240]. Modern dermatologists have reached the

---

238. By some reports, Marat married her in 1792. In any case, Simone's relationship to Marat was closer than that of the mistress some writers describe her as. By all reports, Simone was beautiful and it is hard to understand her attraction to the repellant Marat.

239. Non-pulmonary tuberculosis.

240. Marat reportedly suffered from severe polydipsia, but it is unclear whether this symptom predated his dermatitis. His doctors treated his polydipsia with clay mixed in almond water. His headaches, which had bothered him from childhood,

conclusion that no accurate diagnosis can be made from the information presently at hand. Regardless of what it actually was, his skin disease forced Marat to seek relief in a tub of cold water. He did much of his writing on a board across the tub with a vinegar-soaked rag tied around his head as a treatment for his now continually present headaches.

In September, 1789, he began his own radical paper. Originally named the *Patriotic Watch,* then *Paris Political Journal,* it soon became *The Friend of the People.* Using this forum, he denounced everyone in power and everyone he disliked. He reserved his most venomous attacks for the nobility, the most influential and powerful individuals, the Academy of Science and Lavoisier. He not only attacked their political views, but attacked them personally, frequently describing them as blood sucking. During this period he slept about two hours a night and had to be reminded to eat. He seemed to be manic in his denouncements.

In 1790, Marat's attack on the popular commander of the National Guard, Lafayette, backfired on him and he had to escape to

---

also became worse after the onset of the skin disease.

London[241] to avoid arrest. Five months later, popular support allowed him to return and resume his attacks, not only against the rich and powerful, but now all but the most radical of the revolutionaries. His paper called for a revolutionary dictatorship and decried that so few heads had been taken.

In September of 1792, he was elected to the National Convention. When the Convention declared France a republic on September 22, 1792, Marat changed the name of his paper to *Journal of the French Republic,* but continued his tirades against the rich and powerful, his personal enemies, and all but the most radical of his fellow politicians. Within the Convention, he was aggressively confrontational and frequently carried a pistol with him and often stated he would die before compromising.

From January to May, the fights between the Girondins , who wanted a constitutional republic modeled on the United States, and the Jacobins, who wanted a revolutionary dictatorship, consumed the Convention. The Girondins appalled by Marat's vicious attacks, ordered

---

241. Marat may have escaped to London twice to escape prosecution.

him tried before the Revolutionary Tribunal, but his popular support was so vast the Tribunal was forced to acquit him. Marat returned to the Convention with an increased following and overwhelming popular support. Finally, on May 31, 1793, the Jacobins wrested control of the Convention from the Girondins and the scene was set for the ensuing terror. Marat was now at the peak of his power. His revolutionary dictatorship was now in place with Robespierre, Danton and Marat in the leadership positions.

Marat's political triumph was cut short by his assassination on July 13, 1793.

He was soaking in a tub, as usual, trying to get some relief from his terrible dermatitis when a young female Girondin supporter, Charlotte Corday, gained entrance by saying she had information about the Girondins in Normandy. When Marat said he would have them all guillotined, she stabbed him in his chest with the five inch blade of a kitchen knife. Marat died almost instantly. His autopsy revealed the knife entered the chest on the right[242] through the first intercostal space and

---

242. Almost all contemporary reports state he was stabbed in the left chest and the art work of the time all show the entry wound on the left.

penetrated the lung, the aorta and left auricle. The pericardial sac was filled with blood, but there was no hemothorax because the pleural cavity was obliterated by adhesions.

Corday was caught before she could leave his rooms. Although Charlotte Corday continually maintained she had acted alone, Marat's death sparked dramatic reprisals from the Jacobins and thousands of their political opponents were guillotined. Charlotte Corday herself was executed on July 17, 1793.

The entire National Convention attended Marat's funeral and he was venerated as a saint during the time of the terror. In many ways Marat was more useful to the Jacobins as a martyr to the revolution than he would have been alive. He was worshiped by the poor he championed. Poems and songs were written about him and Marat became a favorite name for French babies. He became a symbol of the "battle" against counter revolution and an argument for the Great Terror.

Marat's death was commemorated in the painting *The Death of Marat* by Jaques-Louis David. He was buried in the Pantheon and his heart displayed elsewhere as a shrine. However, as Marat's popularity waned after the terror subsided, he was disinterred, and his coffin was moved from burial site to burial site until he was finally buried for good in the cemetery of the Church Saint-Etienne-du Mont[243]. His heart was thrown away. At the height of his popularity, thirty-seven towns and villages in France were named for him. A Russian battleship was named after him in 1921 and he still occupies a revered position in left-wing histories.

---

243. There are unconfirmed reports that his coffin had disappeared over the years and what was finally buried were two urns with his lungs and intestines that had been removed at autopsy.

JOHN KEATS (1795-1821)

Hadst though lived in days of old,
Oh what wonders had been told
Of thy lovely countenance,
And thy humid eyes that dance
In the midst of their own brightness,
In the very fane of their lightness,
Over which thine eyebrows leaning,
Picture out each lovely meaning:
In dainty bend they lie,
Like streaks across the sky,
Or the feathers on a crow,
Fallen on a bed of snow.[244]

John Keats was an early addition to my list of physicians who made their mark outside of medicine. Nonetheless, painful memories of struggling through the English romantic poets in high school English class made me continually push the name of John Keats lower on my "to

---

244. Keats' poem to Mary Frogley sent on Valentine's Day, 1816. While most sources agree John Keats was romantically attracted to Mary, there is no consensus as to the actual course of the romance or how serious it was.(As is also the case with the Jeffery sisters and Jane Cox) Many writers believe Mary was far more attracted to John's brother George and that John abandoned the romance when his affection was not returned. However, Mary kept all the poems Keats wrote to her and defended him all her life.

do" list. It wasn't that I just did not like Keats' poetry; that English class made me actively dislike his poetry. His brief life span also seemed to make him a poor candidate for a biographical sketch. However, a short time ago, I became interested in the Apothecary Act of 1815, a historic milestone in medical and medical education history. I found that John Keats sat for and passed the first examination under that Act. That fact finally put John Keats back on the top of my list.

John Keats was born October 31, 1795[245] in Moorgate[246], then a district in the Eastern outskirts of London. Although biographers continually stress the poverty of his origins, the facts of the matter indicate he came from a successful commercial family. His maternal grandfather, John Jennings, originally ran a livery stable alongside an inn, *The Swan and Hoop*. He prospered and eventually bought the inn. He ran both ventures successfully and profitably. John Jennings joined the Innholders Company, and became a successful investor and money

---

245. Although Brown, his closest friend and biographer, gives his birth date as October 29, 1796. A curious error, among many, by Brown.

246. Also called Moorfields in some sources.

lender as well. Thomas Keats, Johns Father, worked for Jennings and, at age twenty, on October 9, 1894 married nineteen year old Frances Jennings, John Jennings' daughter. Sometime between 1797 and 1802, when Jennings retired, management of the stable and inn were turned over to Thomas and Frances Keats. Thomas Keats provided well for his family and there is no indication they suffered any sort of privation.

John was the oldest child born to Thomas and Frances Keats. George born February 28, 1797; Tom born November 18,1799; Edward born 1801 died 1802; and Frances Mary (Fanny) born June 3, 1803 followed.

John's early education was in a local dame's school. In 1803, John and George were enrolled John Clarke's school, a politically very liberal school in nearby Enfield. Clarke pushed the humanities, music, poetry and made politically liberal papers and tracts available for students. John, small for his age, had a quick temper was continually getting into fights with his schoolmates and had to be bailed out by his younger but bigger, tougher, stronger, and more stable brother, George. John excelled at French and rapidly became proficient in that language.

Thomas and Frances visited regularly. On April 15, 1804, when John was eight years old, his father was thrown from a horse while returning from the school. He died from a head injury. His mother became mentally unstable following Thomas's death. She entered a disaster of a marriage to one William Rawlings two months later[247], then disappeared. Exactly what transpired during this disappearance is, today, speculation at best[248], but whatever happened, Frances was disgraced and the Jennings family reputation seriously damaged. John, who had been close to his mother, was particularly influenced by his mother's fall from grace. He never felt he had escaped her black mark on his character.

Sometime in late 1804 or early 1805, the four surviving children became charges of the maternal grandparents, John and Alice Jennings, who now lived in Edmonton. However, John Jennings died in 1805 and the burden of raising the four children fell on sixty-nine-year-old Alice Jennings. John Jennings death also resulted in each of the Keats

---

247. Two weeks later in one source.

248. Usually unverified accounts of alcoholism and promiscuity.

grandchildren inheriting £1000.[249] Unfortunately, this legacy was tied up in litigation for years and resulted in the Keats children's estrangement from their extended family. Nonetheless, Alice seems to have been a loving and considerate grandmother even though she had disowned their mother. The two younger boys, George and Tom, were devoted to their grandmother and praised her for the rest of their lives. John could never fully forgive her for disowning his mother. All three of the boys seemed to be united in their love and protection of their little sister, Fanny.

John became close to the Clarke family and in many ways they became closer and more influential than his grandmother. Charles Cowden Clarke, John Clarke's son, eight years John Keats senior in particular became his protector and mentor. Except in French, John was not a very good student. He was restless and impulsive. Charles Cowden Clarke and George Keats constantly worked to keep John on an even keel and in school.

In 1809, after an absence of some five years, Frances Keats reappeared at the grandmother's door. Now thirty-four, she was worn

---

249. There was also an annuity set up for Frances Keats.

out, destitute and dying of consumption[250] and other unknown diseases. Despite the disgrace Frances had brought on the family, the grandmother took her in, and John, now thirteen, took it upon himself to be her care giver. He read to her, cooked her meals, fed her, changed her bedding, medicated her and even bathed her. The episode, brief as it was, turned him into a reader and probably infected him with tuberculosis. Frances died in March, 1810, some six months after her mother took her in. Her annuity from her father passed to her children.[251]

As the grandmother aged, she became worried about what would happen to the children if she were to die or become unable to care for them. She appointed co-guardians for the children, Richard Abbey and N. Sandell[252]. Abbey, a successful tea broker from London, was a

---

250. As tuberculosis was known in the early 19th century. AKA as *phthistis* from the Greek. Still using the reasoning of the 16th century, phthistis was thought to be caused by stagnant blood in the lungs that had turned malignant. It was diagnosed by fever, wasting and hemoptysis. The treatment was usually fasting, laxatives, phlebotomy, and opiates.

251. Roughly £800, but it isn't clear if this was the total amount or the amount per child.

252. Sandell is a shadowy character that evidently moved away and took little or no part in running the Keats children's affairs.

neighbor and friend of Alice Jennings. He was a conservative man and felt the children had been unduly influenced by John Clarke and his liberal politics. He was not a bad man, but one who was completely unable to accept anyone who held beliefs contrary to his own. Alice Jennings knew he was old-fashioned and set in his ways, but admired him for his success, standing and charitable giving. Unfortunately, Abbey was incapable of being a father figure to any of the children, but his relationship with John was particularly stormy. Literary biographers tend to paint a picture of him as a villain, but there is no evidence he was anything but a rigid, conservative man who could not identify with John Keats as a poet, a foppish dandy, or a political liberal.

At age 14, John left school and entered an apprenticeship with Dr. Thomas Hammond[253], a well qualified Guy's-trained surgeon in Edmonton, a village close to Enfield.[254] Much has been made of the role his guardian played in Keats leaving school and starting on a medical career. The usual line taken by literary biographers is that Keats was

---

253. At least one source claims Hammond treated Frances Keats.

254. George also left school about the same time as did John. George became a clerk in Abbey's firm.

forced out of school and into an unwanted career. However, they fail to take into account the following: (1) under any circumstances Keats would have left school sometime within the year; (2) his mother's death and his role in nursing her had made him interested in medicine; (3) he knew and most probably had been treated by Dr. Hammond; (4) the apprenticeship allowed him to remain close to his grandmother his only hint of a parental figure; (5) medicine offered a measure of financial security the boy thought he desperately needed; (6) Thomas Keats' close relative was a surgeon[255] (7) medicine was in the midst of change, and the Napoleonic wars had greatly increased the prestige of surgeons. All the objective evidence supports the idea that medicine was a career chosen by Keats himself and supported by his grandmother and Abbey.

Medicine in England at that time was really a three-tier system. Apothecaries were the drug compounders and distributers and the

---

255. Variously described as a brother, cousin or uncle who worked as an inspector of Regimental Infirmaries or as a Regimental Surgeon. The best we can say is that there probably was a surgeon relative that John knew about.

unlicensed, but not illegal, physicians to the poor[256]. The surgeons were the general practitioners of medicine and dentistry. The physicians were university trained and the specialists of their day. However, there was a political undercurrent proposing changes in medical education and licensing.

John Keats did well in his apprenticeship and from all accounts was happier and more stable than he had been in school. He lived in quarters above Dr. Hammond's surgery. His duties included cleaning the surgery and caring for Hammond's horses as well as assisting in the surgery and learning to compound Hammond's remedies. All through his budding medical career, Keats found time to return to Enfield and keep up his contacts with Charles Cowden Clarke, who was striving to make his mark as a poet. As Keats entered his final year of apprenticeship, new legislation was in the works requiring time on the wards of a teaching hospital. Many literary biographers have mistaken the move required by the new legislation as a disagreement with Dr. Hammond. However, there is no evidence of such a disagreement. In fact, Dr.

---

256. Although unlicensed as physicians, the Rose decision in 1704 permitted their practice of medicine.

Hammond wrote letters of recommendation to Guy's for John Keats. Keats was admitted to the Apothecary/Surgeon program at Guy's/St. Thomas hospital in London on October 1, 1815.

St. Thomas Hospital was the older of the two hospitals. It was originally founded in the 12th Century with forty beds as a charitable hospital for the sick and needy. Thomas Guy, a Governor of St. Thomas, a Member of Parliament, and a successful bible publisher and seller, founded Guy's in 1721 because of the overcrowding and aging facilities of St Thomas. The new hospital was adjacent to St Thomas on St. Thomas Street. Guy died in 1724 before his hospital was completed in 1725[257]. The two hospitals functioned without a medical school until Benjamin Harrison founded a school at the combined hospitals. That medical school functioned from 1768 to1825 when the schools separated.[258] Certainly it was the most prestigious hospital possible for John Keats to attend to further his career as an apothecary-surgeon. In Keats' day, the most famous surgeon in England, Sir Astley Cooper,

---

257. Originally, Guy's had 60 beds.

258. The schools reunited in 1982 as the United Medical and Dental Schools.

operated out of Guy's. The school at Guy's required a healthy tuition fee, which Abbey readily supplied.

Keats began his day at 7:30 in the morning with lectures Monday, Wednesday, and Friday at Guy's and Tuesdays and Thursdays at St. Thomas in chemistry, compounding, dentistry, midwifery, and experimental philosophy. After the morning lectures, Keats worked on the wards. From 2:00 to 4:00 in the afternoon, there were anatomy lectures followed by one hour of dissection.[259] Medical and surgical lectures were held in the evenings. Keats' medical career had auspicious beginnings. Keats seems to have been promoted rapidly, even though most sources hint that he was not the most attentive or that he excelled. No one even hints the promotions were based on merit, but no one gives real evidence as to why the promotions were given. In any event, John Keats rapidly became the dresser for William Lucas, a surgeon of no

---

259. The dissection of human bodies for the teaching of anatomy was still illegal in England. Bodies were bought from grave-robbers or "resurrection men", a practice supported by the Guy's staff, including Astley Cooper, who frequently paid the body snatchers' fines and even supported their families when they were sent to prison.

particular note[260]. There were only twelve dressers chosen out of over 700 students. The duties of a dresser were varied. The dresser attended rounds with the surgeon, took notes, carried the plaster box, acted as assistant at surgery, became resident surgeon for a week at a time on a rotation with other dressers, and did minor surgical procedures. Because Lucas had more complications than most surgeons of his day, Keats was an extremely busy dresser.

On July 25, 1816, John Keats successfully passed the prescriptions and Pharmacopeia, the theory and practice of medicine, pharmaceutical chemistry and materia medica parts of the Society of Apothecaries examination. Passing the examinations made John Keats a licentiate of the Society of Apothecaries, and thus fully licensed to practice medicine[261]. Most of his contemporaries and many of his literary biographers fail to realize the significance of Keats' medical credential.

---

260. Keats recognized Lucas' shortcomings, and attended Astley Cooper's surgeries whenever possible. There is some evidence that Cooper had a special interest in Keats and might have been responsible for his rapid rise to the rank of dresser.

261. Actually he would not have been able to activate his license until October 31, 1816, his 21st birthday.

He was a fully qualified physician, not just the pill counter his early critics were apt to label him. In fact, contemporary accounts reveal that Keats had expressed some plans to continue another year of training at Guy's to become a full-fledged surgeon[262]. Therefore, his abrupt decision to leave medicine and devote himself full-time to poetry has become a source of conflicting stories.

The account most often expressed is that Charles Cowden Clarke was enthusiastic about Spenser's recently published *Fairie Queen,* and interested Keats in it. Keats attempted to imitate Spenser with a few poems and Clarke was amazed to find Keats' poems were superior to Clarke's own. The second version has Charles Cowden Clarke reading him Chapman's *Homer* and Keats realizing the tremendous power of the poetry. In either case, most literary biographers report that Keats experienced an epiphany, and realized his true calling was as a poet and not as a physician. His closest friend, Charles Armitage Brown, however, gives a much different account of why Keats left medicine.

He ascribed his inability to an overwrought

---

262. Bannerjee states that Keats actually practiced as Lucas' full time assistant for a short time after passing the examination.

apprehension of every possible chance of doing evil in the wrong direction of the instrument. 'My last operation', he told me, was the opening of a man's temporal artery. I did it with the utmost nicety; but reflecting on what passed through my mind at the time, my dexterity seemed a miracle, and I never took up the lancet again.[263]

Whatever the reason, Keats left medicine to try his hand at poetry[264]. There is no evidence that he ever thought to question the economic consequences of his action, and it was doubtful he had anyone's commercial opinion about his poetry. Charles Cowden Clarke was trying to interest Leigh Hunt in his own poetry and delayed showing Hunt anything by Keats. Finally, Charles Cowden Clarke showed Keats' poems to Leigh Hunt. Leigh Hunt was co-owner and editor of the *Examiner,* a friend and supporter of Shelly, and had published many of Shelly's poems. Leigh Hunt was a well known political liberal who had

---

263. From Brown at 48.

264. Numerous sources relate that he had not totally dismissed the idea of returning to medicine if all else failed.

served a prison term for sedition. He was also a poet, and was taken with Keats poems. The two finally met on October 9, 1815. Hunt agreed to publish Keats' poetry, and immediately Keats became part of Hunt's politically liberal artistic circle; consisting of Thomas Barnes, editor of the *Times;* Charles Lamb, writer; John Scott, editor of *London Magazine;* William Hazlett, writer for the *Morning Chronicle;* Vincent Novello, organist at the Portugese Church; Charles and John Ollier, publishers; Benjamin Robert Hayden, painter; and John Hamilton Reynolds, poet; among others. Hard as Keats tried, he could never overcome playing second fiddle to Shelly within the group Hayden seems to have become his closest friend within that circle.

Keats affected Byron's look with an open collar and a foppish man-about-town attitude. Many contemporary accounts comment on his effeminate appearance and imply that he was a homosexual[265]. He had problems surviving in London on the sums his guardian, Abbey, would give him now that he had left medicine. For the rest of his life, Keats felt Abbey was withholding his due. In Abbey's defense, it is important to

---

265. Keats' closeness with his male friends has always led to questions about his sexual preferences and speculations that he was bisexual.

bring out that much more had been spent on John Keats' medical training than on his siblings' training, and that Abbey was raising Fanny in his own home. Abbey felt Keats was foolish for abandoning a profession that could earn him a living, and selfish for demanding so much more than his siblings. Abbey also detested both Keats' liberal politics and his poetry. Much as Keats complained about and demeaned Abbey, he never once investigated the state of his finances, the terms of his inheritance, or the state or amount of his mother's annuity.

In late 1815 or early 1816, John moved in with his brothers George and Tom, both of whom worked as clerks in Abbey's firm. George was still the leader and dominated the brothers' social life. He introduced his brothers to Mrs. Wylie, the widow of an infantry officer. She had a daughter, Georgiana, with whom George was smitten. As was frequently the case, John was also attracted to Georgiana. He wrote her sonnets, and even though it soon became obvious that George was the object of her affections, Keats and Georgiana had a deep and poorly understood relationship for the rest of his life.

Seeking cheaper lodging, in 1817[266], the three Keats brothers moved to Hamstead, where they took the first floor of a postman's house. Keats soon decided he needed more privacy to write and took a brief trip to the Isle of Wight. It didn't work out, and he soon left the island for Margate where Tom joined him. George had started a business with a borrowed £50. It rapidly failed.

Sometime in the interval between moving to Hamstead and returning from the Isle of Wight, John Keats had met Isabella Jones, a lady whose virtue and character has long been questioned by his biographers. There seems to be no doubt that they had a hot and heavy affair, and many sources maintain she was the source of Keats' case of gonorrhea[267]. It was Isabella Jones who received the first word of Keats death in Italy.

At about this time, Tom's consumption became obvious and he was sent to the South of France for his health. John returned to

---

266. The exact date of this move is questionable. It could be as early as 1816.

267. John Keats had been treated extensively with mercury and the evidence points to a case of gonorrhea. However, Ms. Jones may be falsely accused. Keats frequented prostitutes both in London and on the Isle of Wight.

Hamstead. On one of his walks, he was introduced to Charles Armitage Brown. Brown was seven years older than Keats. He had joined his brother in a business in Russia, returning to England when that business failed. Since his return, he had worked as a bookkeeper and tutor. He had written a comic opera about his Russian experience that had been well received. In addition to his wages and royalties, he had received a £10,000 inheritance from his brother. He owned a large house nearby. Brown and Keats bonded almost immediately, and Brown took on the same sort of protective role that George had served while John was in school. Brown soon became Keats' closest friend. George was Tom's real care giver at this time. As he became more concerned with his own career, and contemplated marrying Georgiana Wylie and emigrating to the United States, John became less central to his life. Brown, in turn, took on an ever larger role in John's life.

Brown's description of Keats and their meeting is worth repeating.

> Still, as in that interview of a minute I inwardly desired his acquaintanceship if not his friendship. I will take this

small in stature, well proportioned, compact in form, and though thin, rather muscular; – one of the many who prove that manliness is distinct from height or bulk. There is no magic equal to that of an ingenuous countenance, and I never beheld any human being's so ingenuous as his. His full fine eyes were lustrously intellectual, and beaming (at that time) with hope and joy. It has been remarked that the most faulty feature was his mouth; and, at intervals, it was so. But, whenever he spoke, or was in any way, excited, the expression of the lips was so varied and delicate, that they might be called handsome.[268]

Keats' early poems attracted little notice except in Hunt's circle and provided essentially no income for Keats. His first volume, *Poems*, was published in 1818 by the Ollier brothers, Charles and John, part of Hunt's circle and publishers of Shelly. It was a critical and financial failure. As part of Hunt's circle, Keats had expected to be tagged as a radical and receive a poor reception for his poems by the Tory press, but he did not expect the personal attacks that developed.

---

268. From Brown at 44.

He is at present a very amiable, silly, lisping, and pragmatical young gentleman – but we hope to cure him of all that – and should have much pleasure in introducing him to our reader in a year or two speaking the language of this country, counting his fingers correctly, and condescending to a neckcloth.

(*Blackwood's Magazine*, vi December 1819, 239-40)[269]

The result was that no mainline publisher would touch his work. Keats was a radical and was published almost exclusively in radical publications that paid him a pittance. Keats found some income by acting as the temporary theater review columnist for the *Champion*. Keats now spoke out whenever possible, damning the new emphasis on science and mathematics in education and society. Even though he still expressed the occasional statement about returning to medicine, this new attitude showed he really had made the split from his former life irreversible.

By July of 1818, George had purchased 1440 acres of farm land in Illinois for $2.00 per acre and had married Georgiana Wylie. He was

---

269. From Brown, Notes at 46 #28 at 99.

newlyweds to Liverpool and then set off for a foot tour of Scotland[271]. The walking tour of Scotland was one of the high points of John Keats' short life. They climbed Ben Nevis, the highest of Scotland's hills, visited some of the islands and tramped the highlands. Keats developed a fever and sore throat and on August 6, 1818, saw a physician in Inverness who told him he was too ill to continue the walking tour[272]. In retrospect, many observers believe this fever was the initial symptom of his tuberculosis. John took the stage with Brown to Cromarty and then went by ship to London. By the time he returned to Hamstead on August 18, 1818, Tom was terminal. He had repeated episodes of hemoptysis and even coughed up fragments of lung. John spent the next month caring for Tom as he had for his mother[273].

---

270. George never farmed the Illinois property. He went into business with James Audibon in Cincinnati and when that business sold (at a loss) moved to Louisville and started a lumber business that prospered. John never forgave George for taking capital from the estate to start the business.

271. It is hard to determine who cared for Tom while John was away. It is also interesting to note that John did not wait to see George off. He resented George's easy way with women and seems to have been far more interested in Georgiana than most of his biographers have noted.

272. Keats had been dosing himself with mercury, thinking his sore throat was a syphilitic ulcer.

273. Keats met Jane Cox in September, while he was still caring for Tom. The exact nature of their relationship has never been truly explained. It is difficult to understand why almost every biographer mentions it.

When Charles Armitage Brown and Keats had left for the trip to Scotland, Brown had rented half his house to Mrs. Brawne and her three children. Sometime between his return to Hamstead in August and November of 1818, Brown introduced John to Mrs. Brawne's pretty eighteen-year-old consumptive daughter, Fanny. Fanny was small, sensuous, and a flirt. She spoke and read French and German, was witty and lively and addicted to romance novels, card playing and dressmaking. Later in life, she became a successful author. According to Motion, she considered men too stupid to post a letter. John was smitten.

Tom died at the end of November 1818, and John, unable to afford the house he had shared with his brothers, moved in with Brown. John Keats was perpetually broke. His poetry didn't sell; he lived beyond his means; borrowed from whoever would lend him money; and still loaned money to his friends. His poetry was not critically successful at any time during his lifetime. It was only his circle of friends, like Brown, Hayden, and the Ollier brothers who kept him afloat.

His romance with Fanny Brawne flourished, and he spent Christmas with the Brawnes. At some point he gave Fanny a ring as a token of his commitment, but it is unclear if the ring signified an engagement or something less. Over the ensuing years their unconsummated love affair continued to grow and ended only with his death in 1821.

John Keats seems to have realized he was a symptomatic consumptive by 1819, even though his physicians were still making other diagnoses. Throughout 1819 and 1820 his health steadily deteriorated. He continued to write poetry and Hunt and the Olliers[274] continued to publish it, despite losing money in the process[275]. He developed what appears today to be a major depression. He became obsessed with his lack of money and felt certain George and Abbey had cheated him in some way. He wanted to marry Fanny Brawne, but his financial insolvency and deteriorating health kept him from acting. Mrs. Brawne also strongly opposed the marriage on much the same grounds. Keats seems to have reveled in his misery and some aspects of his depression

---

274. Taylor relieved the Olliers on Keats' final volume.

275. Hunt apparently did it out of friendship and loyalty. The Olliers apparently did it because they thought he was a great poet who would eventually be appreciated. Taylor evidently agreed with the Olliers and was willing to take the chance of relieving them of another loss.

appear theatrical in retrospect. His physician, William Lambe, FRCM, could do nothing for him.

By the summer of 1820, Keats' hemoptysis and fever had reached the point that Lambe feared he could not survive another English winter. Lambe suggested that Keats go to Italy, where the mild weather might possibly accomplish a recovery. His friends[276] pitched in and raised the money for a trip to Italy and enough to sustain him over the winter. By this time, Keats was too ill to travel alone and a companion was necessary. Brown was the logical choice, but Brown was disinclined to go and away on another trip to Scotland when arrangements were made. Finally the painter, Joseph Severn, was chosen to accompany Keats. Severn had known Keats for four years, had no serious commitments in England and wanted to see Italy.

After their twenty-three months of courtship, Keats and Fanny Brawne made a pact to marry when Keats returned from Italy. Mrs. Brawne doubted Keats would survive to return from Italy and agreed to their pledge. Fanny Brawne also agreed to correspond regularly with

---

276. The Ollier Brothers, Taylor (successor to Ollier as his publisher), and Hayden are thought to have been the major contributors.

Fanny Keats and keep John informed about her. Keats sent Fanny Keats a lock of his hair and said goodbye via letter. He left his books and a miniature portrait Severn had done of him with Fanny Brawne[277].

Keats and Severn sailed for Naples aboard the two-masted brigantine *Maria Crowther* on September 17, 1820. It had very limited accommodations. Almost immediately after putting to sea, the ship was caught in a storm and had to put in at Portsmouth. They did not reach open sea for at least two weeks. The ship was caught in another storm in the Bay of Biscay and suffered another delay. Keats suffered a major hemorrhage and was racked with violent night sweats. They finally reached Naples thirty-four days after leaving London. The port authorities quarantined the boat for another ten days and Keats did not get ashore until October 31, 1820. Keats rested in Naples before the pair continued to Rome via carriage. They arrived in Rome on November 15, 1820.

In Rome, Keats' care was provided by James Clark, an

---

277. Motion notes that Keats gave Fanny Brawne's younger sister an amethyst broach that might have belonged to his mother. Rather strange considering his concern for his sister, Fanny.

Edinburgh trained, ex naval surgeon who had post-graduate training in major European medical centers. He was familiar with, and had used, the stethoscope long before it was introduced in England. For some unknown reason, Clark doubted the diagnosis of consumption (tuberculosis) and thought Keats had a gastrointestinal disease. Clark arranged for Keats and Severn to stay in rooms at the foot of the Spanish Steps near his surgery. On December 9, 1820, Keats had another major hemorrhage, which continued intermittently until Christmas. Keats realized he was not going to recover and began making arrangements for his death.

He requested that Fanny Brawne's letters and a lock of her hair be buried with him along with a purse Fanny Keats had made for him. He wanted his headstone to be engraved with a broken lyre and the inscription, "Here Lies One Whose Name Was Writ In Water."

John Keats died on February 23, 1821. Severn notified Brown, who notified Isabella Jones, Abbey, Fanny Keats, and Fanny Brawne, and spread the word to Keats' circle of friends. Dr. Clark and a fellow physician performed an autopsy. Dr. Clark called it the worst case of tuberculosis he had ever seen, with the lungs almost totally destroyed. John Keats was buried in the Protestant Cemetery In Rome.

Fanny Brawne reportedly wore mourning clothes for three years. She finally married in 1833. Fanny Keats could not forgive Fanny Brawne for not remaining faithful to John and ended their friendship. George did much to promote John in America and was responsible for publishing his poems there. The English literary critics damned his poetry even after his death. Despite heroic promotion efforts by Keats' circle of friends, including Shelly and Byron, it took another fifty years before his poetry was accepted in England.

JOHN HENRY HOLLIDAY 1851-1887

John Henry Holliday, better known as "Doc Holliday" is one of the Legends of the Western Frontier. However, his life has been badly distorted by the popular media, and, almost invariably, his biographers have offered poorly researched, poorly written, conflicting pictures of the man. What follows is as objective a picture of the man and his life as one can draw from existing sources.

John Henry Holliday's father, Henry Burroughs Holliday, was a veteran of both The Cherokee Removal[278] and the Mexican War. He settled in Griffin, Georgia, a small southern Georgia town, and opened

---

278. It is quite possible that he took part in the Cherokee Wars as well.

a drug store[279]. The store became successful and its owner achieved some status in the town. Henry Holliday ventured into land speculation both in the town of Griffin and the surrounding countryside. He soon courted and married Alice Jane McKey, the daughter of a prominent Georgia planter. Their first child, Martha, died at six months. Their son, John Henry, was born August 14, 1851. He was delivered by his uncle, Dr. John Siles Holliday, a Fayetteville physician who came to Griffin for the occasion.

One family source reported that John Henry was born with a cleft palate that was repaired by John Siles Holliday and Dr. Crawford W. Long. However, there are no contemporary accounts by either John Siles Holliday or Dr. Long of repairing the cleft palate. At that time, successful repair of a cleft palate was rare enough that one of the two was bound to have reported it. This is especially true of Dr. Long. Roberts, for one, doubts the accuracy of the family report.

When John Henry was five, upon the death of his McKey grandparents, his mother's siblings moved into the Holliday's Griffin home. Tom McKey, only nine years older, became John Henry's mentor.

---

279. By all reports, Henry Holliday was a slave-holder by the time he arrived in Griffin. It is rather rare for a landless veteran to hold slaves.

Georgia was known as the "southern frontier" at the time, and John Henry grew up as much a frontier child as a child of the south. He rode, hunted, shot, fished, wrestled and roamed the area with Tom McKey. He had much more independence than would be granted a child of today. It is reported that Henry spent little or no time with his son and that they were never close. Many writers believe John Henry always considered himself more a McKey than a Holliday.

With the onset of the Civil War, Tom McKey joined the 5th Georgia Volunteers and Henry Burroughs Holliday was commissioned a major in the 27th Georgia Infantry. John Henry was left the only male in a household consisting of his mother and her female siblings. He became very protective of his mother and aunts. To make matters even worse, his mother fell ill with consumption. By 1863, Major Henry Holliday could see the handwriting on the wall and decided to move his family to safer territory. He sold enough property in and around Griffin to transport his family to Valdosta in Southern Georgia. Henry saw something that he thought spelled a future in the area and bought 2450 acres on Cat Creek ,just outside of town.

John Henry attended Professor Varnedoe's Valdosta Institute, a school that offered a classical education. He was an outstanding student, and well liked by both his classmates and teachers. Of medium height and slight build, with sandy hair, he was considered handsome and something of a catch among the local belles. He was also extremely popular with his female cousins and young aunts. John Henry was completely given to the Confederate cause and followed the dispatches carefully, marking changes in positions on the map. There are rumors he was among the night riders that tried to frustrate reconstruction efforts following the war.

The family was reunited with the end of the civil war. Major Holliday took a position with the Union Reconstruction Administration, which offended his neighbors and further alienated John Henry. On September 16, 1866, Alice Jane Holliday died of her tuberculosis. John Henry was devastated. His hurt was intensified when, only three months later, Major Holliday married Rachel Martin, the daughter of his next door neighbor. John Henry considered this an overt insult to his mother. The relationship between father and son was forever strained[280].

---

280. From later interviews with the Martin family, it doesn't appear that the relationship between John Henry and Rachel was any better.

Influenced by a young Valdosta dentist who offered to be his preceptor, and his uncle John Siles Holliday, John Henry decided to attend the Pennsylvania College of Dental Surgery in Philadelphia when he graduated from the Valdosta Institute. It offered him an escape from his strained family situation and a profession that would allow him to be independent of his father. John Henry started his dental studies on October 3, 1870. By all reports, John Henry was a brilliant and skilled dental student who easily completed the two-year course on schedule. However, he was five months short of his twenty-first birthday when he completed the course and could not receive his degree immediately. While awaiting his diploma, he accompanied one of his classmates to St. Louis where the classmate set up practice with John Henry as his assistant.

St. Louis was where the Doc Holliday legend began. Besides being a practicing dentist, he began to be known as a gambler and a drinker. It was probably in St. Louis that he first met his long-time paramour, Kate Fisher.[281] After a five-month stay in St. Louis, John

---

281. Later known as Kate Elder, more frequently called "Big Nose Kate" by contemporaries. A dance hall girl and more than likely a prostitute, she was

Henry received his diploma[282] and returned to Georgia to join the dental practice of Dr. Arthur Ford in Atlanta.

Shortly after beginning practice in Atlanta, John Henry was diagnosed with consumption (tuberculosis). Most biographers give this as the reason he left Georgia and headed west. However, the more likely motive for leaving Georgia in a hurry was that he had shot a black man he thought had offended him. Georgia under a reconstruction administration was bound to bring charges. In any case, John Henry took off in some haste for Texas.

By September of 1873, he had opened a dental office at 56 Elm Street in Dallas, Texas. He supplemented his start-up practice income with gambling. He was arrested and fined for gambling in the spring of 1874. In January of 1875, he was arrested for trading gunshots with another man in a saloon, but because no one was injured, he was not

---

extremely loyal to John Henry and nursed him through relapses.

282. It is interesting to note that as a graduation present John Henry received a Colt Navy revolver.

prosecuted[283]. However, sometime in the spring of 1875, Doc shot and killed an AWOL black soldier and left Dallas before charges could be brought. From then on Doc was constantly on the move between Denison, Fort Griffin, and Fort Clark[284] Texas. Somewhere on these moves he re-encountered Kate Fisher/Elder and the two joined in a monogamous relationship. Doc's well-known fiery temper and willingness to die by the knife or the gun, rather than from his tuberculosis, kept him in continuous scrapes. Two incidents with his knife[285] in which he cut one man's throat and disemboweled another spread his reputation as a dangerous man. Nonetheless, Doc continued to practice dentistry throughout this period.

Sometime in 1878, Doc opened up his dental practice in Dodge

---

283. Although almost all of his contemporaries attest that Doc was the fastest draw in the West, his accuracy was terrible. Most of the men who traded shots with him lived to tell the tale. In most of his fully documented shootings he either missed altogether or wounded the man. Most of the people who knew him feared his knife more than his gun. Certainly Looper's claim that he shot and killed thirty men is an exaggeration.

284. It was probably in Fort Griffin or Fort Clark that Doc first met Wyatt Earp, although they were both gamblers there is no indication of any particular friendship at that time.

285. Thought to be a knife made by his uncle, Tom McKey, and carried by McKey during the Civil War. The knife was known as the "Hell Bitch".

City Kansas. At that time, Bat Masterson was the local sheriff and Wyatt Earp was the town marshal. Far more interested in gambling than being a practicing dentist, Doc bought a partnership in a local saloon and gambling house. One day when Doc was dealing faro in his saloon, he glanced out the window and saw Wyatt Earp trying to arrest a group of cow boys. One of the cowboys was to Earp's back and was about to draw on him. Doc raced out the door with a borrowed revolver in his hand and rescued Earp. Wyatt Earp always credited Holliday with saving his life, and the two developed a long, warm friendship.

Sometime in late 1789, Doc's tuberculosis took a decided turn for the worse. He and Kate packed up and moved to a spa in Las Vegas, New Mexico. One of Doc's best documented gunfights took place there on July 19, 1879, when Doc traded shots with a former Army scout named Mike Gordon and killed him. Doc was placed on trial, but acquitted when the shooting was ruled self defense.

Exactly why Doc decided to leave Las Vegas and join Wyatt Earp in Tombstone, Arizona is unknown. It is clear that Kate was against the move and didn't approve of Doc's friendship with the Earps. But in September, 1880, John Henry Holliday and Kate Fisher/Elder showed up in Tombstone. The town was wide open for a gambler like Doc, and he made no attempt to set up a dental practice[286]. He continued to have violent encounters, but was fully protected by the Earps. In turn, he became embroiled in the political battles between the Earps and the cowboys as an Earp partisan.

The popular reason given for the gunfight at the OK corral is that it was a culmination of the political fight between the town forces represented by the Earps and the cowboys, represented by the Clantons and McLaurys. However, little note has been given to three facts: (1) that the gun fight followed a bitter argument the night before between Ike Clanton and Doc; (2) that the OK Corral was next door to Doc's boarding house, Fry's; and (3) all witnesses attest to the fact that when Ike Clanton came into town his widely voiced intention was to kill Doc Holliday. Therefore, the alternative theory that the Clantons and McLaurys were there to kill John Henry Holliday, and that the Earps stepped in to repay Doc for saving Wyatt's life in Dodge City, may have some validity.

---

286. There is no indication that he practiced dentistry after he left Dodge City.

In any case, on October 26, 1881, three Earp brothers[287] and Doc encountered the five cowboys in front of the OK Corral and in the ensuing gunfight Doc shot two of the McLaurys and was grazed by a pistol shot[288].

The Earps and Doc all testified at the subsequent inquest and court proceedings and were acquitted of the murder charges brought by the sheriff, Johnny Behan[289]. Following the acquittal, in December of 1881, Virgil Earp was ambushed and shot. Virgil was crippled for life. In March 1882, Morgan Earp was killed by "unknown gunmen".

Warren Earp, Wyatt Earp and Doc left Tombstone to escort the badly wounded Virgil Earp and his family to California. As they were about to board the train in Tucson, Frank Stilwell (one of Johnny Behan's sometime deputies and a cowboy partisan) and Ike Clanton reportedly tried to ambush the party. Frank Stilwell ended up dead in the

---

287. Wyatt, Morgan and Virgil. Warren and James were not involved.

288. Ironically, Ike Clanton who undoubtedly was responsible for the confrontation was unarmed and turned and ran. He was unhurt.

289. It was sometime during the court case that Kate Fisher/Elder quietly slipped out of Tombstone and out of Doc's life.

railyard with both buckshot and pistol wounds[290]. Wyatt Earp admitted killing Stilwell with the shotgun blast, but legend has it the pistol shots came from Doc Holliday.

Exactly what role Doc Holliday played in the Earp vendetta that followed Virgil's trip to safety is unclear. Most biographers state that Doc joined Wyatt, Warren Earp, Sherman McMasters, Jack Johnson, and Jack Vermillion in their three week ride that killed at least three men suspected of the ambushes of Virgil and Morgan Earp. However, others believe Doc's health was too fragile for him to have been on that ride, and attribute these claims to legend builders. However, warrants were issued for all six, including Doc, of those on the vendetta and they all left Arizona. It appears that Wyatt and Doc went first to Las Vegas, New Mexico and then to Colorado.

At some point between the time they left Tombstone and the time they arrived in Colorado, Doc and Wyatt Earp had a falling out. Some sources claim Doc was appalled at Wyatt's cold-blooded vendetta, but that hardly seems likely, given Doc's own frontier code. A more likely

---

290. If Ike Clanton was really there as both Wyatt Earp and Doc claimed, he again avoided the action and disappeared in the rail yard.

cause was Wyatt's intention to marry Josephine Sarah Marcus, convert to Judaism and move to California. Doc did not like Josephine, and probably made his feelings known to Wyatt. Regardless of the cause of the break up, they went their separate ways when they reached Trinidad[291], Colorado in May 1882.

Doc spent a few days in Pueblo and then moved on to Denver. He was arrested there on trumped up charges until the Arizona warrant could be served to try to return him to Arizona[292]. After a well publicized[293] and lengthy legal battle, the Colorado Governor refused to extradite Doc. After his release he had an approximately one month reunion with Wyatt and Warren Earp in Gunnison, Colorado, and apparently re-established his friendship with the Earps. From there he moved on to Leadville.

---

291. Bat Masterson was the marshal in Trinidad.

292. Strangely, no effort was made to extradite the Earp brothers.

293. The tabloid-style stories printed about him in Denver are probably the source of most of the myths and legends that sprang up about him. Those stories made him a character far better known than Wyatt Earp. It was only after Lake's biography of Earp was published in 1931 that Earp's name became better known.

Leadville was booming. With more than seventy working claims (mines) it was the queen of the mining camps. It boasted a population of close to 40,000, with 120 saloons, 119 gambling halls, 110 beer gardens and 35 brothels. However, Leadville was almost 5000 feet higher than Denver. To function well at 10,000 feet above sea level, one has to have an almost perfect ability to oxygenate their blood. It was hardly an ideal environment for a "lunger" like Doc..

Nonetheless, Doc settled in for a long stay. He rented a hotel room, found a job as a faro dealer in the Monarch Saloon, and let his family in Georgia know where he could be found. He seemed determined to keep his temper under control and become a model citizen. Whether this new attitude was some self-remodeling, aging, his poor oxygenation, or a change forced upon him by the Governor in exchange for safety from the Arizona warrants is unclear. The only charge brought against him in these early days in Leadville was one for being drunk and carrying a concealed weapon in late 1882.

By the winter of 1884, Doc's drinking, use of opiates[294] and

---

294. The local druggist supplied him with opiates to control his cough, free of charge.

disease were making it difficult for him to hold a job in the gambling houses. We know he lost his job at the Monarch and moved to Mannie Hyman's saloon. However, his repeated bouts of pneumonia prevented him from keeping that job also. After he left Hyman's, there is no record of him having a regular table. He seems to have wandered from place to place, sitting in on a game whenever he could find one and had enough cash to play. However, he was losing his judgment along with his strength, and he was too broke to play much of the time. Many of his old enemies from Texas, Kansas and Arizona were now in Leadville and sensed Doc was vulnerable and could not retaliate. He began being hazed openly, and had to ask the Leadville police for protection.

By the summer of 1884, Doc was living on borrowed money and handouts. One of the men he owed money to was William J. Allen, an ex-policeman, bartender and hanger-on with some of Doc's old enemies from Tombstone. When Doc was unable to repay the loan, Allen threatened to "knock him down and kick his brains out."[295] Doc, unable to carry a concealed weapon, stashed a revolver in Hyman's saloon.

---

295. Roberts at 347.

When Allen came into Hyman's looking for Doc, Doc retrieved the revolver and fired two shots at Allen. Per usual, his aim was poor. The first shot missed Allen completely. The second shot hit Allen in the arm. Doc was disarmed before he could fire a third time.

Doc was arrested on a charge of assault with intent to kill and jailed. Friends put up bail money for him and he was freed to await a preliminary hearing. At the preliminary hearing, the judge bound Doc over for criminal trial and remanded him to jail on a larger bond. The trial was eventually held on March 21, 1885, and Doc was acquitted.

There are unconfirmed rumors that Doc visited his father or cousin in New Orleans following his trial, but given the state of his finances and health those claims are suspect. If he did go to New Orleans, it was a quick trip. In June of 1885, Doc collected $50.00 owed him by another gambler in Leadville at the point of a gun.

By the fall of 1885, Doc had moved to Denver, where the breathing was a little easier. He was able to find a regular table[296] and his finances seemed to improve somewhat. It was in Denver, probably in the

---

296. Although now it was at a much seedier gambling hall.

early spring of 1886, that Doc and Wyatt Earp saw each other for the last time. After that time, a reform movement in Denver pushed Doc out to Pueblo and Silverton, but Doc was unable to develop a favorable situation in either place. After an unsuccessful attempt to return to Denver, Doc came back to Leadville. Mannie Hyman gave him a table, more out of pity than anything else. Doc spent the 1886-1887 winter in Leadville, but knew the end was near. In May 1887, Doc took the stage to Glenwood Springs, Colorado. It was lower than Leadville, and the sulphur springs were reputed to be healthful. Doc moved into the Glenwood Springs Hotel and found work as a faro dealer and bartender. For the first four months he was able to earn enough to sustain himself. He was quiet and his temper was under strict control. However, in September he developed chest symptoms, that were diagnosed as pneumonia, that forced him to bed. He never really recovered. He went downhill rapidly and was out of bed only twice before he died on the morning of November 8, 1887[297]. He was barely 37 years old.

---

297. Most reports state he died in a Glenwood Springs sanitarium, but the most reliable sources seem to indicate that he was never an inpatient, and died in his hotel room.

A collection had to be held to pay for Doc's funeral. His only correspondent at the time of his death was his cousin Mattie McKey, a Sister of Charity in Atlanta. Mattie was rumored to have been a romantic interest of Doc's when he was still in Georgia and he had obviously kept in touch with her all those years.

It is hard to give an objective summation of a man with so many contradictory characteristics. Apologists want us to consider his slight physique and illness as factors that forced him to resort to knife and gun; they allude to his genteel manners, and intelligence as the signs of the underlying Southern gentleman. However, it is hard not to conclude that John Henry Holliday would have gone down the same path to his world of gambling, violence, alcohol[298] and drugs even without his diagnosis. Gambling and alcohol were factors in his life before he had a hint of consumption. He killed his first two men before his disease had caused much or any debilitation, and, in the frontier West, a fiery temper made violent encounters inevitable. He undoubtedly was loyal and intelligent, and could even be charming when he chose to be, but the remainder of

---

298. Some sources claim that in his prime he could consume three bottles per day.

his baggage was his own.

ANTON PAVLOVICH[299] CHEKHOV

Anton Chekhov ranks high on my list of favorite physician authors. It is not because his stories are necessarily my favorites,

---

299. Also found as "Pavelovich".

although I like many of them, but because he demonstrated many qualities that I admire. Even after he became a famous writer, he continued practicing medicine. He was an avid fisherman and an unapologetic dog lover. Probably his most admirable quality was his ability to describe the desperation and poverty of the Russian masses, and expose the repressive Russian regime, despite every word he wrote being subjected to government censorship. To this day, his guide for fishermen, dated as it is, remains my favorite put down of pompous fishing writers and editors.

Anton Chekhov was born on January 29, 1860[300] in the Sea of Azov Port of Taganrog, a town founded by Greek merchants imported to Russia by Peter the Great. His father, Pavel Yegorovich Chekhov, was a religious fanatic and unsuccessful grocery merchant. There is no doubt that some of his failure in business was due to the excessive amount of time he spent on religious matters. His only education and reading had been in religious scriptures, but he had high regard for education and each of his surviving children had college educations. Pavel's word was law, both in the store and at home. He played the violin and directed the

---

300. January 17, 1860 by the Russian Calendar.

local church choir, and forced Anton to sing in it. He crammed his store and home with religious icons, and insisted his family attend church almost daily, surely on every religious holiday[301] in the extensive Russian Orthodox calendar of such holidays. Religious fasts were rigorously enforced, and priests and monks treated like royalty[302].

Anton Chekhov's mother, Yevgeniya, was the daughter of an equally unsuccessful merchant. She was far less rigid than Pavel and delighted her children with her stories. As the son of a serf, becoming a merchant was the only road open to a higher rank. Therefore, Pavel was justly extremely proud of his rank[303] as a merchant even if it was the lowest of the three merchant classes, and he worked as tirelessly for the Society of Merchants as he did for the church. In 1871, he was awarded

---

301. A classic story about the father relates that after a rat fell into his supply of olive oil, Pavel called in the priest to bless the oil and then offered it for sale. There is no record of how successful he was in disposing of the oil.

302. Anton Chekhov's frequent references to the drunk priest or monk date from his work behind the counter at his father's store, dispensing vodka at reduced prices to the local monks.

303. The Russian table of ranks was established by Peter the Great in 1722 and was based on a rough social order, with the first rank being the nobility, and the serf or rural peasant being the lowest.

the Saint Stanislaw Medal for service to the Society of Merchants[304]. Pavel considered it the ultimate achievement of his life.

The family originally lived in a four-room house on Police Street[305], but they moved frequently as the father tried to find ever cheaper lodging[306]. Besides Anton, his four brothers, Mihail (Misha), Ivan, Nikolai and Alexander;[307] and older sister Masha[308]; the household included Anton's widowed aunt, Feodossa, and his cousin, Alexi; two apprentices from the grocery store; and occasional boarders. Under these crowded conditions, it is no wonder why Anton's best days were spent outdoors away from the paternal harassment present in the house and store. The outdoors and particularly the steppes meant freedom to him. He loved to swim and fish. He also loved to play practical jokes. He must

---

304. The merchants were the element of the population most supportive of the repressive regime – another point of conflict between Anton and his father.

305. Moscow's red-light area.

306. The family had at least six different residences in Taganrog.

307. The actual number of siblings and their respective names varies between biographers. However, the usual statement is that Anton had four brothers and one sister. These would appear to be the living siblings.

308. A younger sister, Eugina, died at two years.

have been a charming young man because the Russian Orthodox Priest, Father Bandakov, befriended him and became a life long friend, and his teachers went out of their way to help him.[309]

Anton and his siblings were forced to work in Pavel's store throughout their childhood. All the siblings were subjected to periodic beatings for violations of the father's rigid, ill-defined, ever-changing, moral code.

Because the Greek merchants dominated the commerce in Taganrog, when Anton reached age seven, Pavel enrolled Anton and his older brother, Nikolai in the local Greek school. He was hoping to give them a leg up in the local business world. The school was poorly run by the almost illiterate Greek Orthodox priest, and even Pavel was soon able to determine that the two boys were not getting the type of education their older brother, Alexander, was receiving at the local gymnasium. In 1869, Anton was transferred to the gymnasium and educated in what was considered one of the best of the Russian territorial schools. The students were required to wear uniforms and held to rigorous standards in a

---

309. There is a report that as an adolescent he had an affair with a female teacher.

classic education. Superior work was rewarded by financial subsidies to higher education.

In 1876, his father's crumbling business finally went bankrupt. Pavel's poor business practices were not the only factor that led to the bankruptcy. The town was initially left off the regional rail line, and the harbor at Taganrog became too shallow for ships to use.

Pavel was devastated. The loss of rank and the embarrassment of failure were overwhelming. Pavel fled town hidden on a cart to avoid debtor's prison. He moved in with Alexander and Nikolai, both studying at Moscow University[310]. The rest of the family soon followed Pavel to Moscow, but Anton was left behind to finish his studies at the gymnasium and dispose of the family's abandoned property[311]. Anton boarded with various families, and worked as a tutor. He also developed a thriving trade by trapping and selling finches and other birds in the local market. He remained fond of Taganrog for the rest of his life. He

---

310. Alexander was a mathematics and science major, while Nikolai was a very talented art major. Ivan was also at a university training as a teacher, but it is unclear where he was enrolled.

311. Some reports say Ivan also remained behind and left in 1877.

supported the local library and his school generously, but it appears doubtful he ever returned after completing the gymnasium.

Chekhov may have begun selling comic articles to the local newspapers at this time, because he was well-versed in doing so by the time he finished with the gymnasium in 1879 and moved to Moscow to rejoin his family. He registered with the Moscow police as a merchant.

Chekhov immediately enrolled in the Moscow University Medical School. He had shown little interest in medicine before this, and his reasons for choosing it as a profession are cloudy. His parents approved of the choice, but there is no evidence that they influenced his decision. He undoubtedly chose Moscow University for his studies because his brothers were so fond of it.

Alexander and Nikolai were contributing nothing to the family. Nikolai was both a talented musician and artist who managed to sell his work, but had a severe problem with alcoholism and literally drank up what he made. Alexander also had an alcohol problem, and spent whatever he made on women and alcohol. The family regarded Anton's arrival in Moscow as their salvation. Anton had a scholastic subsidy from Taganrog[312] that paid his tuition and school expenses, and he supported his family by writing comic sketches for the Moscow newspapers. He remained the principal bread winner of the family for the rest of his life.

At first finances were strained because Anton only received five kopecks per line, and the family again was forced to move from house to house[313]. Things improved greatly as Anton became more prolific and his stories sold regularly. In 1881, Pavel managed to get a low paying job in a haberdashery firm. About the same time, Ivan got a teaching job, and the family began to climb out of poverty.

All Anton Chekhov's stories at this time were written under pseudonyms. He hoped to keep his real name for the serious writing of medical articles[314]. By 1882, his reputation as a writer of Russian life had grown to the point he was writing for *Fragments,* one of the leading

---

312. The fact that his subsidy was local rather than national meant that Chekhov was not forced to practice in the government system.

313. One source states the family moved twelve times in the years they were in Moscow.

314. There is no record of him writing any medical articles.

Moscow weeklies. It is estimated that he had published in excess of 200 stories by the time he graduated from medical school. Anton and Nikolai were very close, and Nikolai illustrated some of Anton's stories. Despite Anton's considerable efforts, he was never able to influence Nikolai's drinking.

Anton left Moscow for the steppes every chance he got, a habit he continued until the final years of his life, when he moved to the Crimea. He loved the outdoors and the feeling of freedom the steppes provided. He thought the steppes themselves and his activities there renewed and refreshed him. He fished in all the regional lakes, creeks and rivers. He clerked for a rural physician on the steppes from time to time and loved it.

Little is known about his medical school career, but his fellow students remembered him as a good student[315]. In 1884, he qualified as a physician. However, by that time he was successful enough as a writer

---

315. For instance Bartlett describes the student uniform of dark green coat with gold buttons and a blue lined fur cap, but offers little insight to his studies. He kept up a friendship with his classmate G.I. Rossolimo, who became professor of Neurology at Moscow University, for the rest of his life.

that it was apparent that the income from that source would far surpass anything he could earn from the practice of medicine[316]. Nonetheless, he devoted a portion of every afternoon to seeing patients, whom he treated without charge. He considered medicine his profession for the remainder of his short life[317].

Coincident with medical school graduation, Chekhov self-published a collection of six stories as a book, *Tales of Mepomene*. 1000 copies were printed, but there is no record of its reception. His second collection of short stories, *Motley Tales,* was published in 1886 by a commercial publisher and was well received.

Chekhov's big breakthrough came in 1886 when he was discovered by Alexy Suvorin, the millionaire publisher of St. Petersburg's *New Times*[318]. The *New Times* was far more prestigious than

---

316. By 1883, the year before he graduated medical school, it is estimated that he was earning 100 Rubles per month, about three times his father's salary or his student stipend.

317. He is often quoted as saying, "Medicine is my wife, literature is my mistress."

318. The *New Times* was one of the most conservative publications in Russia. A rather odd home for the always liberal Chekhov.

Fragments. Suvorin paid him twice what he had been earning at the Moscow publication and allowed him more column space. With his move to the *New Times,* Chekhov began writing under his own name for the first time, and bought the family the first house they had ever owned. Suvorin became one of Chekhov's closest friends and a frequent traveling companion.

After Chekhov's story, *The Huntsman*, was published in the *New Times*, he received a letter from Demitry Grigorovich, a leading Russian writer, telling him he had real talent as a writer and urging him to write serious pieces of literary quality. The letter struck home with Chekhov and his work, always well-written, became more serious. In 1887, Chekhov, encouraged by Grigorovich, published a collection of short stories, *At Dusk.* The collection won Chekhov the Pushkin Prize from the Russian Academy of Science, the highest Russian literary award[319]. Also in 1887, Chekhov's first attempt at a play, *Ivanov,* was produced to rave reviews. It marked a decisive change in Russian theater. Prior plays had

---

319. There are two versions of Chekhov's win of the Pushkin prize. Some sources give his collection an 1888 publication date, and some sources translate the title as *In the Twilight.* In any case, he won the prize.

been overdone melodramatic pieces. *Ivanov* was quietly contemplative, in contrast. However, Moscow theater was really not ready for this type of play. The theater owners put pressure on him for a comedy. To satisfy them, Chekhov wrote a farce, *Bear*. It too was a huge success and his fame as a playwright was established.

His next big project was his novella-length story, *The Steppe*, that was published in *The Northern Herald*. It was the first of his stories to be published in a literary journal and not a newspaper.

The Anton Chekhov of this period appears to have maintained the charm he exhibited as a youth. Women flocked to him and he reportedly had numerous affairs and maintained close friendships with several different women. His sister Masha, who taught in a girls school, continually tried to marry him off to her friends and students who had mad crushes on him, but Anton always left them broken-hearted, without a proposal.

Exactly when Chekhov discovered he had tuberculosis is debated. There is the possibility that he knew his diagnosis as early as 1884 or 1885 and would not acknowledge it. Certainly, he must have made the diagnosis by 1887 when his brother Nikolai became so ill with the same disease[320]. Nonetheless, Chekhov was by all appearances a robust, healthy man until 1890. He certainly maintained a state of denial until the formal diagnosis was made in March 1897, when he had a major lung hemorrhage in a Moscow restaurant and was finally persuaded to visit a chest clinic.

Following Nikolai's death in 1889 and the coincident flop of his play, *Wood Demon*, Anton became depressed and restless. He sought a cause or purpose that would bring meaning to his life and endear him to future generations. His brother, Mihail (Misha) was researching the Russian prison system as part of his law course. He became an advocate of prison reform and rapidly recruited Anton to the cause. Anton decided to go to the Island of Sakhalin on the Siberian Pacific coast and study the penal colony there[321]. He went overland by train, coach, and river boat to reach the island. The trip took an arduous three months, and inflicted a terrific toll on Anton's health. He was delayed at least once with an episode of hemoptysis. From that time on his tuberculosis was overt.

---

320. Anton paid for Nikolai's care until his death in 1889. Anton's aunt died of tuberculosis two months after Nikolai.

321. One of the largest and most notorious of the Siberian Penal colonies.

Prisoners guilty of almost any crime and disobedient serfs had been exiled to Siberia since the Russians began their expansion into the region in the 16th Century. Most prisoners were marched to their penal colonies, guaranteeing that only the hardiest would survive. Chekhov was well aware of reputation of the penal colonies, but, even so, he was shocked at what he saw in his ninety-five days on Sakhalin Island. A local priest helped him gather information. Officials were selling supplies meant for the prisoners; prisoners were starving; prison funds were being diverted; female prisoners were forced into prostitution; and all the prisoners were subjected to brutal floggings and beatings. Chekhov published his findings in *Russian Thought*[322] in 1893 as a serial titled *The Island of Sakhalin*. *The Island of Sakhalin* was published as a book in 1895. It was not popular with the public either as a serial or book, and lacked the depth and statistical analysis necessary to give it any standing as an academic publication. Despite this, Chekhov was pleased with the work and considered it one of his finest. The island also found a role in his story, *The Murder,* where the murderer is sentenced

---

322. The references to floggings and beatings were removed by the censors.

to Sakhalin. Anton returned to Russia via the sea route, an almost equally time consuming trip, but one far less a strain on his health.[323]

Penal reform was not the only social cause Chekhov was active in. Chekhov worked tirelessly for famine relief and cholera control. He also was responsible for the construction of schools and libraries in rural areas, and was a driving force for the construction of a tuberculosis sanatorium. Despite his social liberalism and disgust with the repressive regime, Anton Chekhov never became politically active, or overtly opposed the regime or even government censorship.

In 1891 and again in 1894, Chekhov, accompanied by Suvorin, traveled to Western Europe. They visited Vienna, Venice, Bologna, Florence, Rome, Naples, Nice, Paris and Berlin. The trip seemingly left him unimpressed with the West except for its beer and theater. He appears to have resented the time away from his writing and the steppes.

By 1892, Anton Chekhov was wealthy enough to buy a country estate of 570 acres, Melikhovo, some forty miles south of Moscow and six miles from the nearest railroad station. There was an existing cherry

---

323. Despite this easier route, he had at least one major episode of hemoptysis.

orchard, a house, a barn, a chicken coop and two ponds, the largest stocked with carp and term. The house had eleven rooms, but no inside plumbing. Anton, his father and mother, his sister Masha, and brother Misha moved to the estate, and lived there all year long. Ivan seemingly lived there intermittently when teaching nearby. Living on the estate was much cheaper than living in Moscow. Misha managed the fields. Masha managed the vegetable garden, and, with her mother, did the pickling and preserving. Pavel became completely committed to the estate's upkeep. Nonetheless, Pavel was still a problem. He tried to force his will on the family as he had in Taganrog, and Anton still had confrontations with him. It is clear Anton never liked or respected his father.

Anton Chekhov planted an additional sixty cherry trees on the estate.[324] It is unclear if Anton converted one of the existing outbuildings to a writing studio or constructed a new one, but he had a studio away from the main house. Although he reserved several hours every day to his writing, he devoted several hours a day to providing free medical care to

---

324. Each year Pavel made a huge quantity of cherry jam. There is no record of how this cherry jam was disposed of.

the peasants[325] in the surrounding area. He also set up several schools. By this time, Anton's tuberculosis was blatant enough that his family and close associates were all aware of it. Despite his cough and lung problems, Chekhov remained a heavy smoker for the rest of his life.

The bulk of Chekhov's stories and his plays, *The Seagull* and *Uncle Vanya*, were written at Melikhovo. There were a constant stream of guests at the estate[326]. When guests were there, Chekhov would bemoan the time they took from his writing. When there were no guests, Chekhov would bemoan the fact than no one came to visit. Although Chekhov would complain that winter at Melikhovo lasted nine months and they had bad weather for the other three, it would seem the happiest period of his life was spent there.

Anton began his play, *The Seagul,l* in 1894. The Alexandrinsky Theater in St. Petersburg produced it in 1896. It was a flop of historic proportions. Chekhov was booed by the audience. However, in 1898, the Moscow Art Theater, one of the few private theaters in Russia, was

---

325. Chekhov hoisted a red flag to denote when he was seeing patients.

326. Suvorin didn't like Melikhovo, and would not stay there.

formed by Vladimir Nemirovich-Danchenko and Constantin Stanislavski. Their first production was *The Seagull*. It was a hit and made the theater's reputation as well as boosting Chekhov's standing as a playwright. It was probably during the production of *The Seagull* that Chekhov met Olga Knipper, one of Stanislavski's students and rumored to be Nemirovich-Danchenko's mistress. *The Seagull* was such a success that the Moscow Art Theater requested more plays from Chekhov, and the next season produced *Uncle Vanya*.

Anton Chekhov traveled to Biarritz and Nice in September 1897. Anton stayed on for the entire winter of 1897-98, and joined a large group of Russian tuberculosis patients who congregated there to escape the bitter Russian winters[327]. He became interested in the Dreyfus case, and supported Emile Zola's stand. He traveled to Paris and met with Dreyfus's brother; however he was coughing badly and returned to Nice almost immediately. After his return he coughed up blood almost continuously for three weeks. That shattered any hope he had that the climate in Nice offered him a cure. He returned to Melikhovo in April.

---

327. It was probably at this time that Chekhov sent 300 French classics to the Taganrog, library.

Pavel Chekhov died in 1898. With his father's death, there was no one to keep up Melikhovo, and Chekhov realized his health could no longer tolerate the severe winters around Moscow. Anton decided to move to the Crimea, where the climate was supposed to be beneficial to tuberculosis patients. At about this same time, Olga Knipper became his mistress and single romantic interest. He first bought a lot in Yalta, then a small red roofed house in a Tatar village, Kuchuk-Koy. The house had fig, walnut, olive and pomegranate trees, a small vineyard, and was close enough to the shore that Chekhov could fish. Shortly thereafter, he started construction of a house in the village of Autka. The Autka house became the family residence, and Kuchuk-Koy became the family's dacha. In January 1900, Chekhov was elected to the literary section of the Russian Academy of Science. Also in January 1900, he secretly bought a new house in the village of Gurzhuf on the Crimean coast. The secrecy was probably to avoid visitors and to be able to be alone with Olga Knipper, who was now visiting from Moscow regularly. The house in Kuchuk-Koy was subsequently sold.

It was in the Crimea that he wrote *Three Sisters* and *The Cherry Orchard*. *Three Sisters* was written specifically for the Moscow Art

Theater and with a role for Olga Knipper in mind. *The Student,* which Chekhov considered the best of his stories, was also written in Crimea, but he wrote little else after leaving Melikhovo.

In 1901, he finally married Olga Knipper. She remained in Moscow and he remained in the Crimea. They met for brief periods when he returned to Moscow for his plays or when she vacationed in Gurzhuf. Chekhov seems to have tolerated Olga's well-known infidelities with more grace than anyone would have expected from the outspoken author. When Olga developed peritonitis following surgery for an ectopic pregnancy, where Anton was obviously not the one who inseminated her, Anton nursed her faithfully and the union seemed to only grow stronger.

By 1904, Chekhov was gravely ill. His friends and family could tell he was not going to recover from this relapse. Chekhov, however, appeared to maintain his sense of denial even at this late date. He decided to enter a sanatorium in the Black Forest, and, accompanied by Olga, set off for Badenweiler in Germany on the third of June. They stopped in Berlin, where Chekhov was seen by Dr. Evald, a pulmonary specialist. Evald considered his case too far advanced for any hope of a cure. It was probably the first time Olga realized the seriousness of Chekhov's tuberculosis. Nonetheless, Chekhov was undaunted by Evald, and the couple continued on and arrived at Badenweiler on June 9, 1904.

Although he wrote letters to his family about how much better he was getting, he was steadily becoming weaker. He died in the early morning hours of June 30, 1904, three weeks after his arrival.

His body was smuggled out of the sanatorium by the Russian consul under the cover of darkness the following night, and taken to a local chapel. A funeral service was held there by a Russian Orthodox priest. His body was then taken to Berlin, where a second Russian Orthodox service was held, and finally sent to Moscow via St Petersburg in a refrigerator car[328]. His body arrived in St. Petersburg on July 7th. A third service was held in the St. Petersburg station with Suvorin, Alexander Chekhov and Alexander's family in attendance. Chekhov's body finally arrived in Moscow on July 9, 1904. Thousands marched in his funeral procession. The procession stopped for prayers at the Moscow Art Theater. Chekhov was buried beside his father in Moscow's Novodevichy Cemetery. As word spread of his death, memorial services

---

328. Reportedly the refrigerator car was one used for the transport of oysters.

were held all over Russia.

In Russia, at the time of his death, Chekhov was regarded as a great writer, but perhaps not quite as great as Tolstoy. However, as translations of his work traveled outside of Russia, the outside world came to regard him as the greatest of all Russian authors. He is now, next to Shakespeare, the most popular playwright in the English speaking world. In Russia, his homes became shrines and Moscow's Chekhov station was named after him.

Olga inherited the home in Gurzhuf and used it until 1953. Masha inherited the Autka house and occupied it with her mother until her mother's death in 1919, and then alone until Masha died in 1957.

FRANZ FANON

Franz Fanon is not well known in the United States. Perhaps a few of the American psychiatrists concerned with social and political psychology would recognize his name as that of one of the pioneers in their field. However, in large areas of Africa, he is well known for his written calls for violent revolution. Over the years, he has assumed the same legendary status in Africa that Che Guevara enjoys in South America.

Franz Fanon was born in Fort-de-France, the capital of Martinique, on July 20, 1925. He was one of eight children born to Casimir and Eleanore Fanon, descendants of slaves. Casimir was active in Masonic affairs and employed as a customs agent. Eleanore ran a shop. Some reports indicate that Eleanore was of mixed race. By Martinique standards, the family was upper middle class. They were rich enough to employ domestic servants and pay for piano lessons for Franz's sisters. Education was important to Casimir and Eleanore, and five of their children went to France for higher education. From contemporary reports, Eleanore appears to have been the dominant force in this family and presumably a great influence on Franz[329].

Neighbors describe the young Franz and his brothers as unruly and prone to random acts of vandalism. None of them describe Franz as being an outstanding student or even of being studious. In 1940, when Franz was fifteen, Martinique came under the control of the Vichy Government. Admiral Robert, Commander of the French West Indies Fleet, and an overt Nazi collaborationist, became Commissioner of the French West Indies. The allies' blockade of Martinique resulted in material shortages of all kinds. The French soldiers and sailors occupying the island soon assumed the role of a racist occupying force. The islanders came to view the Vichy government as racist colonizers, and the Free French forces as their liberators. Franz seems to have been an ardent supporter of the Free French cause, and there are unconfirmed

---

329. Unfortunately, Fanon himself wrote almost nothing about his childhood or early education and most of his childhood background is secondhand at best.

reports that he took part in anti-Vichy demonstrations and street violence. In any case, he made three attempts to reach the island of Dominica to join the Free French forces there before finally succeeding in 1943. By the time he finally reached Dominica, Admiral Robert was overthrown in Martinique. Franz returned to Martinique and joined the all-black Fifth Infantry Battalion.

In late 1943 or early 1944 the Fifth Infantry Battalion sailed for North Africa. Franz Fanon ended up in a combined black and Arab unit, but because of his origin in Martinique was regarded as a "Frenchman". His biographers differ. Some stating that he became a commissioned officer[330] and others that he served as a noncommissioned officer. Fanon's unit landed in France[331] in November of 1944 as part of the Southern France invasion force. As they pushed north, Fanon was wounded in battle and awarded the Croix de Guerre for bravery. By this time, Fanon had become cynical. He felt he had almost died while he was decolonizing the colonizers. He now, as never before, resented the

---

330. Postel states clearly that he went to officers training school.

331. One report states he saw action in Oran as well.

French colonization of Martinique and Algeria.

Following his demobilization, Fanon returned to Martinique to finish his interrupted education. He found little in Martinique's limited educational facilities that would meet his needs[332]. He became active in Aime Cesaire's election campaign. Cesaire was a former teacher of Fanon, and a veteran left-wing politician and advocate for independence. While active in the campaign, Fanon learned the French were giving grants to war veterans. Fanon qualified. Franz left for France with the intention of studying dentistry in Paris. For reasons we are not certain about, he enrolled in the Faculty of Medicine in Lyon instead. He seems to have managed a heavy extracurricular load in addition to his medical studies. He was a member and contributor to philosophy, poetry, and dramatic groups, and edited a small magazine called *Tam Tam*. He courted several white French women[333]; joined the Presence Africaine, a group of intellectuals; and met Jean-Paul Sartre, who remained his

---

332. It would seem he completed whatever secondary school credential he needed by 1946.

333. He fathered a daughter, Mireille, in one of these relationships. According to Wikipedia, Mireille married Bernard Mendes-France, son of French Politician Pierre Mendes-France.

friend until Fanon's death.

In his fifth year at Lyon, he elected the psychiatry track instead of the medicine or surgery track. The psychiatry department at Lyon was organically oriented and there was virtually no interest in social psychiatry or analysis. Franz Fanon submitted the text of his book, *Black Skin, White Mask,* as his thesis. It was Fanon's personal theory of the social and political psychology of the colonized nonwhite. He contended that the colonizer socially instilled the nonwhite with an obsessional neurosis to become white. Because this is impossible, it resulted in an inferiority complex within the nonwhite that was then reinforced by the colonizer. In other words, to Fanon, it was the colonizer who creates the inferior black. He further argued that the North African school of psychiatry was clueless as to the realities of colonization. The thesis was rejected, and Fanon eventually won his degree in 1951 with a thesis entitled *A Case of Friedrich's Disease With Delusions of Possession.*

Black Skin, White Mask was published by Fanon in 1952. At the time of its publication, it made no great impact. Also in 1952, Fanon married Marie-Josephe (Josie) Duble, one of the white women he had courted while a medical student[334]. While Fanon was preparing for his medicat des hopitaux psychiatriques[335], he worked at the St. Albans Psychiatric Hospital, a progressive and well thought of institution. After passing his examination, Fanon took a post at Pontorson on the Normandy Coast.

Almost immediately upon reaching Normandy, Fanon applied for and within two months was accepted for a consultancy at Blida-Joinville, Algeria, a town about fifty miles south of Algiers. Within days of his arrival, he felt a strong kinship with the Algerians and their plight. Exactly when he affiliated himself with the Front de Liberation Nationale (FLN) is not known, because for the next three years he remained in his psychiatric post in Blida, and his FLN activities remained clandestine[336]. He gave numerous papers and spoke on racism and culture to both the first and second Black Writers and Artists Conferences in Paris and

---

334. Fanon had a son, Oliver, from this marriage, but no details are available. Presumably, his son still lives in Algeria.

335. The examination that would allow him to act as a psychiatric consultant.

336. Razanajao et al state that he originally affiliated with the FLN by sheltering wounded fighters.

Rome. As he became more and more involved with the FLN, he realized he could no longer maintain his psychiatric role, and in December, 1956, he resigned his position. In February, 1957, he was ordered out of Algeria. However, other than expulsion, no legal action was initiated by the French authorities.

Fanon traveled briefly to France, Switzerland and Italy, and then found his way to Tunis, which was serving as the Algerian rebels' capital. He joined the FLN full time[337]. Because Fanon was neither an Arab nor a Muslim, it is doubtful that Fanon was ever a FLN leader. However, Fanon was editing the FLN paper, *Al Mujahid,* as well as writing articles for the FLN, and seems to have had some role in directing propaganda. He also became the FLN's roving ambassador to black Africa.

At some time after his affiliation with the FLN,[338] Fanon was

---

337. It would appear that he tried to resume a psychiatric practice in Tunis, but he was never accepted by the Tunisian medical community. It also appears from the scope of his FLN activities, that would it would have been highly unlikely that he could have had the time for anything like a regular psychiatric practice.

338. There is no consistent date given for this accident. Razanajao et al give 1954 as the date, before Fanon moved to Tunis, but others state it happened after he arrived in Tunis, but do not give a specific date.

badly injured in a motor vehicle accident and was sent to Rome for treatment. It is reported that he survived two attempts on his life while he recovered in Rome. There appears to be little doubt that General Salan, Commander in Chief of French forces in Algeria, had put Fanon on his hit list at one point in time[339]. Salan was ruthless and fanatic in his desire to put down the FLN. Therefore, his agents are the most likely to have made attempts on Fanon's life in Italy, although contemporary reports indicate the "red hand" made the attempts. Fanon returned to Algeria or Tunis, depending on the date you accept for the accident, after his recovery.

In 1960, Fanon was appointed the provisional government's ambassador to Ghana. In December, 1960, while in Ghana, he was diagnosed with leukemia. He was immediately flown to Moscow for treatment. The Russian physicians were unable to help him and, surprisingly, recommended treatment in the United States. However, Fanon failed to follow up on the Russian physicians' advice. Instead, he began a series of political lectures for FLN activists.

---

339. Ironically it was Salan who had awarded Fanon his Croix de Guerre.

Finally, in the fall of 1961, he became too ill to continue. To the surprise of most writers, it appears that the CIA helped him gain entrance to the US and care at the National Institutes of Health (NIH). He was admitted to the Clinical Center of the NIH on October 10, 1961, under the name of Dr. Omar Ibrahmin Fanon, and died on December 6, 1961. He was 36 years old. Reportedly, he was confused, agitated and paranoid at the time of his death.

Fanon's most famous book, *The Wretched of the Earth*[340], was written while he was traveling in search of a cure for his leukemia. He began writing it in April of 1961, and copies of the published book reached Fanon less than a week before he died. *The Wretched of the Earth* is an appeal to Colonial Africa to expel the colonizer with violence. Fanon essentially rejects any other course of decolonization once negotiation has failed, and believes the violence is therapeutic to the colonized mind. The following excerpt is a typical passage from the book:

> At the individual level, violence is a cleansing force. It

---

340. The title was taken directly from the communist anthem, the *Internationale*. "Arise ye prisoners of starvation, arise ye wretched of the earth."

rids the colonized of their inferiority complex, of their passive and despairing attitude. It emboldens them, and restores their self confidence. Even if the armed struggle has been symbolic, and they have been demobilized by rapid decolonization, the people have time to realize that liberation was the achievement of each and every one and no special merit should go to the leader.[341]

On December 6, 1961, the book was declared seditious by the French authorities and seized. Fanon's body was flown to Tunis where it lay in state[342]. Later, it was buried in Algeria. After Algerian independence, Fanon was re-buried in the Martyrs Graveyard at Ain Kerma. Fanon is still considered an Algerian national hero. His widow, Josie, committed suicide in Algeria in 1989. The hospital in Blida is now named after Franz Fanon, an unapologetic revolutionary.

---

341. Fannon, *The Wretched of the Earth,* at 51.

342. It is also reported that the CIA arranged for the transport of Fanon's body to Tunis.

BIBLIOGRAPHY

ABOUL-ENEIN, Youssef, *Aymam al-Zawahiri,* The Counterproliferation Papers -Future Warfare Series No. 21, Air University, Maxwell Air Force Base Alabama 2004.

ADAMS, *The Social Psychiatry of Franz Fanon,* American Journal of Psychiatry 127(6):809-114 1970

AL-ZAYYAT, Montasser, *The Road to Al-Qaeda,* Pluto Press, London 2004.

AMBROSE, *Nothing Like it in the World,* Simon & Schuster, New York, 2000.

ANDERSON, *Che Guevara, A Revolutionary Life,* Grove Press, New York, 1997.

ANONYMOUS, *" Where satisfaction is not given, money will be refunded" John H. Holliday, Dentist, Dodge City, Kansas 1878,* J. Americ an Dental Association 108(4):488 1984.

ANONYMOUS, *Thomas Dover (1662-1742) - Rescuer of Robinson Crusoe,* JAMA
189(3):142-3 1964.

APPLEYARD, *Jean Paul Marat(1743-1793). Revolutionary and Doctor of Medicine,* Practitioner 206(236):826-35 1971.

BANERJEE, *John Keets: his medical student years at the United Hospitals of Guy's and St Thomas'* Journal of the Royal Society of

Medicine 82(10):620 1982.

BARTLETT, *Chekhov: Scenes from a Life,* Free Press, London 2004.

BARTON, *Who Ever Heard of Doctor Keats?,* New York State Journal of Medicine 77(2):244-6 1977.

BEHRMAN, *The Ailment of Dr. Anton Chekhov,* Journal of The Royal Society of Medicine 82(3):163-4 1989.

BENSLEY, *Gertrude Stein as a Medical Student,* The Pharos, Spring 1984:36-37.

BOURNE, *Essays in Historical Criticism,* Charles Scribner's Sons, New York 1901.

BRODY, *Doctors Afield; General Hugh Mercer,* New England Journal of Medicine 252(18):770-2 1955.

BROWN, *Life of John Keats,* Oxford University Press, London 1937.

BUCKNER, *Overview of the History of Medical Malpractice,* Graduate Group, Hartford, 2002.

BUTLER, *The Liberal Party and the Jameson Raid,* Clarendon Press, Oxford 1968.

CAILLOU, *South From Khartoum,* Hawthorn Books, NY 1974.

CALDER, *Willie: The Life of W. Somerset Maugham,* St. Martin's Press, NY 1989.

CARR, *The Life of Arthur Conan Doyle,* Harper, New York 1949.

CLARKE, *Chekhov's Chronic Tuberculosis,* Proceedings of the Royal Society of Medicine 56(11):1023-36 2001.

CLIFTON, *Dr. Thomas Dover,* Nursing Times, Feb. 8: 247 1978.

CLAMAN, *Emin Pasha - Confusion in the Jungle,* New England Journal of Medicine 261(1):37-8 1959.

COHEN, *Asthma Among the Famous,* Asthma and Allergy Proceedings 18(2):128-32 1997.

COOPE, *Mania Sakhalinosa,* Medical History 23(1):29-37 1979.

COULEHAN, *A Writer Well-Versed in Patient Care,* American Journal of Medicine 119(1):99 2006.

COULEHAN, *Adventures in Medicine,* American Journal of Medicine 119(7):622 2006.

DEWHURST & DOUBLET, *Thomas Dover and the South Seas Company,* Medical History, 18:107-121 1974.

DOBERNECK, *Sun Yat Sen: Surgeon and Revolutionary,* Surgery 122:101-04 1997.

DODD, *From Medicine to President,* The Practitioner, 225(9):1342-3 1981.

DONEGAN, *Dr. Guillotin-Reformer and Humanitarian,* Journal of the Royal Society of Medicine 83:637-9 1990.

DOTZ, *Jean-Paul Marat: His life, cutaneous disease, death and depiction by Jacques Louis David,* American Journal of Dermatopathology 1(3):247-50 1979.

DOYLE, *Memories and Adventures,* Little, Brown, Boston 1924.

DOBOVSKY, *John Keats (1795-1821) -- poet, physician and tuberculosis patient,* South African Medical Journal 59(24):875-8 1981.

DUKE, *Thomas Dover-Physician, Pirate and Powder, as Seen Through the Looking Glass of 20th-Century Physicians,* Connecticut Medicine 49(3):179-183 1985.

ENGLISH, *General Hugh Mercer,* Vantage Press, New York 1975.

ENGLISH, *Gertrude Stein and the Politics of Literary-Medical Experimentation,* Literature and Medicine 16(2):188-209 1997.

FANON, *The Wretched of the Earth,* Grove Press, New York 2004.

FARWELL, *Queen Victoria's Little Wars,* W.W.Norton, London 1985.

GARLAND, *Joseph Ingnace Guillotin,* New England Journal of Medicine 248(23):983-4 1953.

GARLAND: *Oliver Goldsmith,* New England Journal of Medicine 247(19):718-9 1952.

GEISMAR, *Fanon: The Revolutionary as Prophet,* Grove Press, New York 1971.

GIANAKOS, *Tolstoy, Chekhov, and Self Knowledge,* Chest 112(3):575-6 1997.

GUEVARA, *The Motorcycle Diaries,* Verso, London 1994. (For a remarkably accurate visual treat, see the movie of the same name.)

HARPER, *Ernesto (Che)Guevara. Physician - revolutionary physician - revolutionary,* New England Journal of Medicine, 281(23):1285-89 1969.

HEMMING, M., *Jean Paul Marat: physician, philosopher, patriot,* New England Journal of Medicine, 254(23):1087-9 1956.

HILL, *Apothecary in Arms,* Practitioner 219(1310):268-70 1977.

HOCHSCHILD, *Doctor Durant and His Iron Horse,* Adirondack

Museum, Adirondack Park,1961.

HOFFMAN, *Gertrude Stein,* University of Minnesota Press, Minneapolis 1961.

HOFFMAN, *Gertrude Stein*, Twayne Publishers, Boston 1976.

HOLTZENDORF, *Letter: More on Doc Holliday,* Journal of American Dental Association 88(1):30 1974.

HOOK, The Literature and Medicine Movement, Pharos, Summer 1996:35-38.

HOPKINS, *The True Genius of Oliver Goldsmith,* Johns Hopkins Press, Baltimore 1969.

IGIC, *Anton Pavlovich Chekhov (1860-1904)* American Journal of Psychiatry 162(12): 2248 2005.

JACKSON, *A World on Fire,* Viking, New York 2005.

JAMES, *The Savage Wars: British Campaigns in Africa 1870-1920,* St. Martins Press, NY 1985.

JAMES, *Che Guevara*, Stein and Day, New York 1970.

JARCHO, *Auenbrugger, Laennec and John Keats*, Medical History 5:167-72 1961.

JELINEK, *Jean-Paul Marat: The differential diagnosis of his skin disease,* American Journal of Dermatopathology 1(3):251-2 1979.

JOHNSON & STEPHENSON, *The Gatling gun and flying machine of Richard and Henry Gatling,* Johnson Publishing, Murfreesboro, NC 1979.

KAUFMAN ET AL, Dictionary of Medical Biography, Greenwood Press 1984.

KELLER, *Clinician and Revolutionary: Franz Fanon, Biography and the History of Colonial Medicine,* Bulletin of the History of Medicine 81(4):823-841 2007.

KELLY & BURRAGE, Dictionary of American Medical Biography, Appleton, New York 1928.

KERSHAW, *A History of the Guillotine,* Barnes & Noble, New York 1993.

KETCHUM, *The Winter Soldiers,* Doubleday, Garden City, 1973.

KLEIN, *Union Pacific: The Birth of a Railroad 1862-1893,* Doubleday, New York, 1987.

KNAPP, *Gertrude Stein,* Continuum, NY 1990.

KRUGER, *Good-bye Dolly Gray,* Pan Books, London 1974.

LAKE, *Wyatt Earp: Frontier Marshal.* Houghton, Boston 1931.

LASKY, *The Paradigm of Religion, Medicine and Capital Punishment,* Medicine Science and the Law, 14(1):26-31 1974.

LEHMAN, *Are We Any Safer,* Navel Institute Proceedings, 132(9):18-22 2006.

LOOPER, *John Henry Holliday, DDS: Georgia's most famous dentist,* Journal American Dental Association 87(2) :250-6 1973.

LOPEZ, *Franklin and Mesmer: An Encounter,* Yale Journal of Biology and Medicine 66(4):325-31 1993.

MA, *Sun Yat-Sen(1866-1925), a man to cure patients and the nation - his early years and medical career,* Journal of Medical Biography 4:161-170 1996.

MACEY, *Franz Fanon 1925-1961* History of Psychiatry vii:489-497 1996

MALCOM, *Gertrude Stein's War,* The New Yorker, June 2, 2003:59-81.

MAJOR, *A History of Medicine,* Thomas 1954.

MERKEL, *Medicine and the Arts,* Academic Medicine 76(1):48 2001.

MILLER, *Poisoning by Antimony,* Southern Medical Journal 75(5):592 1982.

MITCHELL, *Gatling and Guillotin: Two Physicians Far Afield,* North Carolina Medical Journal, 60(5):292-5 1999.

MONK, *Thomas Dover, Physician and Pirate,* Journal of the Royal College of Physicians of London 16(1):60-1 1982.

MONRO, *The Physician as a Man of Letters Science and Action,* E. & S. Livingstone, Edinburgh, 1951.

MOORHEAD, *The White Nile,* Harper & Row New York 1960.

MORA & SANTAMARINA, *Che Guevara the Antihero,* New England Journal of Medicine, 281(23):1289-91 1969.

MOROWITZ, *The Kindly Dr. Guillotin,* Hospital Practice (office ed.) 28(4):14-6 1993.

MORGAN, *Maugham,* Simon & Schuster, New York 1980.

MORTON, *Dr. Thomas (Quicksilver) Dover 1660-1742,* British Journal of Venereal Disease, 44:342-46 1968.

MOTION, *John Keats* Farrar, Straus and Giroux, New York 1997.

MURPHY, *The Itches of Jean-Paul Marat,* Journal of American Academy of Dermatology 3:565-7 1989.

NORDON, *Conan Doyle*, Holt, Rineheart and Winston, New York 1967.

OBER, *Jean Paul Marat, MD 1743-1793,* New York State Journal of Medicine 71(10):125-35 1971.

OBER, *Joseph Ingnace Guillotin,MD (1738-1814),* New York State Journal of Medicine 71(7): 787-90 1971.

PASSCAL, *Arthur Conan Doyle: Beyond Baker Street,* Oxford University Press, Oxford 1999.

PHEAR, *Thomas Dover 1662-1742,* Journal of the History of Medicine and Allied Sciences, April 1954: 139-156.

PORTER, *Richard Gatling and His Gun,* North Carolina Medical Journal, 49(6):332 1988.

PROSTEL, *Franz Fanon -Looking Back,* History of Psychiatry vii:487 1996

QUINTANA, *Oliver Goldsmith,* Macmillan Company, New York 1967.

RADETSKY, *John Keats and Tuberculosis,* Pediatric Infectious Disease Journal 20(5):535-40 2001.

RAINS, *Keats: a tragedy in three acts 1815-1821,* Journal of the Royal Society of London 87(12):743 1994.

RAPHAEL, *Somerset Maugham and His World,* Charles Scribner's Sons, New York.

ROBERTS, *Doc Holliday, The Life and Legend,* John Wiley and Sons, Inc. Hoboken, NJ 2006.

RAZANAJAO, POSTEL & ALLEN, *The Life and Psychiatric Work of Franz Fanon,* History of Psychiatry vii: 499-524 1996.

SATRAN, *Chekhov and Rossolimo,* Neurology 64(1): 121-7 2005.

SCHAMA, *Citizens: A Chronicle of the French Revolution,* Alfred A. Knopf, New York 1989.

SCHIFFRIN, *Sun Yat-Sen and the Origin of the Chinese Revolution,* University of California Press, Berkeley 1968.

SCHIFFRIN, *Sun Yat-Sen Reluctant Revolutionary,* Little-Brown, Boston 1980.

SCHNECK, *W. Somerset Maugham, Capgras Syndrome and Aging,* NY State Medical Journal 92(12):547-50 1992.

SCHNEIDERMAN, *The Good Doctor: The Literature and Medicine of Anton Chekhov,* Family Medicine 33(1):11-13 2001.

SCHOENBERG, *Gertrude Stein's Neuroanatomic Investigations,* Southern Medical Journal 81(2):250-258 1988.

SCHWARTZ, *Healing and Havoc in the Works of T.S. Eliot and William Carlos Williams,* Pharos Fall 1991:35-7 1991.

SCHWARTZ, *"Medicine is My Lawful Wife" - Anton Chekhov, 1860-1904,* New England Journal of Medicine 351(3):213-4 2004.

SHAMPO AND KYLE, *Enesto Guevara de la Serna,* JAMA 235(14):1486 1976.

SHEE, *Dr. Eduard Schnitzer alias Emin Pasha,* The Central African Journal of Medicine12(3):50-5 1966.

STASHOWER, *Teller of Tales: The life of Arthur Conan Doyle,* Henry Holt, New York 1999.

Swinton, W.E., *Physicians in Literature. Part VII: the mortal woes and timeless writing of Anton Pavlovich Chekhov,* Canadian Medical Association Journal 114(4):366-8 1976.

SWINTON, *Physicians in Literature, Part III, Oliver Goldsmith,* Canadian Medical Association Journal 113:1079-81 1975.

UTLEY & WASHBURN, *The Indian Wars,* American Heritage, New York 1977.

WATERMAN, J.M., *With Sword and Lancet,* Garrett & Massie, Richmond, 1941.

WEINER, *The Real Dr. Guillotin,* JAMA 220(1): 85-9 1972.

WRIGHT, Lawrence, *The Man Behind Bin Laden,* New Yorker 9/16/2002.

WRIGHT, Lawrence, *The Looming Tower*, Knopf, New York 2006.

WINEAPPLE, *Gertrude Stein Read JAMA*, JAMA 276(14):1132-1133 1996.

YOUSSEF, & FADE, *Franz Fanon and Political Psychiatry,* History of Psychiatry vii:525-532 1996.

www.ingramcontent.com/pod-product-compliance
Lightning Source LLC
Chambersburg PA
CBHW072131220426
43664CB00013B/2207